IMAGES
of America

KARNES COUNTY

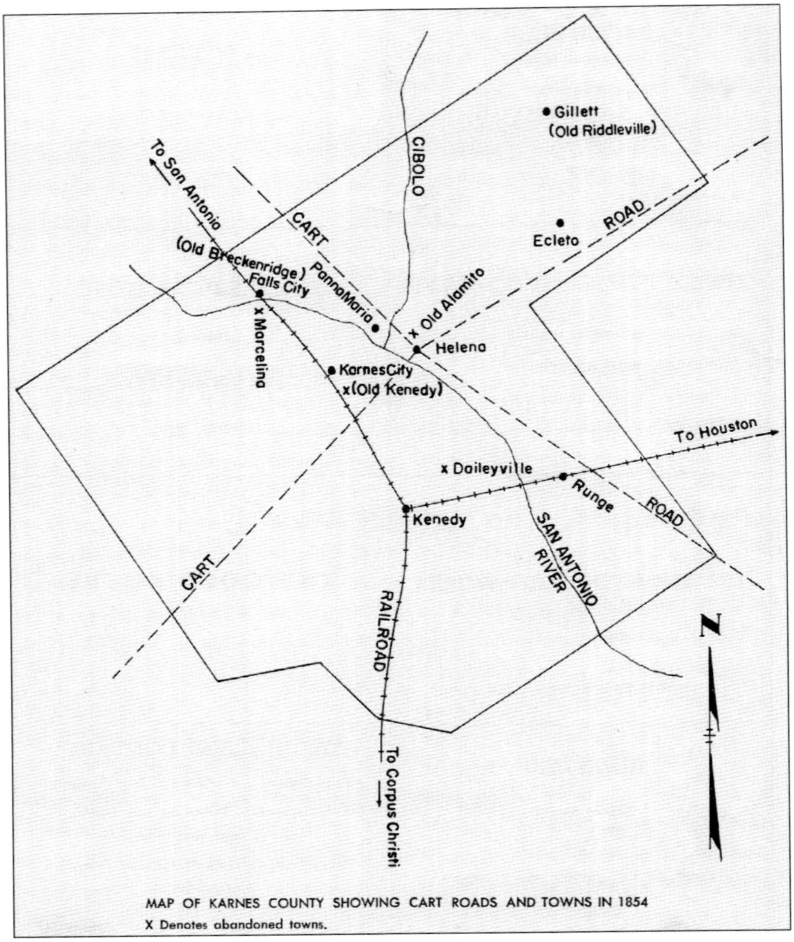

An early Karnes County map showing all of the old trails before there were roads, and the location of many of the small towns are no longer in existence. Also shown is the San Antonio River and Cibolo Creek that defined much of where our newly formed settlements were situated.

On the Cover: Colwell Dilworth enjoyed offering his ranch for hunting and fishing to many of his Karnes County friends. (Photograph by Mason Johnson; courtesy of the author.)

IMAGES
of America

KARNES COUNTY

Catherine Johnson Passmore

ARCADIA
PUBLISHING

ISBN 978-0-7385-8492-8

Published by Arcadia Publishing
Charleston, South Carolina

Printed in the United States of America

Library of Congress Control Number: 2011925334

For all general information, please contact Arcadia Publishing:
Telephone 843-853-2070
Fax 843-853-0044
E-mail sales@arcadiapublishing.com
For customer service and orders:
Toll-Free 1-888-313-2665

Visit us on the Internet at www.arcadiapublishing.com

In loving memory of my father, Mason Johnson, an amazing amateur photographer and lover of history, who let me tag along on many of his picture-taking excursions. He was always searching for just the right moment to snap a picture.

Contents

ACKNOWLEDGMENTS

A special thanks to the Karnes County Historical Society located in the first Karnes County Courthouse constructed in 1853, in Helena, Texas, and to its members. Their sources of pictures and history-laden artifacts were very illuminating. Also, thanks to the Karnes City Community Chamber of Commerce for its treasure trove of pictures and for allowing me access to them. Also, I am grateful for the special encouragement and advice from our own Karnes County historian, the notable and oft-published author Robert Thonhoff, who is acknowledged throughout the state as one of the best historians of our early history. I must not neglect thanking Dan Kleiner, former editor of the *Karnes Countywide Newspaper,* who got me started on this project in the first place. And certainly, last but not least, my acquisitions editor at Arcadia Publishing, Lauren Hummer, who gave such good advice and shared her knowledge. What a lucky happening to get Lauren as my advisor and teacher on this project!

Introduction

Karnes County has a history that speaks of legends and facts right out of a Western movie. Beginning with Spanish Conquistadors, Comanche, Apache, and other Indian tribes, a French pirate, and heroic men and women who came to the area to find a better life, its roots go deep into the heart of Texas. Situated not far south from San Antonio, Texas, it is considered to be geographically the center city of Texas. Karnes County actually began in the 1850s. Its birthplace was a small community named Helena. It was the site of an already well-traveled road, the Spanish Colonial La Bahia Road, also known as the Chihuahua or Ox-Cart Trail. The site gave access to trade and commerce all the way from San Antonio through the Goliad Mission area and eventually to the Gulf Coast.

Early entrepreneurs Thomas Ruckman and Lewis Owings considered the site an ideal place to join forces and build a partnership to develop businesses and a future town site. Changing its name from Alamita, as it had been known, to Helena, after the wife of Dr. Owings, Helen, they began their plans. By 1853, Ruckman and Owings had opened a mercantile, a gristmill, and soon a post office of which Ruckman became the postmaster. As it grew in population, the two men petitioned the legislature for a new county to be formed, named Karnes County, after a military hero and early Texas Ranger, Henry Wax Karnes. After their petition was granted, it is reported that the first election of Karnes County, held in 1854, was on the gallery of their store as Helena had been declared the county seat.

Karnes was a suitable name, as Henry Karnes was a heroic, skilled Indian negotiator, a member of the Texas Cavalry, and an early Texas Ranger. He was dedicated during his short life to peacemaking while helping subdue many of the troubles faced by the earliest settlers. Not only was Karnes County named after him, but in 1942, the USS *Karnes*, a Haskell-class attack transport ship, proudly served in the Navy during World War II under the banner of his name.

Karnes County continued to grow. Many large settlements consisted of ethnic groups who were coming to Texas to escape hardships and deprivations that involved parts of Prussia, particularly the Polish and German peoples of the Silesian region. These groups included the first Polish family groups to settle in America, choosing parts of Karnes County near the junction of the San Antonio River and Cibolo Creek. Subsequent groups of immigrants formed the Karnes communities of Czestohowa, Panna Maria, Pawelekville, and Falls City. German residents found the farming and ranching areas around Karnes City and Kenedy to be ideal for their interests, and many remain there today. Other communities still in existence today from these earliest settlements are Runge, Gillette, Coy City, Hobson, Ecleto, and Lenz.

The coming of the Iron Horse would soon change everything. Due to a mistake in judgment, when the San Antonio and Aransas Pass Railroad were seeking a route to continue its line from San Antonio to the coast, the company laid out its policy and demands that a community must meet to be included on the line. Helena officials did not think it necessary to pay those demands to be part of the sites for the railroad lines, considering Helena to be the biggest and most well-known city in Karnes County anyway. Alas, their logic failed to persuade the railroad officials, so Helena was bypassed and the line went through Falls City, Karnes City, Kenedy, Runge, and other towns on its way to the Gulf Coast. From then on, those cities continued to grow while Helena gradually lost ground and, eventually, its designation as the county seat. Other small communities left behind by the railroad were Daileyville, Marcelino, Breckenridge, and Riddleville. They, too, mostly remain now in the minds of family descendants through their cemeteries, or as scenes of some interesting stories of long ago feuds and gunfights. Riddleville eventually came back to life and is renamed Gillette. In a vigorous and heated election in 1894, Karnes City won to become the county seat, with Runge and Kenedy not far behind.

Kenedy, even though developed to be on the railroad line by Mifflin Kenedy, an associate of the railroad, became infamous for its reputation as a rough and rowdy town. It even earned the nickname "Six Shooter Junction." Because of the Civil War and so many local men being involved in the Confederate effort, Karnes County was deemed easy prey for bandits and deserters. The county also went through a severe drought for three years, from 1862 to 1865. But after the Civil War, it was not long before Karnes County rebounded, especially through its livestock and the greater demand from surrounding areas, which in turn brought about episodes of huge cattle drives. Famous for its herds of Texas longhorns, originally brought into the area by the Spaniards, cattle raising was the main economic source for many farmers and ranchers, as it still is today. Again, when the railroad was brought through the area, large-scale agriculture production began to thrive with easier access to markets. Cotton, sorghum, hay, flax, corn, other grains, and a variety of vegetables began to flourish as crops.

As with the coming of the railroads, with extensive highway and road building, even more avenues of opportunities were opening for Karnes Countians. Highways, good bridges, and county roads all played an important part in the growth and success of many areas. After World War II, employment opportunities through government programs continued to keep the road and highway construction going. It also opened the access and opportunity for businesses that needed growth in the cities. And soon, with new revenues coming in from the discovery and drilling for oil and gas wells, Karnes County had its second growth spurt. Included in this mineral-based dimension was the discovery of uranium in the mid-1950s, that brought in another processing mill that was built near Falls City. And this continues!

A new discovery of large gas-oil shale in just the last few months has recreated the boom that once held our county in the spotlight. The uranium mine, too, has recently reopened. Karnes County has one of the best employment records in the country, with more job availability waiting as production speeds up.

One

A Rough and Rowdy Beginning

The area known as Karnes County, inhabited several thousand years before the arrival of Europeans, has evidence that members of the ancient Coahuiltecan linguistic, hunter-gatherer type of people were here even before the Comanche, Tonkawa, Karankawa, and Apache Indians called this part of Texas home. Along with its battle for independence from the Spanish, French, and Mexican cultures, they created trouble for south central Texans in their search for fertile and rich grasslands to homestead. But with the help of heroic Texans, including Henry Wax Karnes, they determined to stake their claims. Henry Karnes was described as a real frontiersman, a skilled negotiator, and a dedicated peacemaker who worked to subdue many of the troubles faced by settlers in the earliest years with the native Indians and Mexican Spanish coalition. Although Karnes died at 28 years old from yellow fever after having been shot through the upper part of his body with an arrow, he dealt with the fierce Comanche tribe more successfully than any other negotiator had. Karnes was a captain of the Texas Cavalry, second in command of the cavalry forces at the Battle of San Jacinto, and an early member of the early Texas Rangers. When Thomas Ruckman and Lewis Owings petitioned for the town of Helena and the developing areas around it to become a county in its own right, they requested to name the new county Karnes, after the hero who lived such a full life in such a short time. Helena, first settled in 1852, was designated as the county seat.

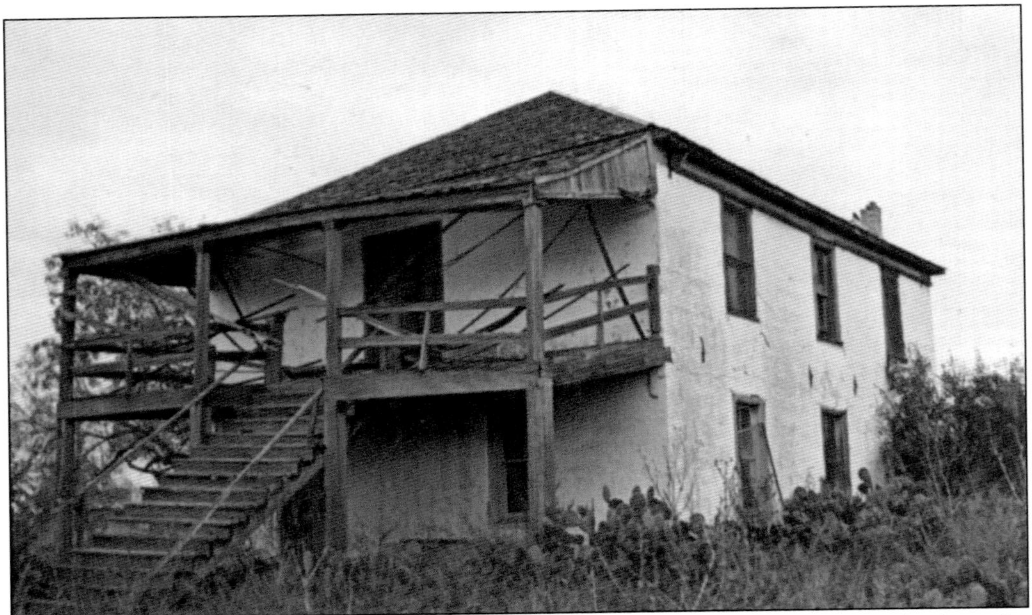

The view of the 1854 Karnes County Courthouse in Helena, Texas, shows the porch where the first official meeting of the county was held. The original building was destroyed in a storm, and the second one was built of stone.

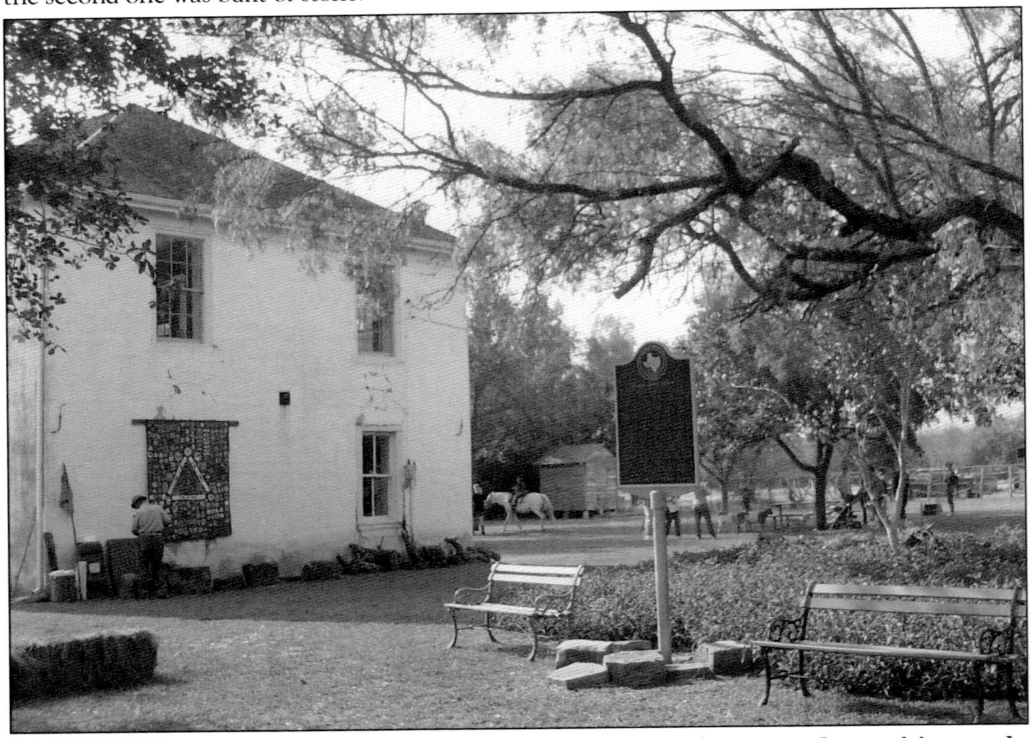

The stone Helena courthouse as it stands today is being used as the Karnes County Museum. In the late summertime, an Indian summer celebration is held on the grounds. A state historical marker is nearby.

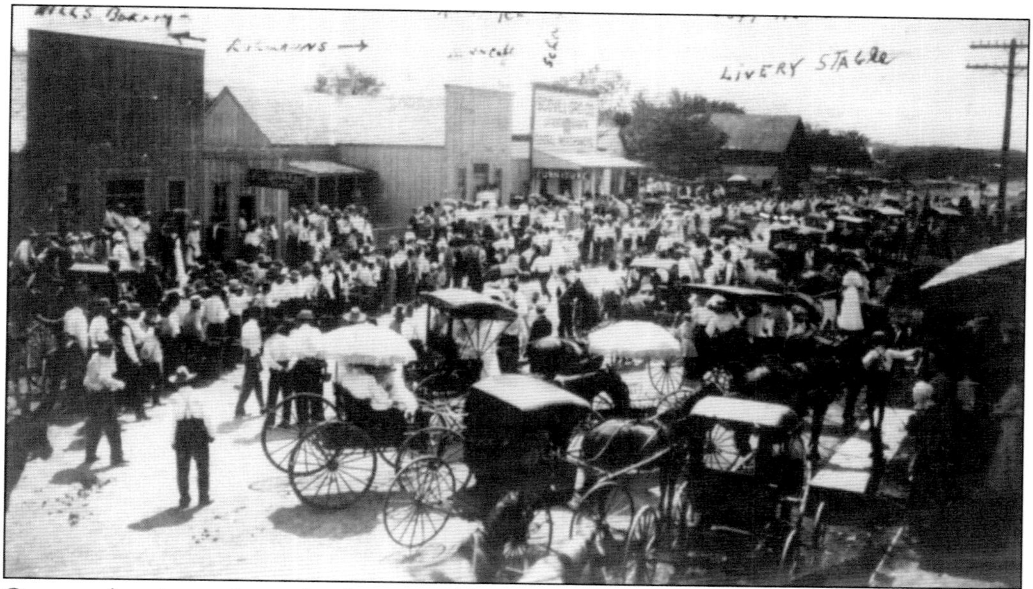

Ox carts, buggies, and crowds of men would gather in the street in Karnes City for the election of a new county seat. This was before women had the right to vote.

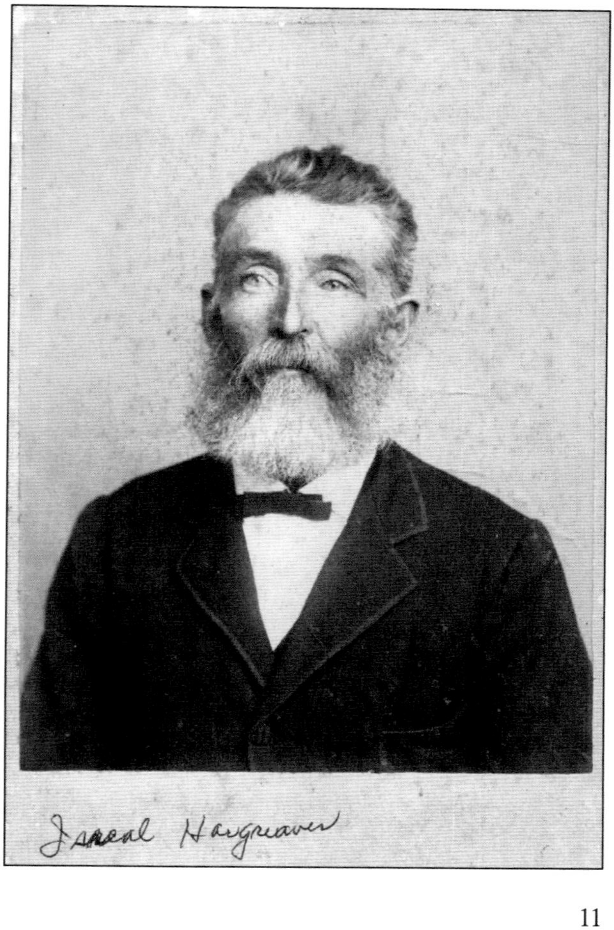

As early settlers began to make their way past the Helena area, other parts of the county were experiencing growth from the newcomers. One family had originally started in Lancashire, England, where their son Isreal Hargreave was born.

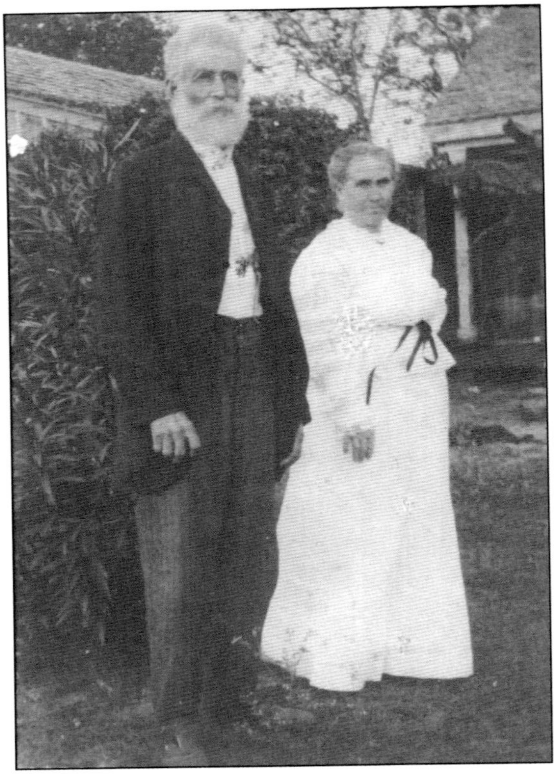

The Hargreaves then left England for Australia, settling in New Zealand. Isreal wanted to move to Texas, so he and his wife, Selina, did. They bought over 1,000 acres of land near Hondo Creek in Karnes County.

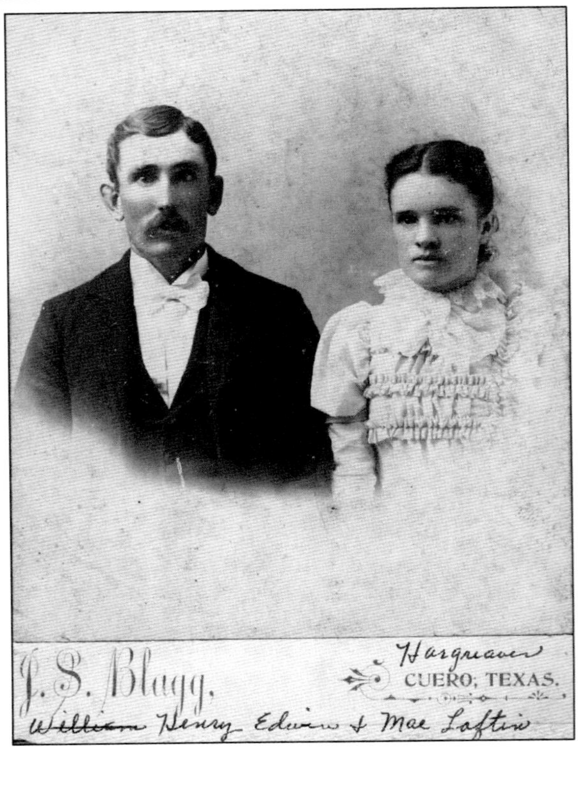

Pictured here is one of Isreal and Selina's sons. Henry Edwin and his wife, Mae Loftin Hargreave, made their home in Runge. At that time, it was one of the fastest growing communities in Karnes County.

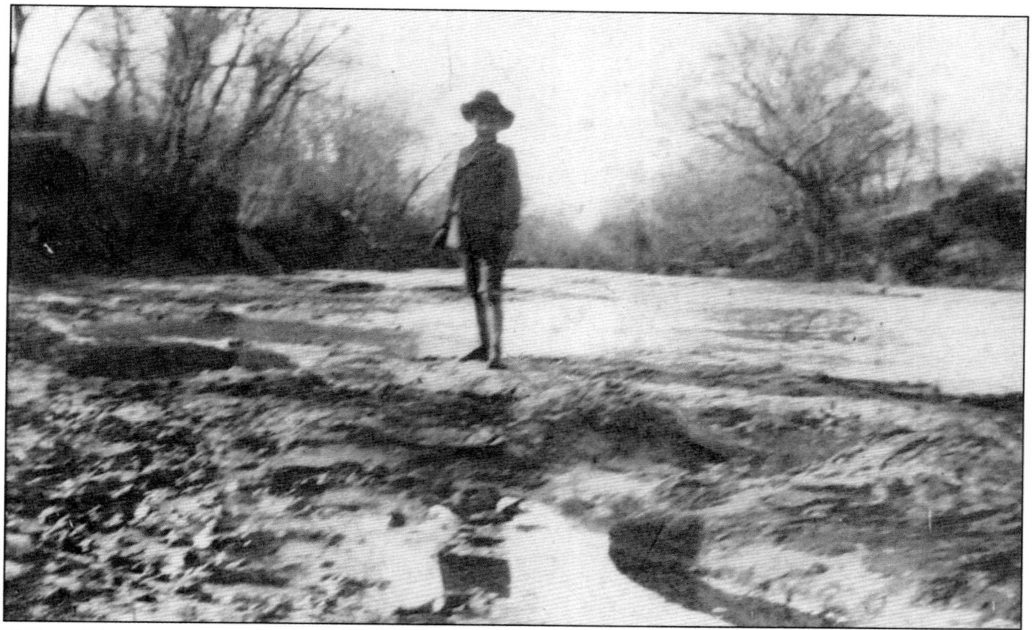

Wilton Hargreave stands at one of the crossings on the San Antonio River.

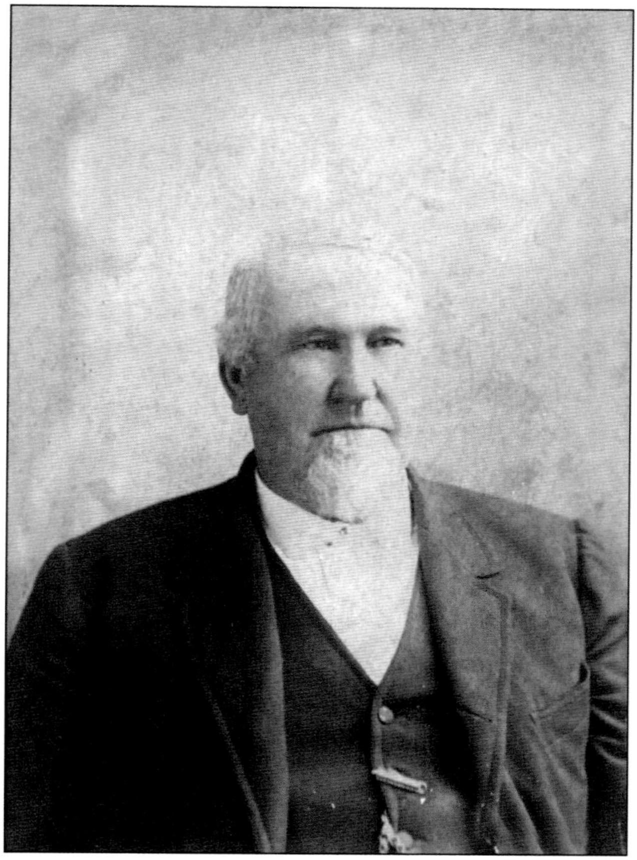

In later years, the Hargreaves, like Wilton, shown at an older age, said they were glad to be in America, and in Texas.

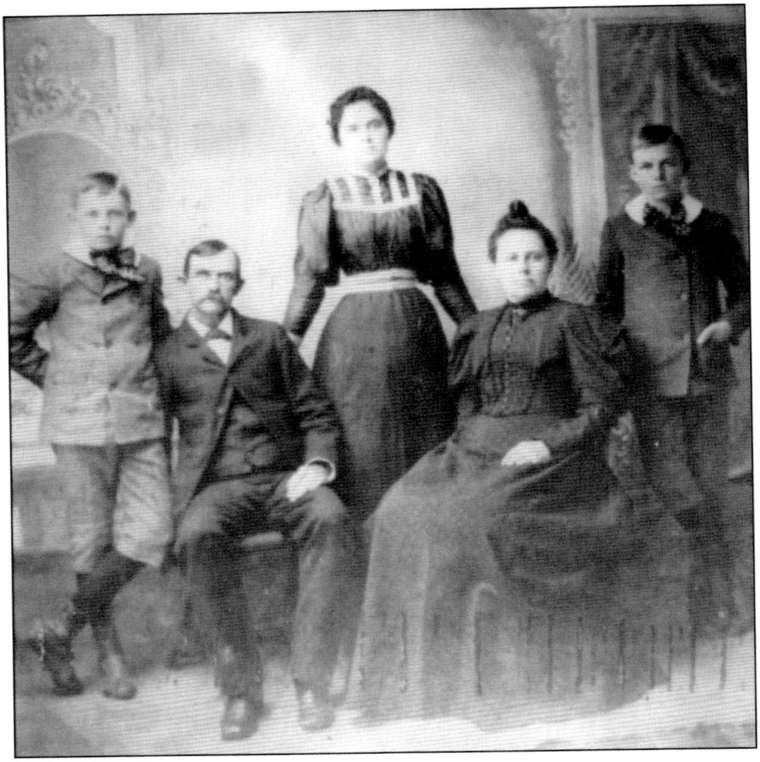

Pictured are members of one of the first families of Karnes City. The main street in the middle of town is named Calvert Avenue, as their family owned much of the land that the city is built on. From left to right are Caldwell Calvert, Tom J. Calvert, Mrs. Will J. Fulbright (Fannie Calvert), Alice Hines Calvert, and Frank Calvert.

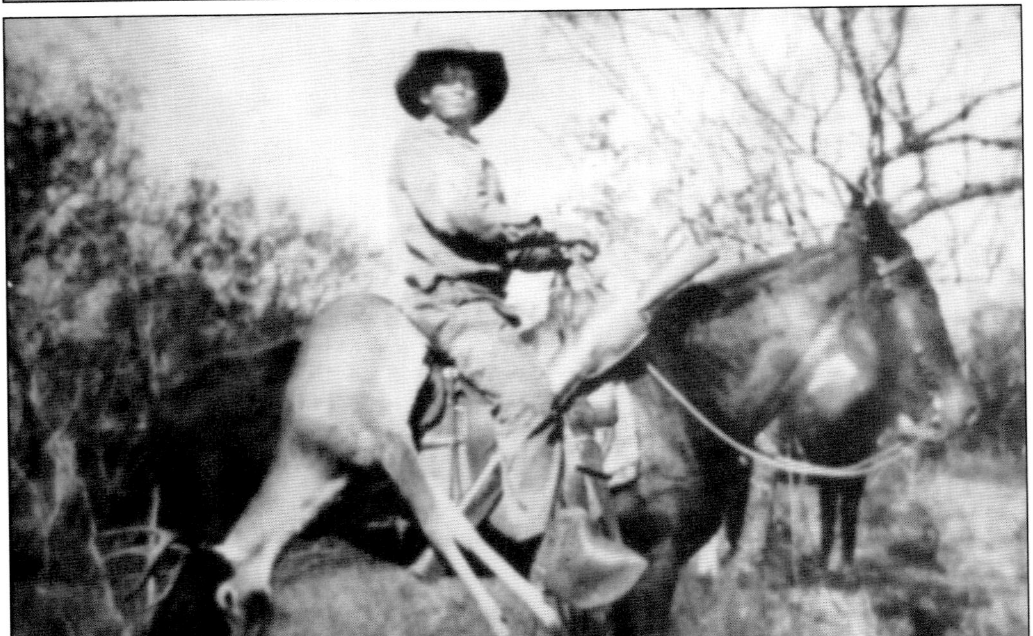

As Caldwell Calvert grew up, he became quite a horseman. He often rode Karnes City Jim. As shown in another image, that horse was featured in races that often went through the middle of town.

Sheriff for more than 20 years and succeeding E.C. Seale, J.F. (Jim) Brown owned Karnes City Jim.

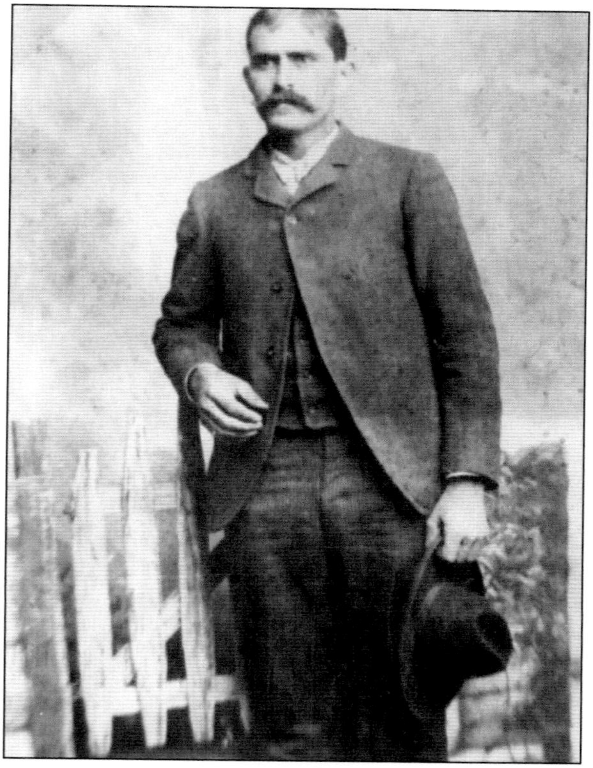

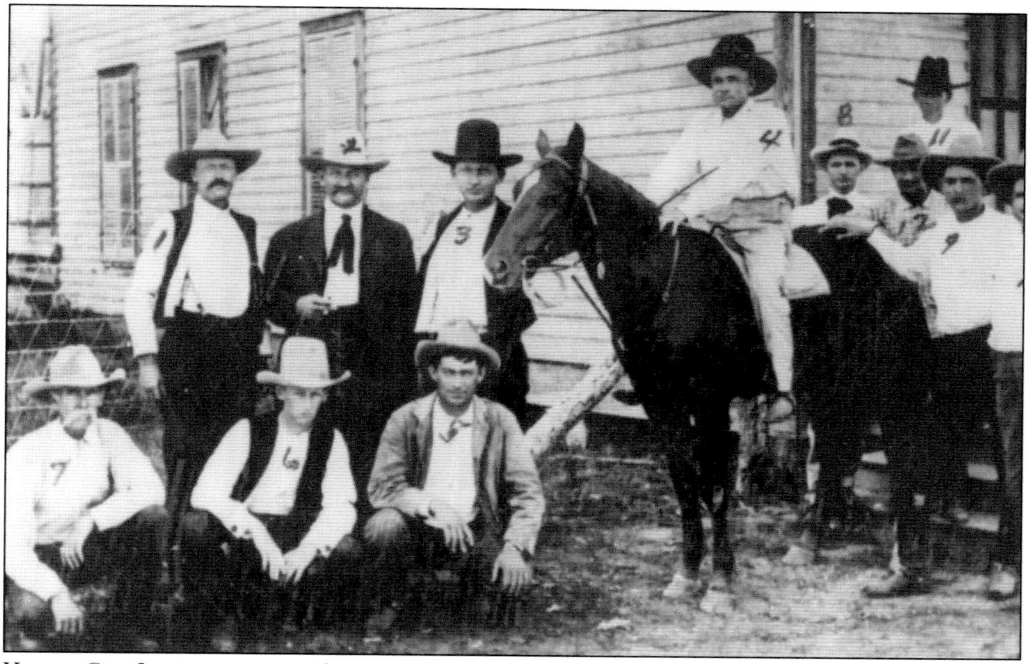

Karnes City Jim is getting ready to race. The rider is Jess Parsons. In front of the horse, from left to right, are Mr. Jones, Jim Seals, Mr. Wilder, Sylvester Shoat, Calaway Seals, and John Elder. Behind them are Bob Lewis and Mr. Jones. Others were not identified.

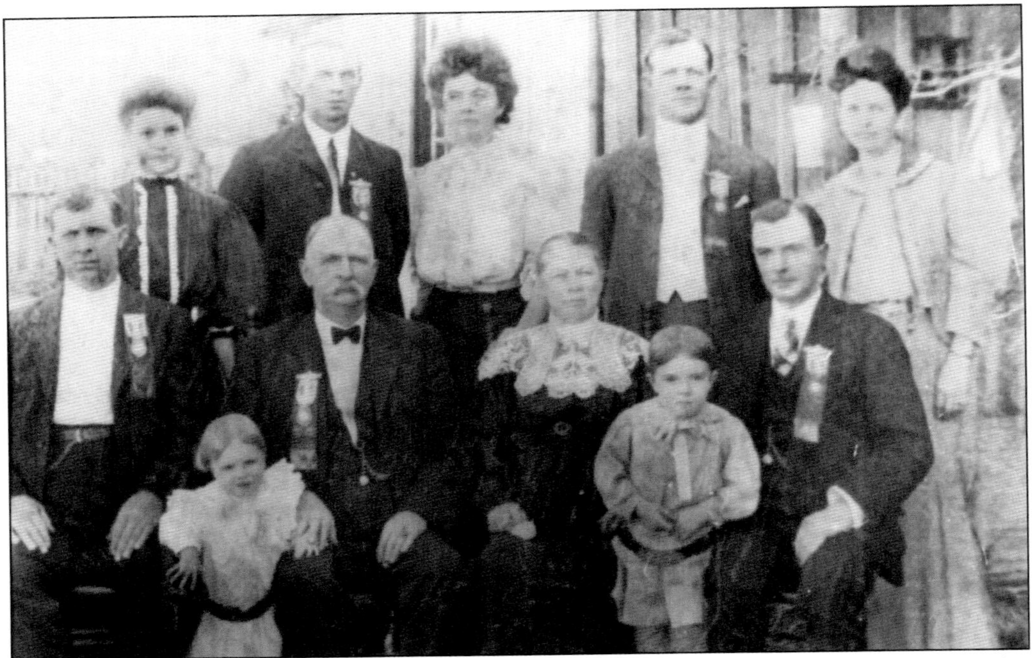

Members of the Tobin family, closely related to the Calverts, are pictured here. From left to right, are (first row) Allen Tobin, Allen Tobin, Lang C. Tobin, Georgia Archer Tobin, Harold Tobin, and John F. Tobin; (second row) Bessie Hall Tobin, Frank Calvert, Lucian Tobin Calvert, Lee Tobin, and Sally Mayfield Tobin.

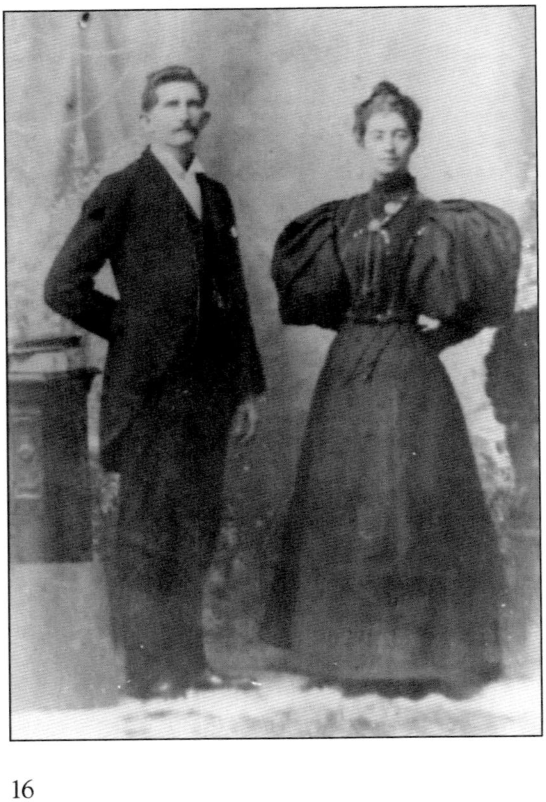

Mamie Whetstone, 17 years old, is pictured with her father.

Molly, Sarah, and Virginia Johnson dressed up for this formal portrait.

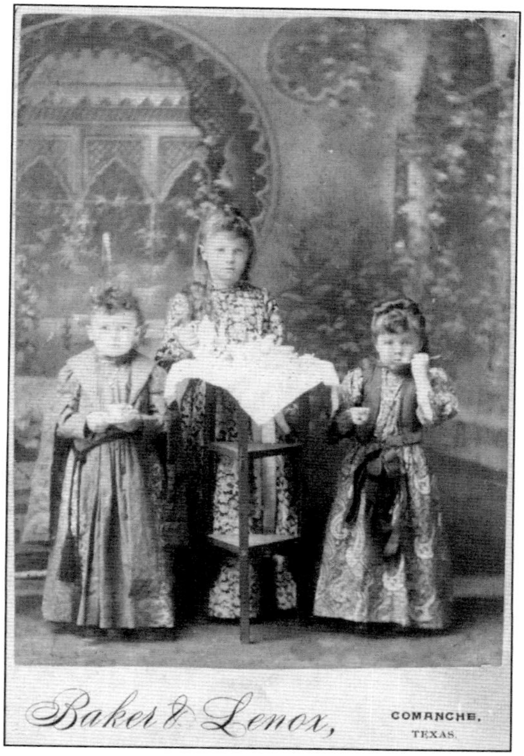

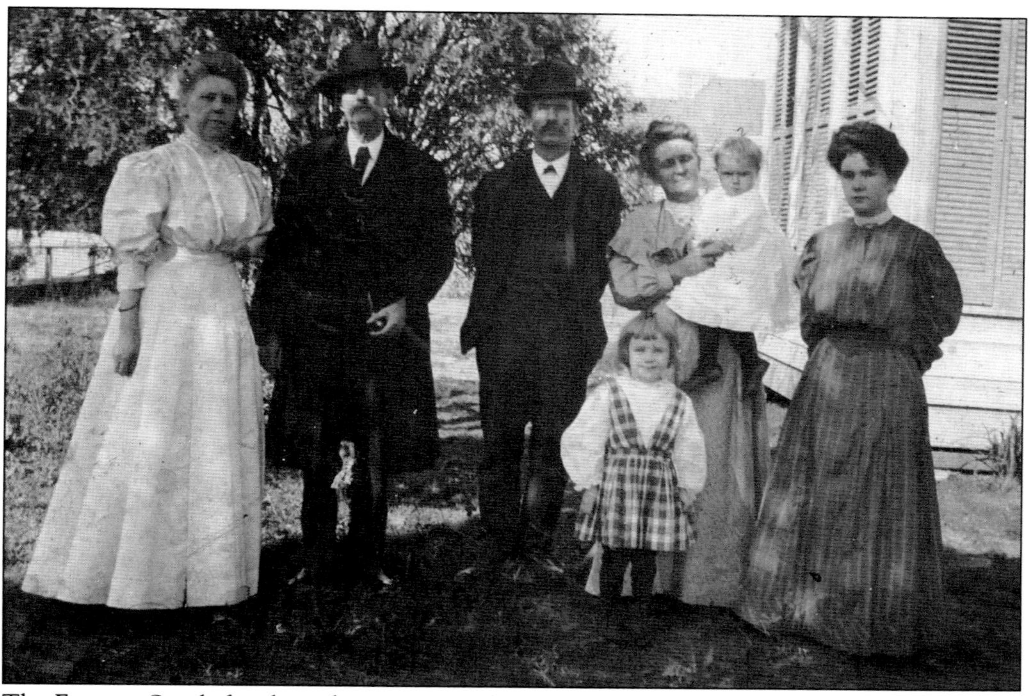

The Emmett Smith family strikes a pose in their backyard, dressed in their finest attire. They were relatives of Mason Johnson.

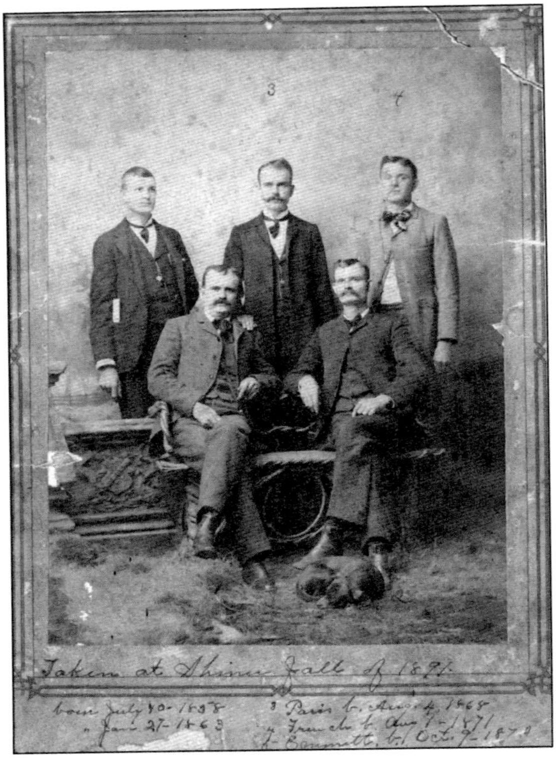

This is a group photograph of the Smith brothers, all born in the 1850s and 1860s. Guy, Cloyd, Paris, French, and Emmett were all uncles of Mason Johnson.

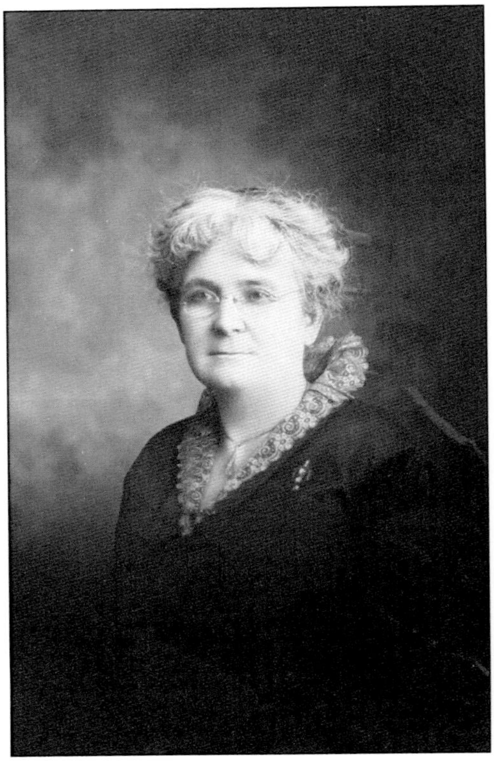

Pictured to the right is the Smith brothers' sister and Mason's mother, Carrie Smith Johnson.

Another member of the Smith family, Merrill, joined his relatives here early on, before moving to Seguin.

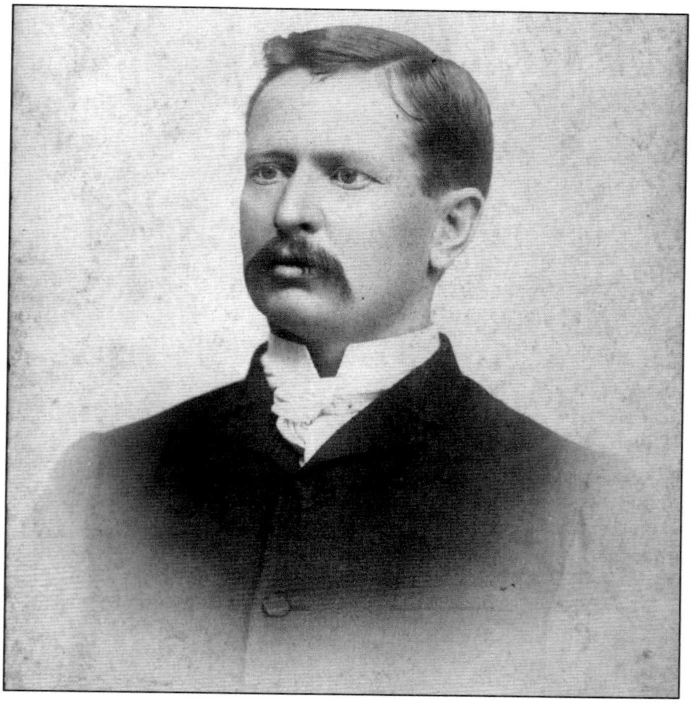

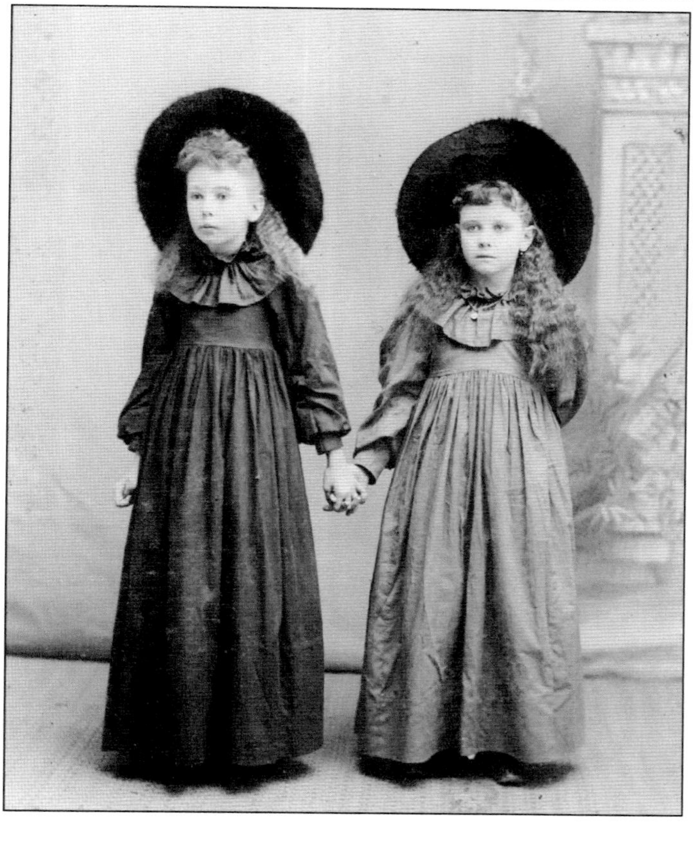

Merrill Smith's daughters Theresa and Susan loved to dress up to have their picture taken.

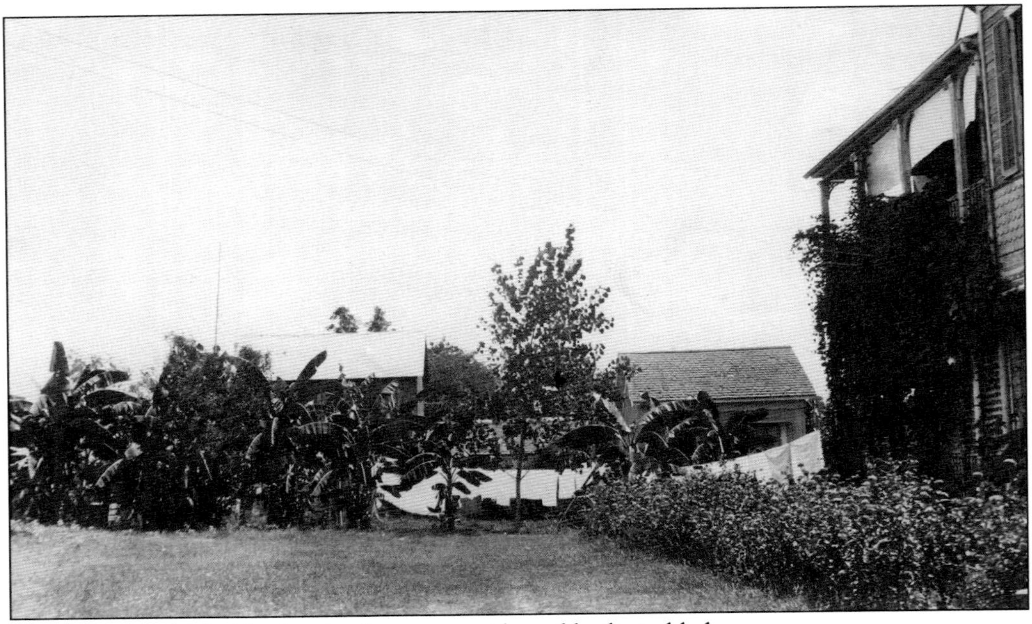

Some families settled farther in the countryside and built sizable homes.

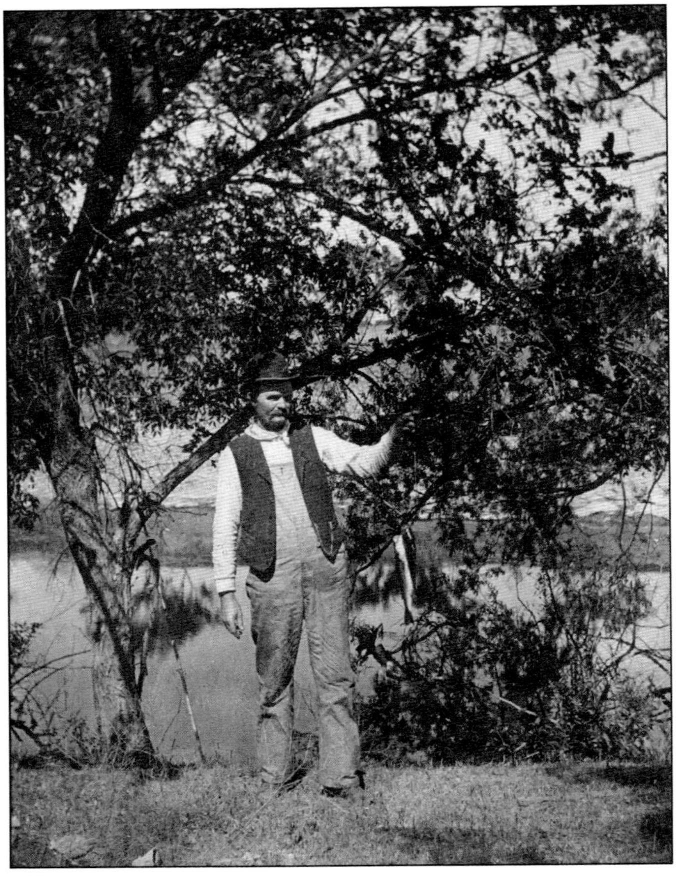

Karnes County was continuing to welcome newcomers as they braved any raids or aggression that might still occur from time to time.

Two

Hardships with Indian and Spanish Aggression

Several battles took place in the early days of Karnes County that involved the newly arriving settlers. One of the earliest battles was over a well-traveled trail that ran through Helena, called the Chihuahua Road or Ox-Cart Trail. This road had been a main artery for those moving from south of San Antonio through the Goliad La Bahia area to the Gulf Coast. And it was filled with much commerce of wagon freight, including gold bullion and one of the founders of Helena, Dr. Lewis Owings's own stage line of four horse coaches. The fight that took place was called the Cart War, between Mexican drivers and their Anglo opponents. The governor at that time, Elisha Pease, called out the early Texas Rangers in hopes of keeping the peace. But, as more often than not, frontier justice prevailed, with lynchings or other forms of solutions being handled on the spot. Karnes County' troubles with the Comanches did not stop, in spite of Henry's skillful negotiations with the ferocious tribe. One of the fiercest battles took place just outside of Karnes County on Plum Creek. It pushed the Indians farther south and west, but they did not give up. Even before the Plum Creek battle, the Spanish had tried to control the raids on their settlements by building several small outposts or forts, including one within Karnes County along the Cibolo Creek. It was called El Fuerte del Cibolo and was first occupied by the Spanish in 1734. Its ruins, not far from Brockman's Crossing on the Cibolo, are now recognized with a historical marker. It gives evidence of the hardships in settling the new frontier.

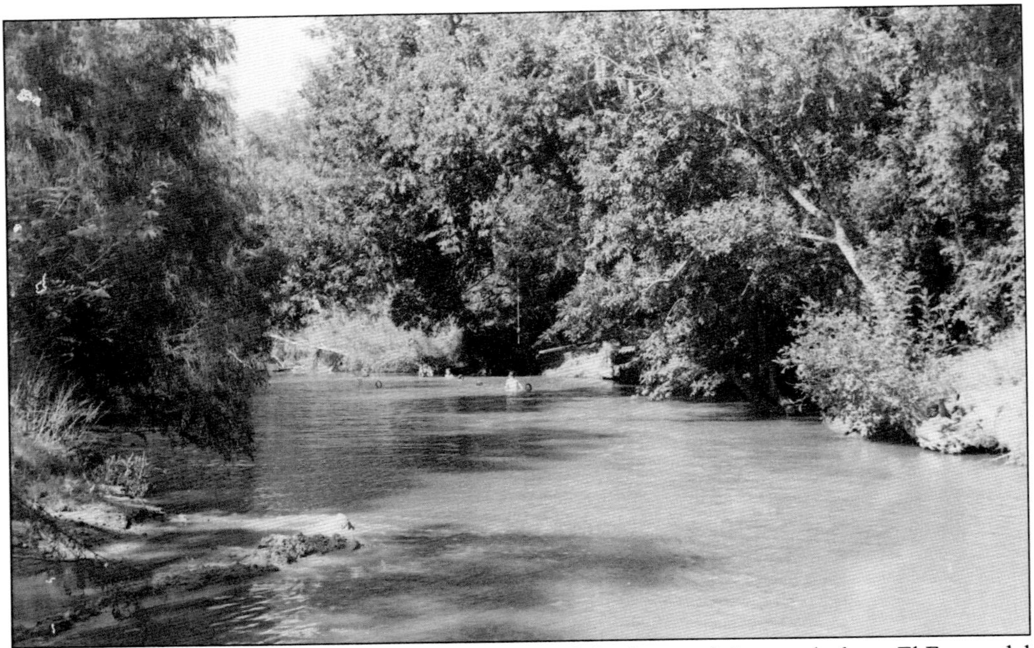

Brockman's Crossing, situated near where the Spanish built one of their early forts, El Fuerte del Cibolo, in an effort to control Indian aggression, had little effect, especially on the Comanches. The crossing did give early settlers a better place to cross the Cibolo Creek to get from one settlement to another.

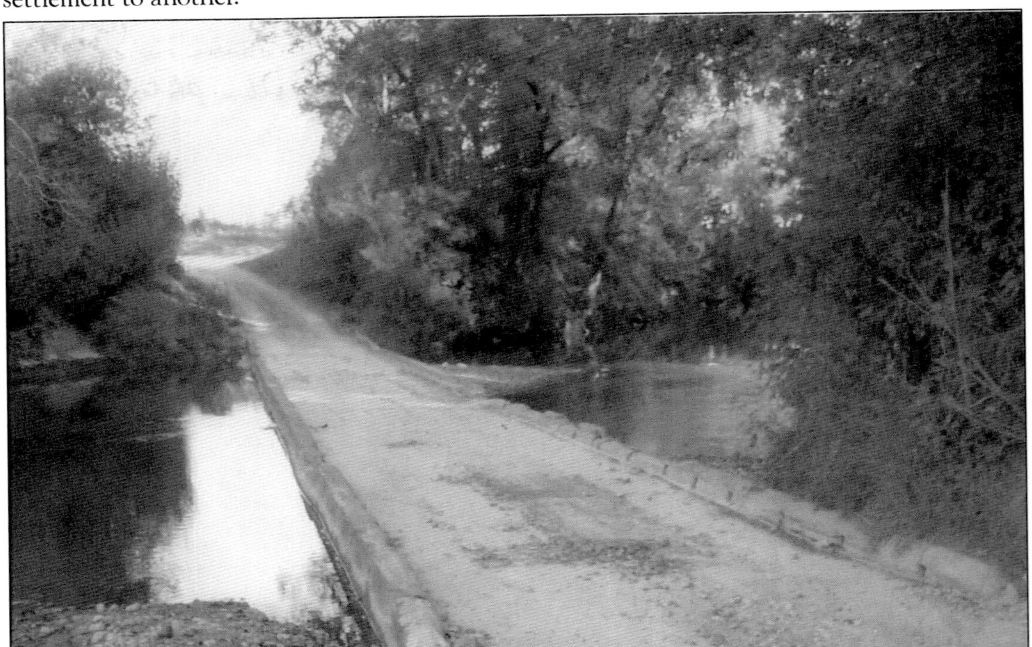

Later, the crossing was used as part of the trail for cattle drives. Inaccessible ruins of the fort are said to still be at that site. After the paving across the Cibolo at Brockman's, it became a favorite picnic spot in later years and still is today.

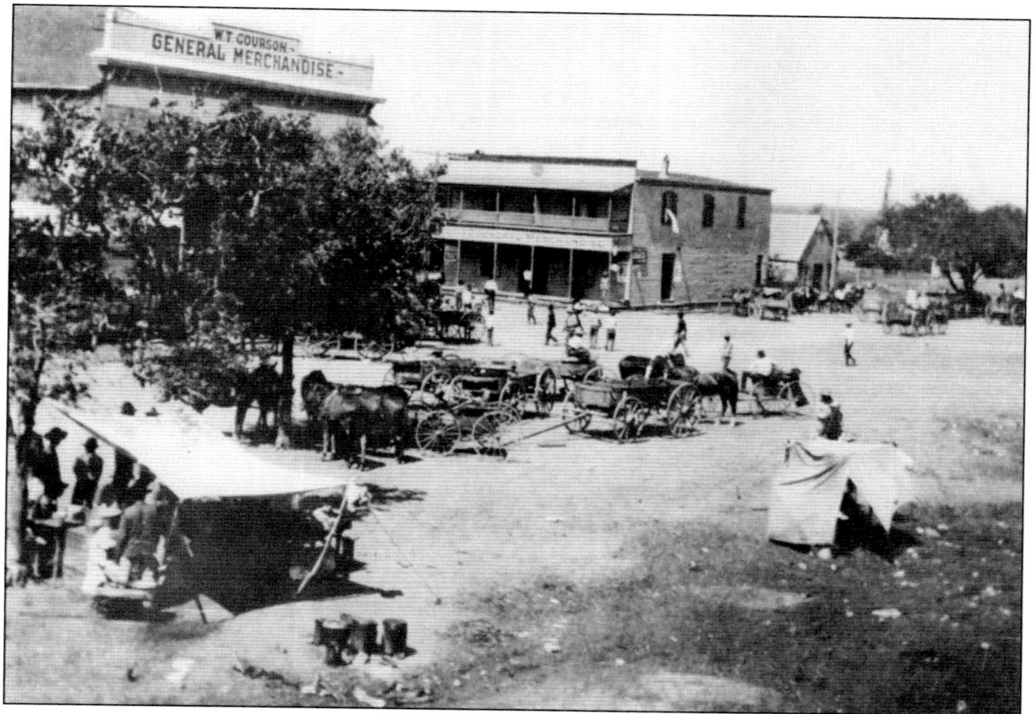

More ox carts and buggies could also be found in Kenedy. It was one of the early cities to grow, due to early settlers coming to Karnes County. The Cart War that happened in Helena between the Anglo and Mexican cart owners traveling the Oxcart Trail was settled with the help of the governor at that time, Elisha Pease, and some early Texas Rangers.

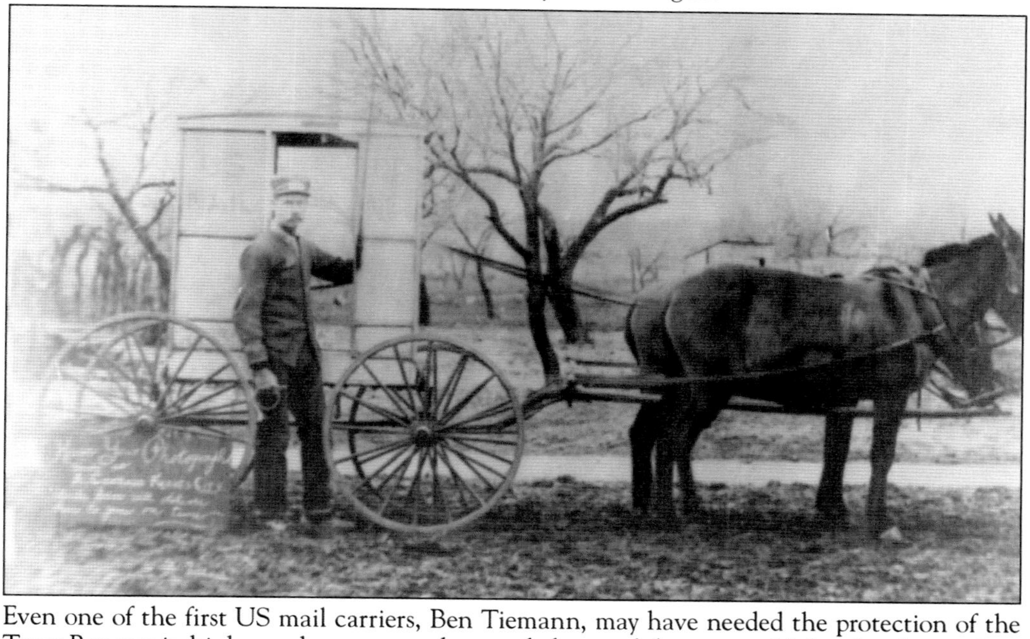

Even one of the first US mail carriers, Ben Tiemann, may have needed the protection of the Texas Rangers in his horse-drawn cart as he traveled around the county. He has family members that still live in Karnes County.

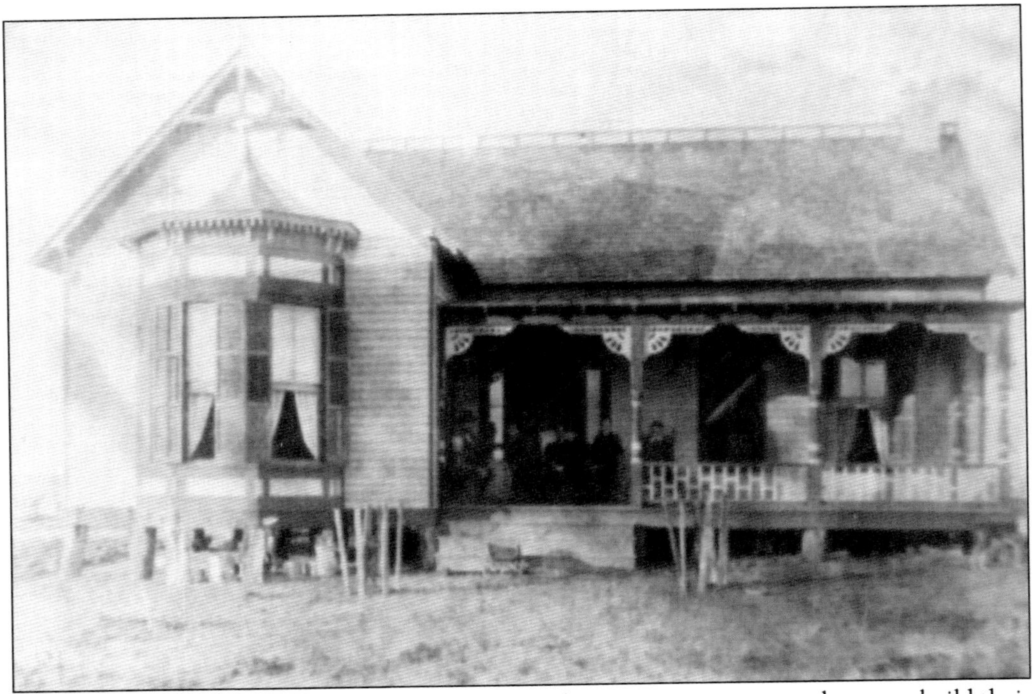

Although a lot of the hostilities that settlers had to face were not over, some began to build their homes both in the towns and out in the country. One of the earliest homes built in Karnes City was the Seale home, shown here.

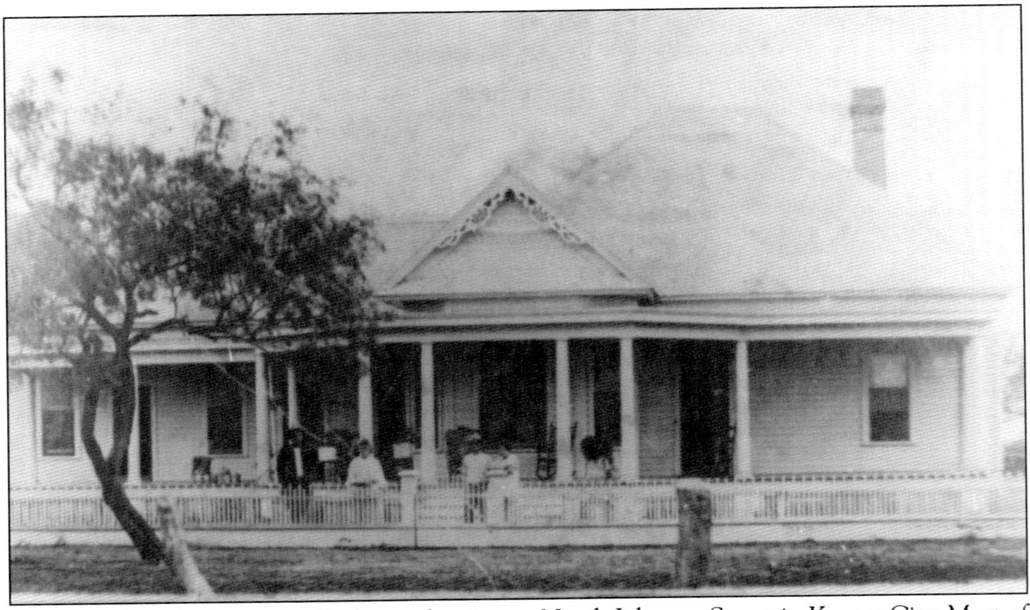

The Alfred Taylor home was built on what is now North Johnson Street in Karnes City. Most of the very earliest homes are no longer in existence.

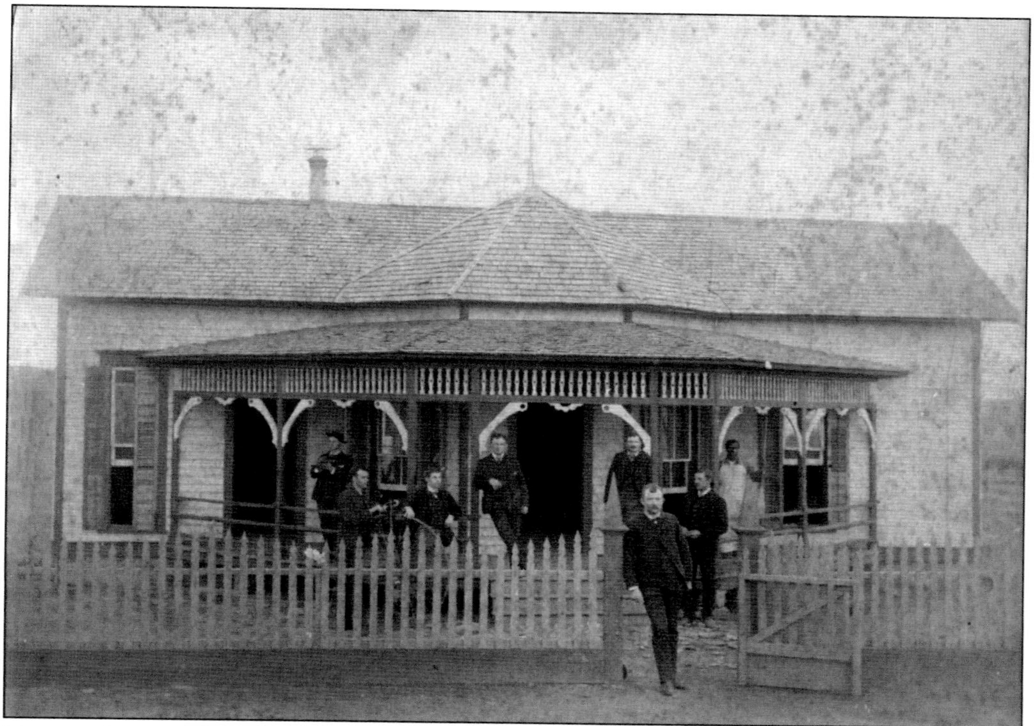

Men are shown gathered on a front porch of a country home in 1854. This image was part of the Smith family collection of their early history.

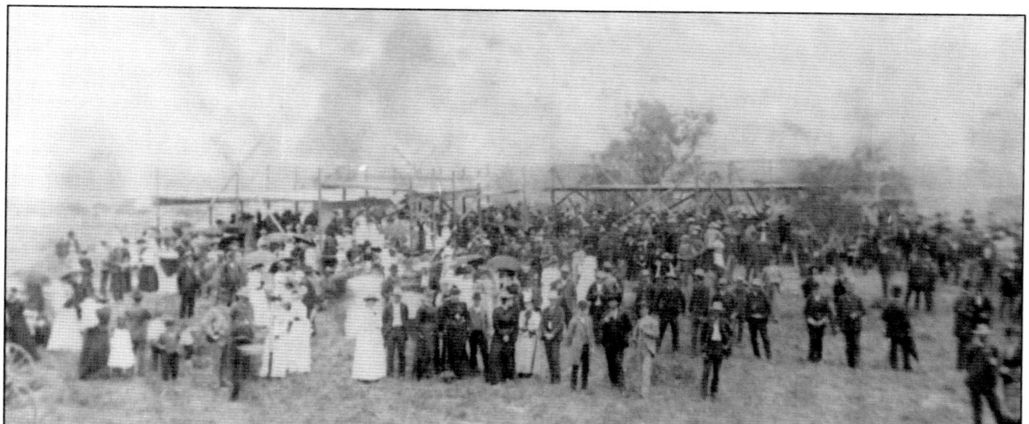

Several years after Karnes City had attracted its first settlers, a gathering was held in conjunction with a barbecue given by city promoters. A drawing was held for single lots from numbered blocks. As pictured, it was quite successful.

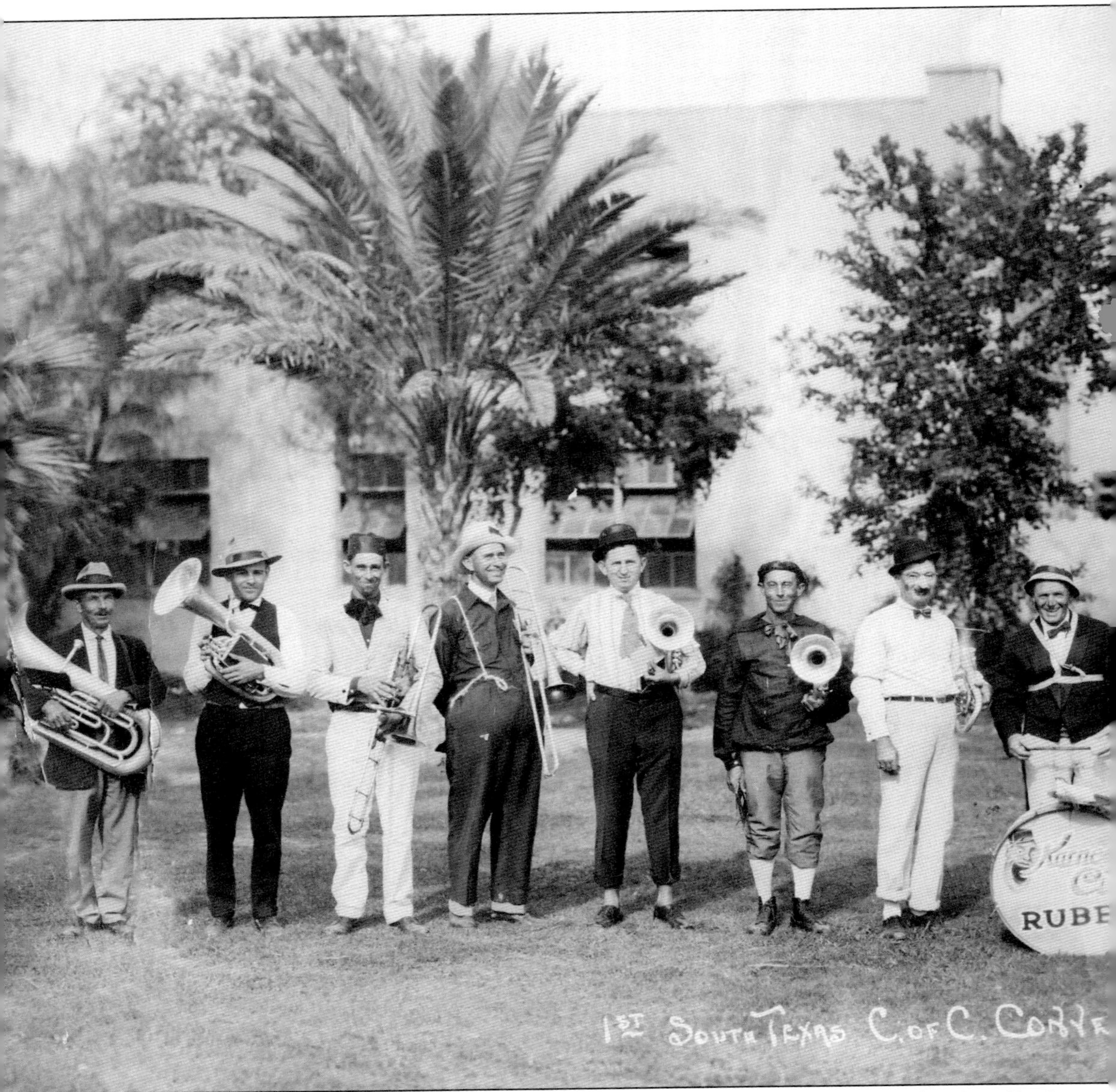

The Rube Band was making a name for itself by 1927. They were featured on the Pathe News Reel at the Texas Theatre in San Antonio. From left to right are Hans Wernli, Milton Keorner, Ed Weigang, Alfred Brieger, J.P. (Jimmy) Rohan, Joe Hons, Hal Lakey, H.J. Niehaus, Tom Polasek,

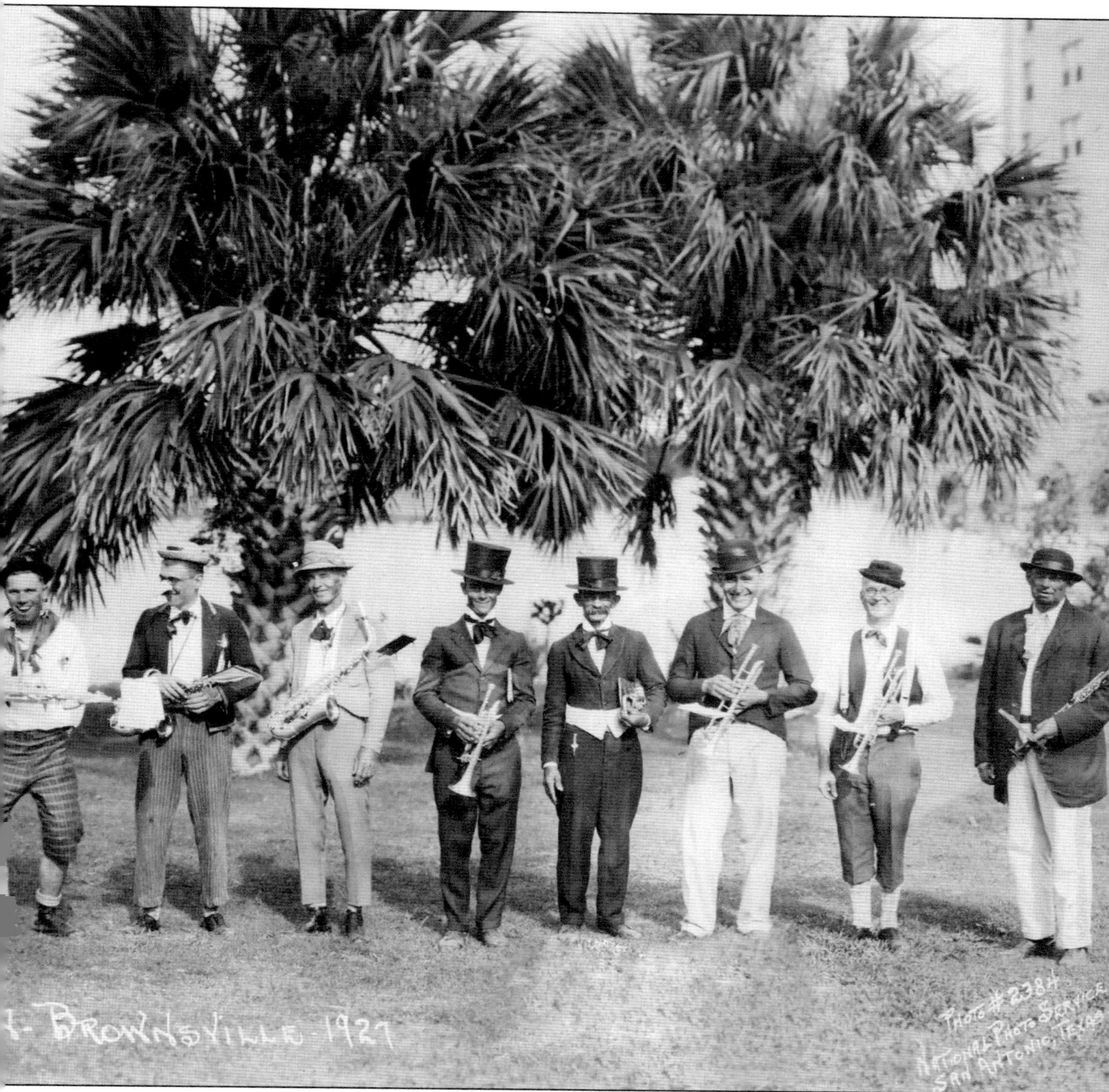

Alvin A. Salge, A.W. McGall, George Weigang, H.J. (Joe) Weigang, Mr. Willard, Mac Miculka, and Mr. Brieger.

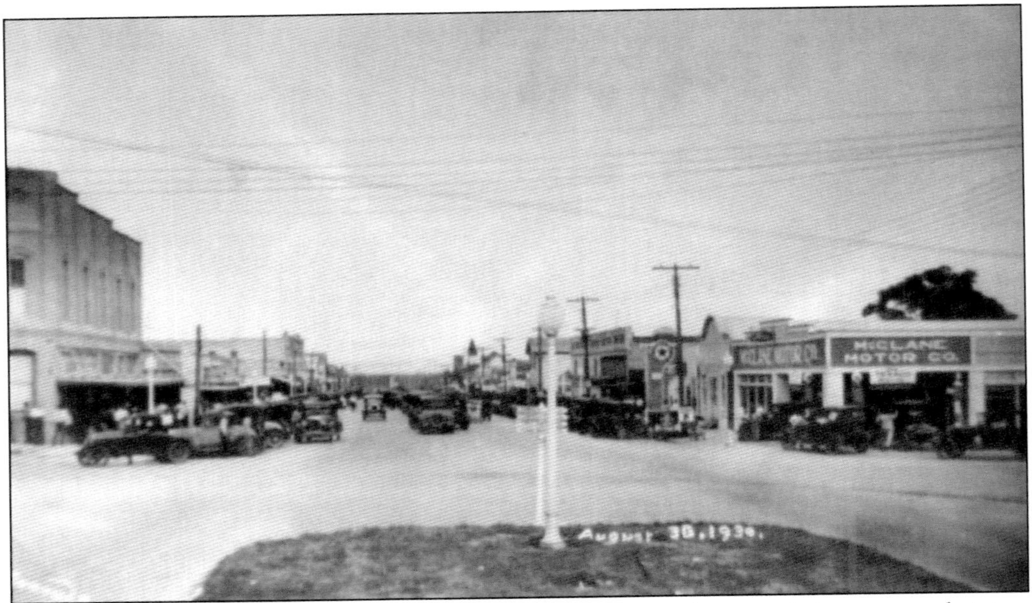

Looking down Calvert Avenue from the courthouse, one can see how much the city was thriving. Note the grassy island and lampposts.

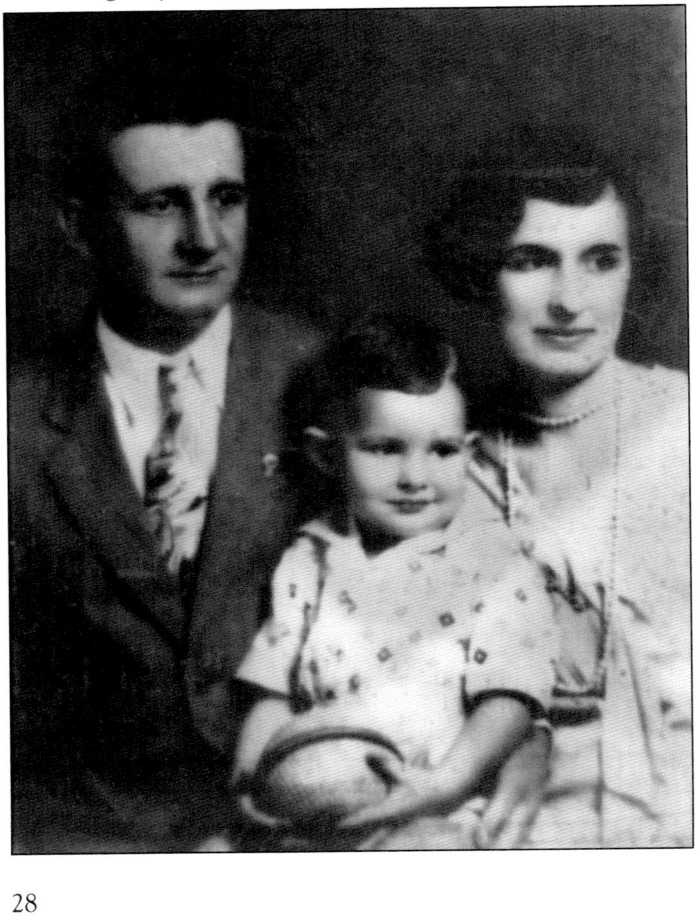

About this time, the Oliver G. Abbott family was arriving and living in Karnes City. They owned and operated a grocery store on the corner of Calvert and Browne Streets for many years.

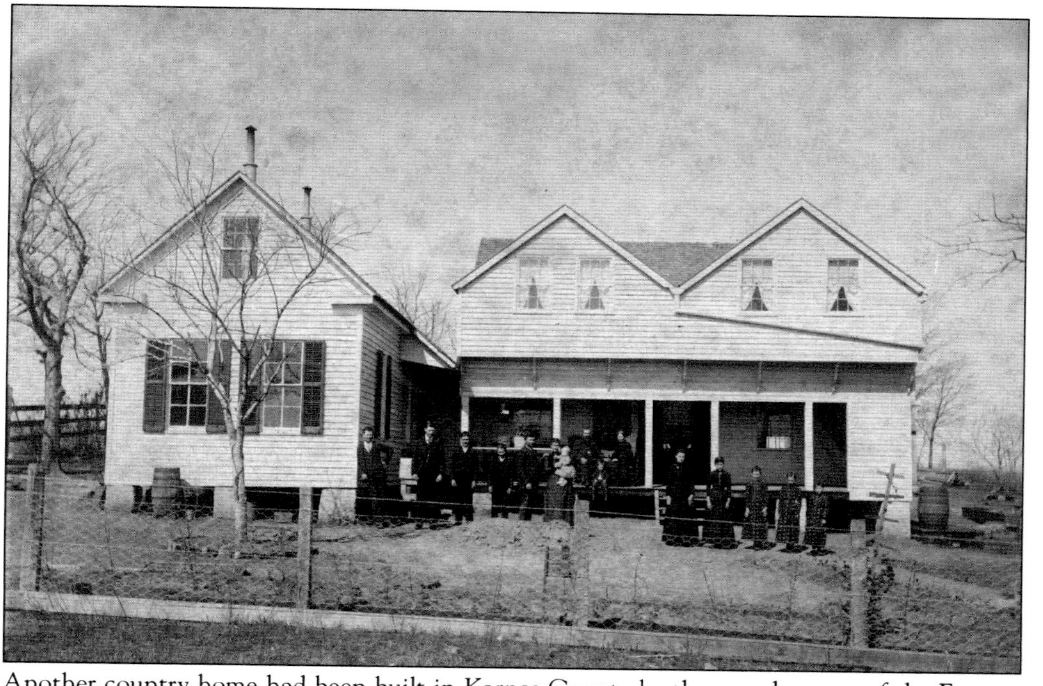

Another country home had been built in Karnes County by the grandparents of the Fenner-Shortner family.

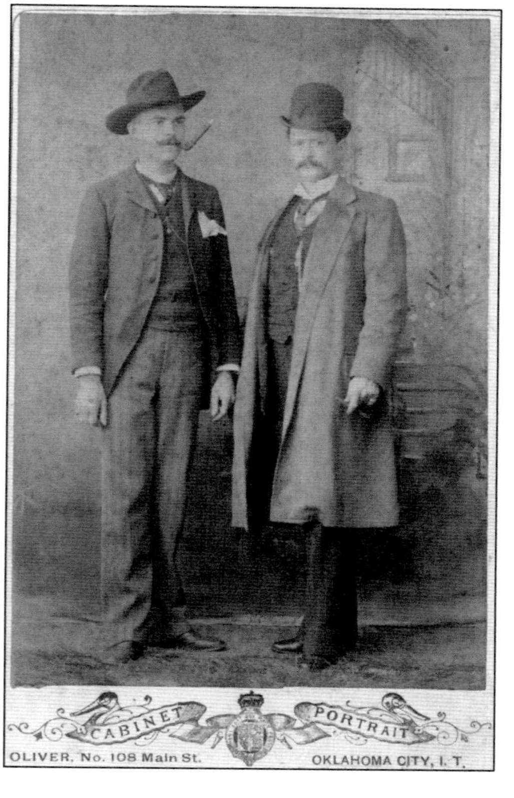

Two gentlemen, Frank Butt and Paris Smith, are ready to face the future in their city attire.

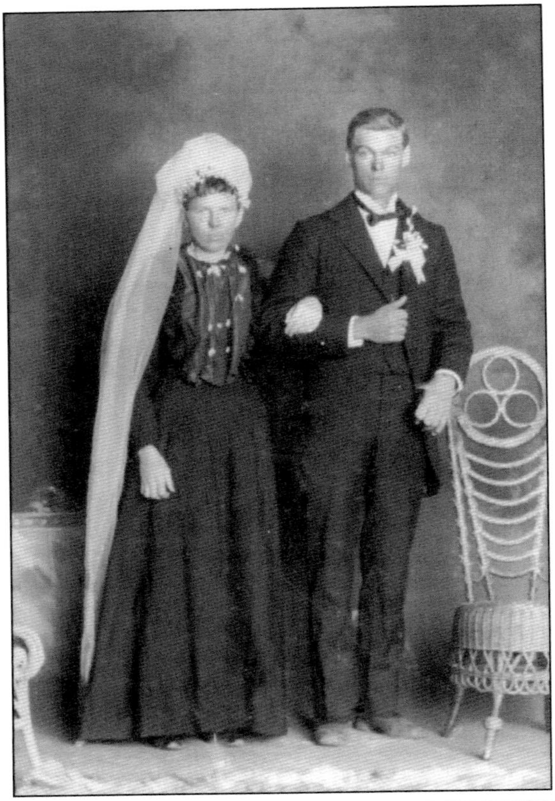

Despite some of the native unrest that occasionally occurred, couples were beginning to feel secure enough to get married. Fritz and Alma Renee Fenner were wed in 1898.

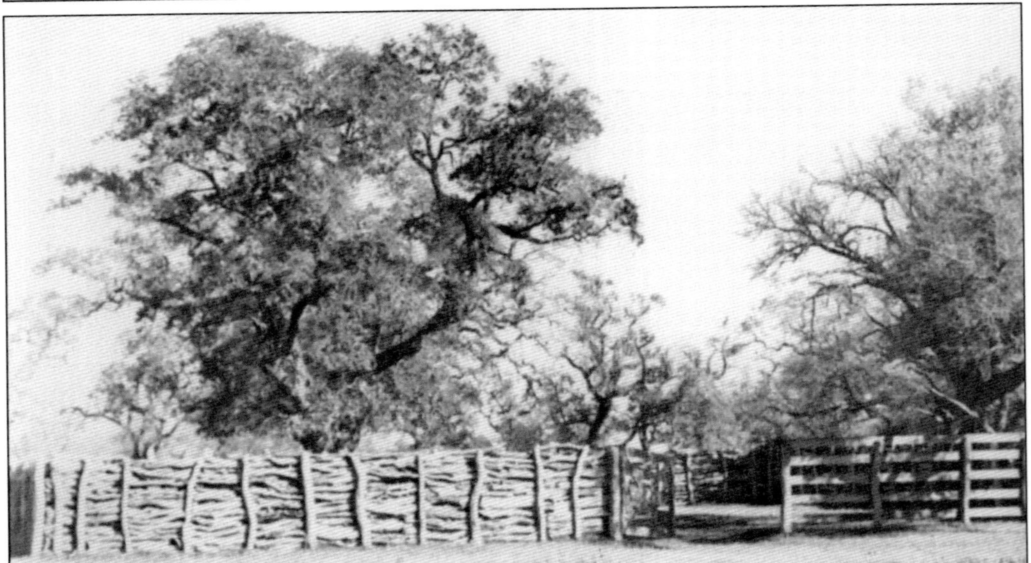

Just as everything that the early settlers had to build was extra hard to do, so were the pens and corrals that were cut and made from logs. The results could truly be works of art, just as the one shown in the picture above. They were built to last.

Three

Earliest Settlers Arrive

The many hardships greeting settlers upon arrival often paled in their struggles just to get here and settle in Texas, having gone through worse times. In 1854, 100 Polish families arrived in Karnes County. They were one of the first groups of families to arrive. Through the direction and encouragement of Father Leopold Moczygamba, they settled on 300 acres of land between the San Antonio River and Cibolo Creek. It was purchased from landowner John Twohig. These families left the Silesian Region of Prussia as Napoleon's conquest rolled through their homeland, negating any rights to live with long held customs and religious beliefs. Arriving in Karnes County, they named their new settlement Panna Maria (Virgin Mary) and celebrated their first communion under a large oak tree. They soon began to build a beautiful stone church in the first permanent Polish community in the United States. Ruins and remnants of the first stone buildings remain today. Other ethnic groups, some from the same Silesian region, largely German and Czech populations, also found their way to Karnes County. They established small communities such as Czestohowa, Hobson, Falls City, Kosciusko, and Pawelekville. St. Joseph's, the first Polish school established in Panna Maria, was constructed in 1866. The Nativity of the Blessed Virgin Mary Church in Czestohowa was also constructed. The families began establishing their lives in their new country, and brought what their families had long treasured to share with their new countrymen, including a recipe for sausage that was brought over by Marcian and Mary Pollok. It did not take long for a demand for their sausages to grow and a family business to take root and flourish in Falls City. The family continues to make use of their delicious family recipe as their business has grown. Each ethnic group settled into the life of Karnes County as new Texans. They established other churches, including some of the earliest churches built in Karnes County, such as the Baptist, Methodist, Lutheran, Presbyterian, Episcopalian, and Pentecostal, in addition to the Catholic churches.

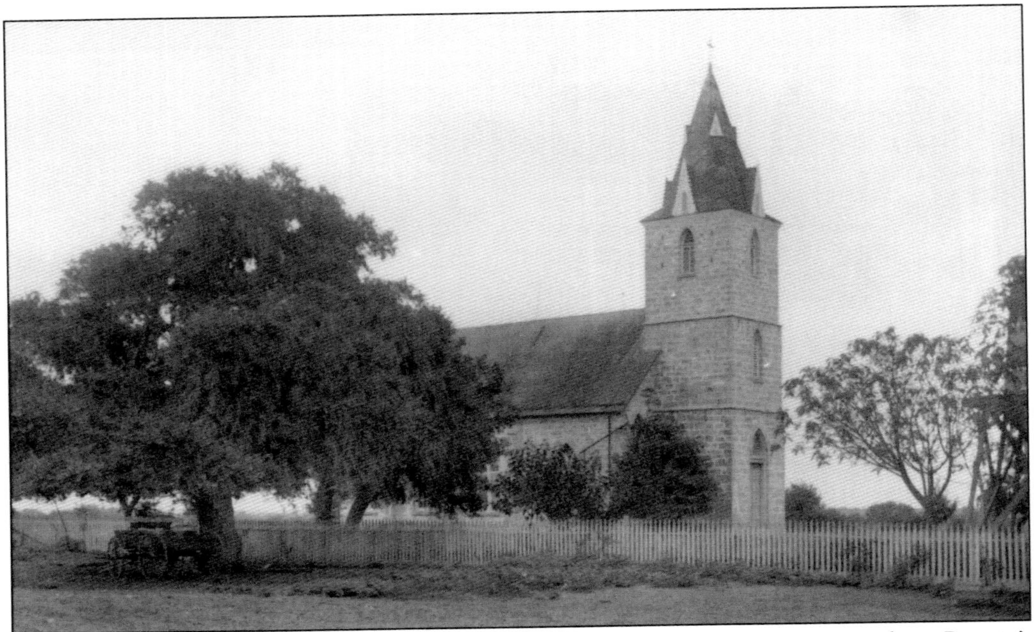

As settlers arrived from all over, they included the first Polish families to come from Prussia's Silesian region. One of the first things they did was construct their church in 1854. It was destroyed in a severe thunderstorm and later rebuilt.

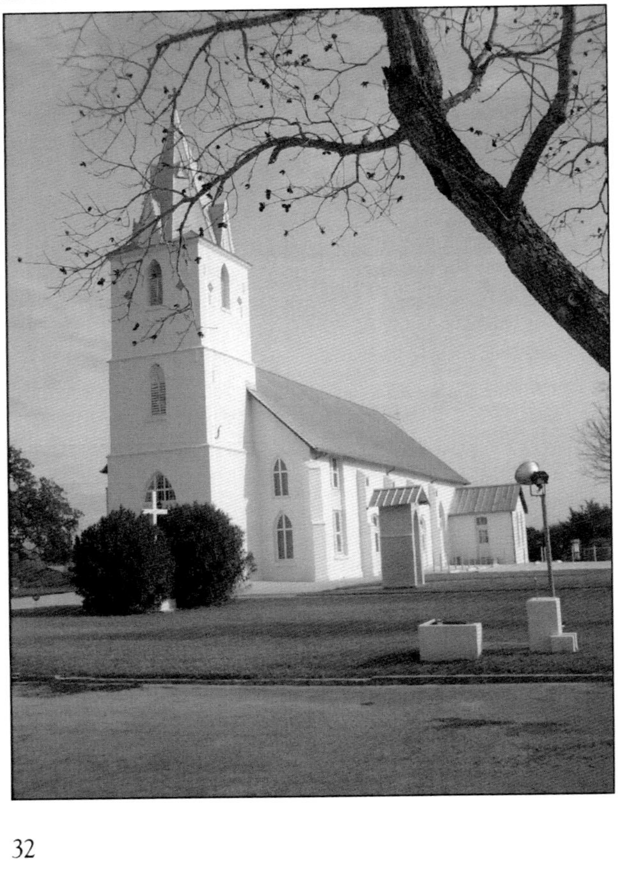

St. Mary's Church is pictured as it is today. Under the tutelage of Father Leopold Moczygamba, many others who formed nearby communities, such as Czestohowa, Hobson, and Falls City, joined the first families.

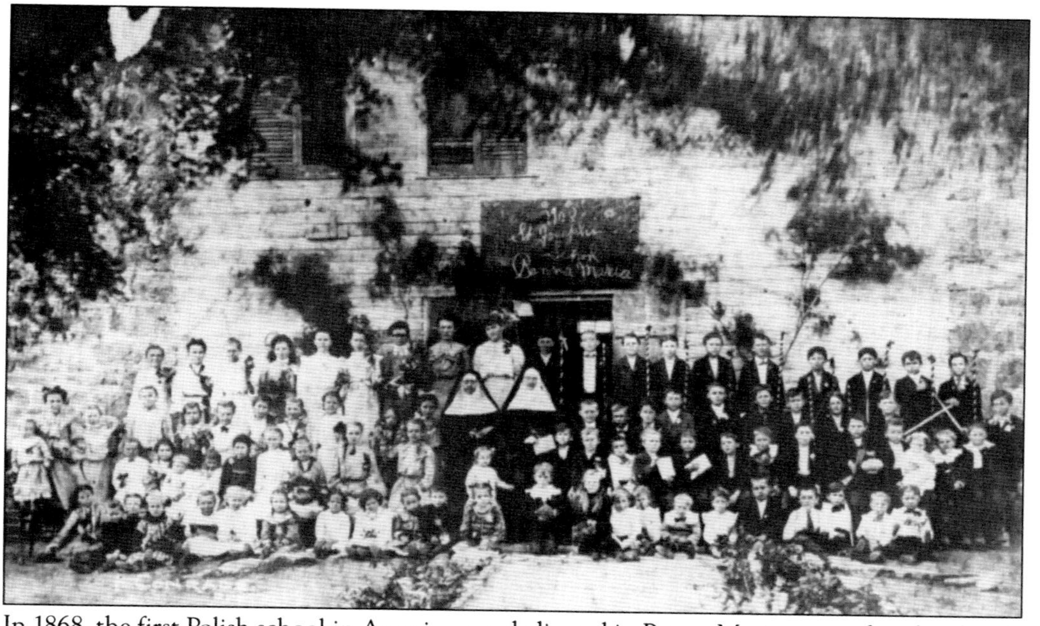

In 1868, the first Polish school in America was dedicated in Panna Maria, soon after the church was completed. In 1866, before the school opened its doors, Father Felix Zwiardowski taught classes in a barn with 32 pupils. The Catholic Order of Sisters taught at St. Joseph's until the middle of the 20th century.

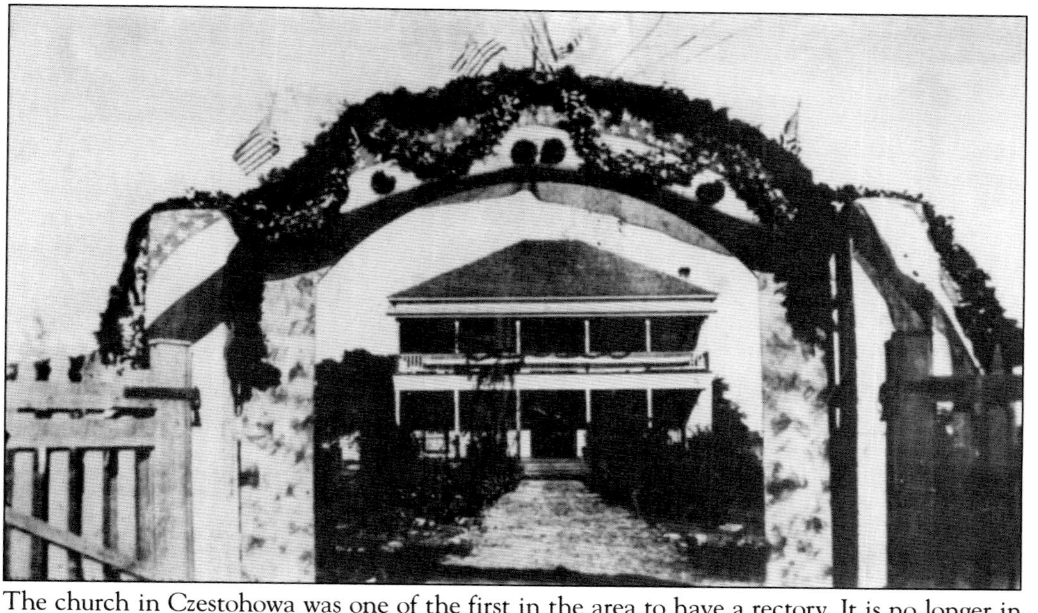

The church in Czestohowa was one of the first in the area to have a rectory. It is no longer in existence. The beautiful gates and entrance were ornately decorated.

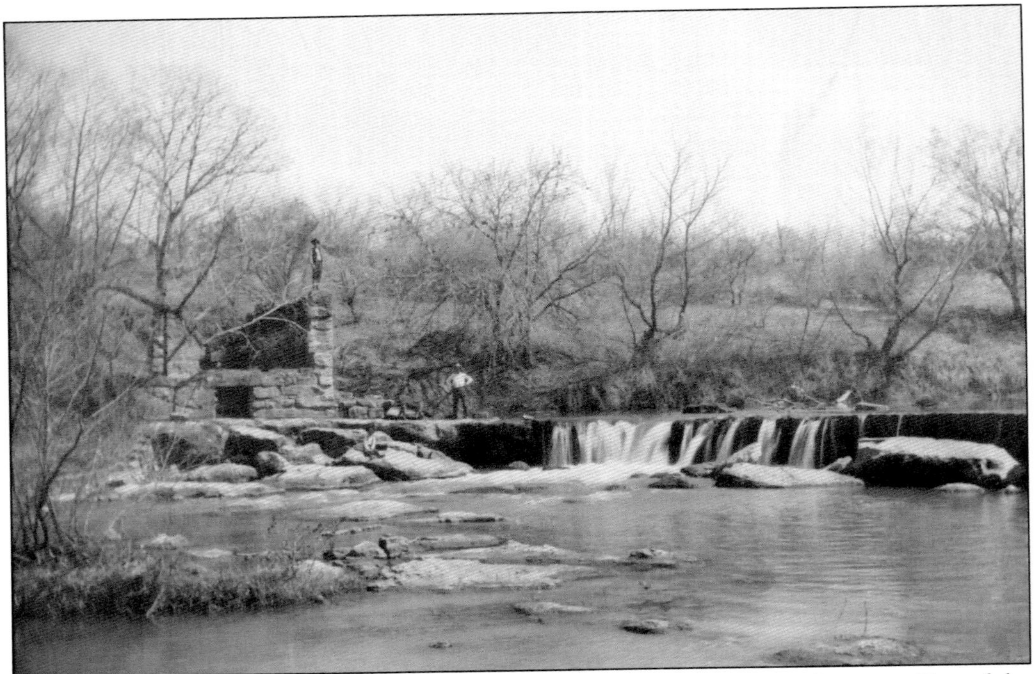

Falls City was named after the Mills Falls, on the San Antonio River near the town. One of the early Polish families, the Polloks, made their home here. They brought with them a delicious sausage recipe that they began to use and shared the results with their friends and neighbors.

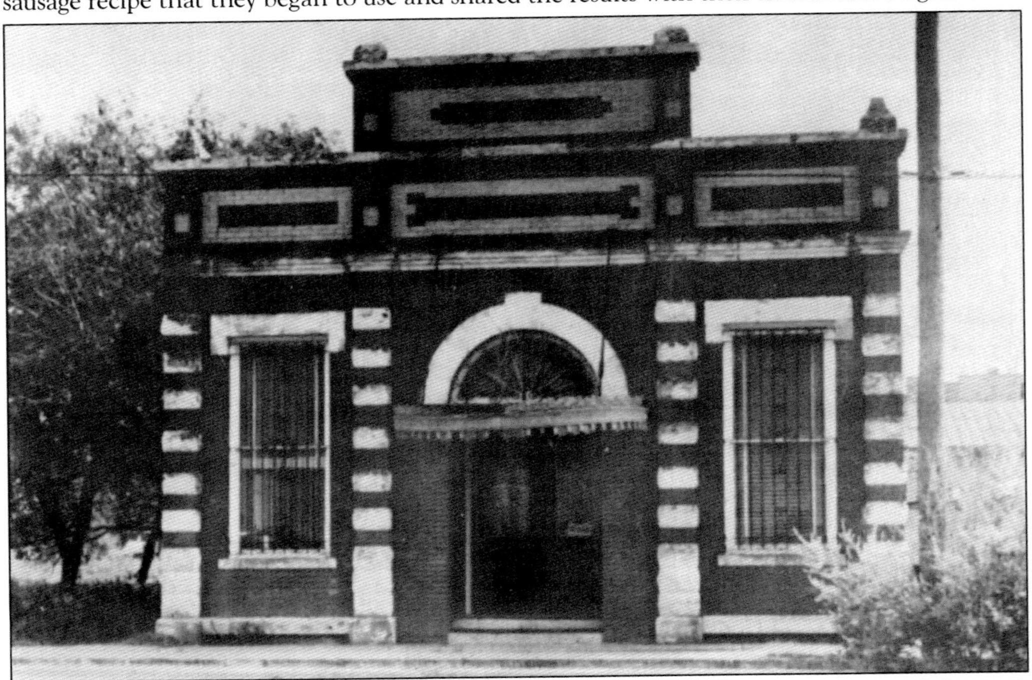

The founding of the Falls City National Bank in 1907 was made possible because of the city's growth due to being on the railroad line. The advantageous location enabled the city to grow while others declined.

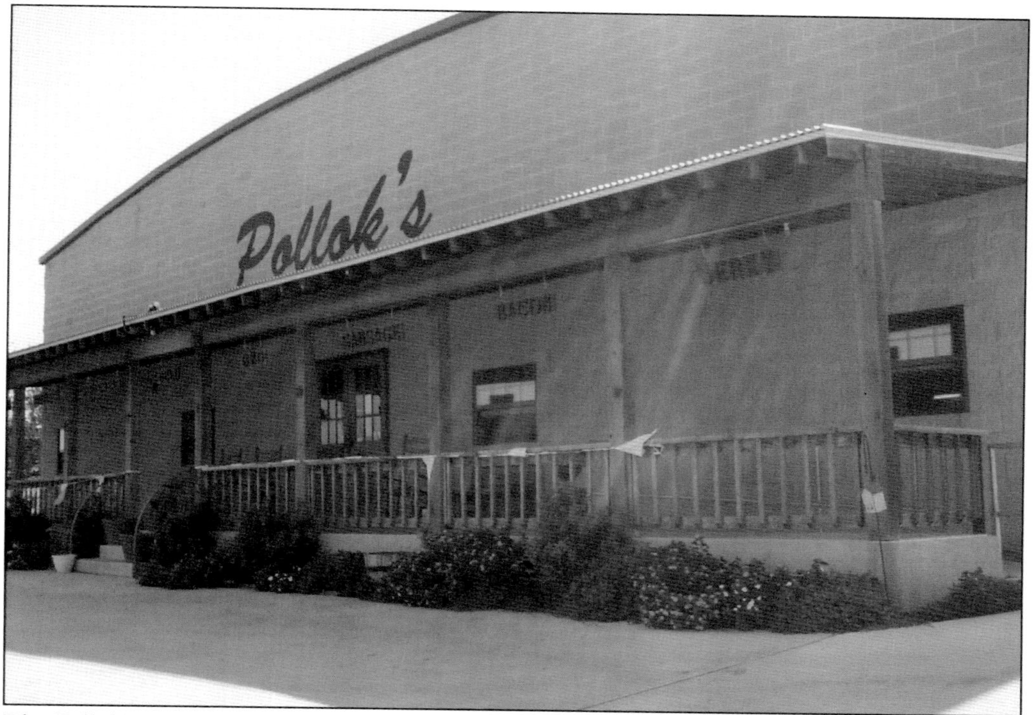

The Pollok's store had to expand as the demand for their sausages grew. Ever since it was first made, it has grown into a thriving business. Their sausages are now available in stores all over South Central Texas.

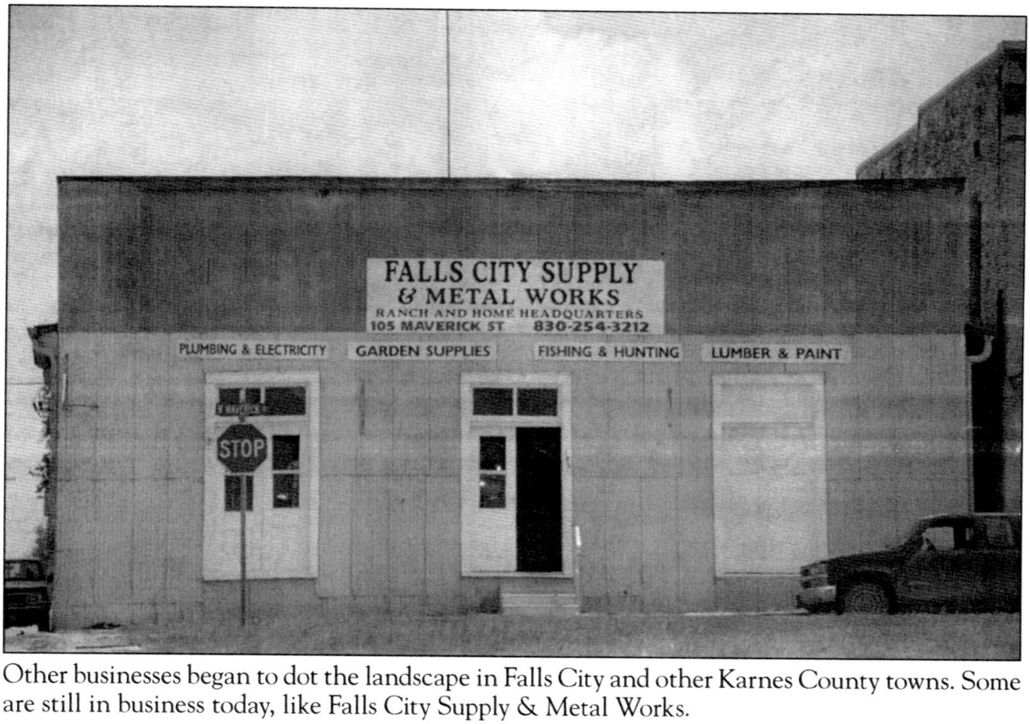

Other businesses began to dot the landscape in Falls City and other Karnes County towns. Some are still in business today, like Falls City Supply & Metal Works.

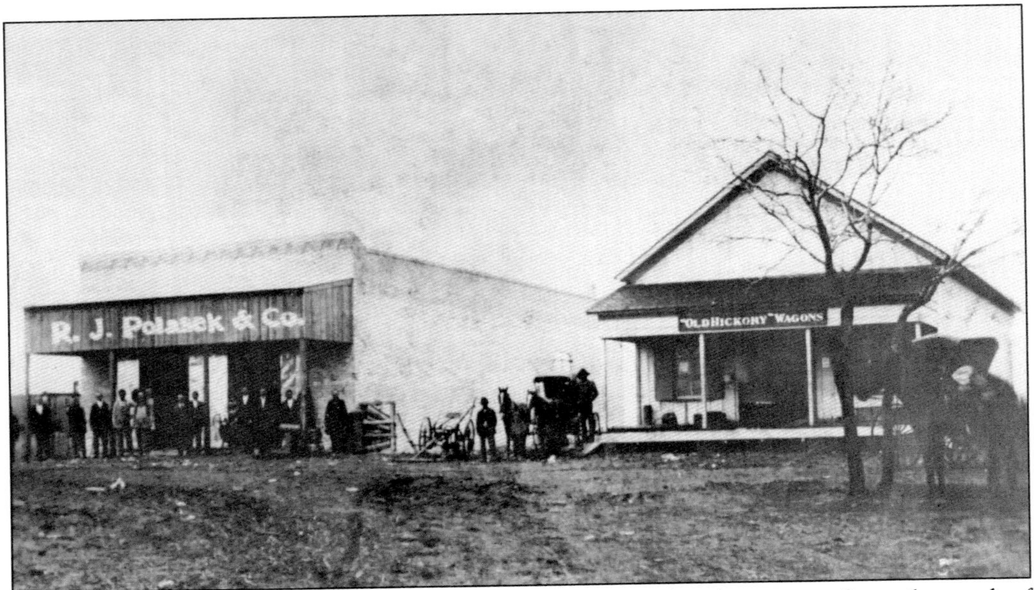

R.J. Polasek & Co., pictured, is actually in a small town named Hobson, just a few miles south of Falls City; it opened in 1895. Polasek became the postmaster here and eventually owned a gin, lumberyard, and a gristmill, as well as this store.

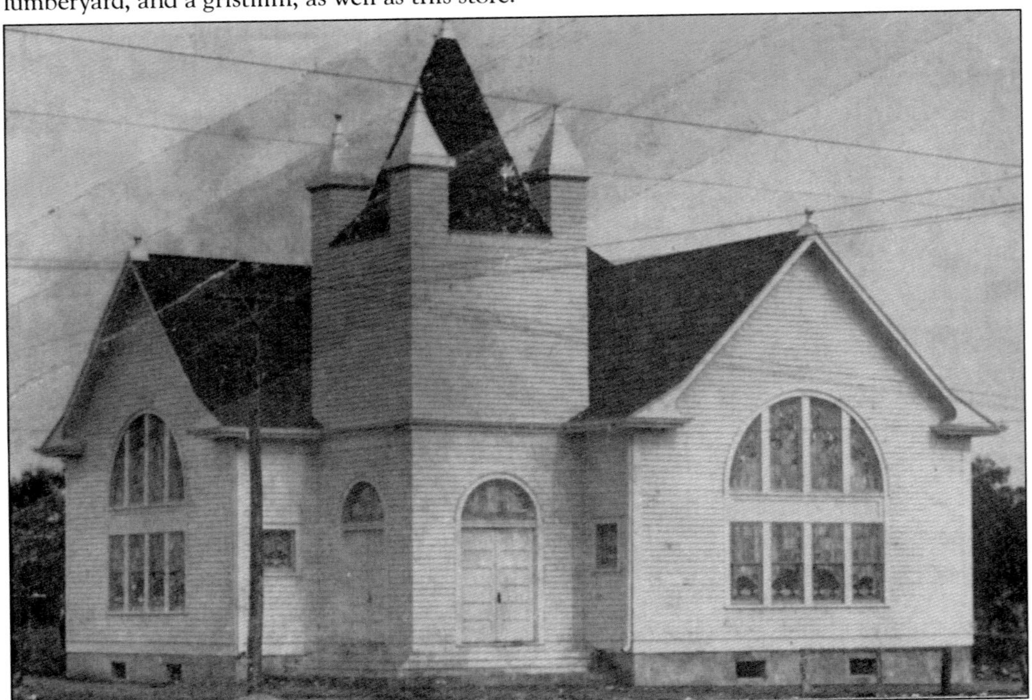

As all kinds of buildings were going up, so were the local churches, including the Catholic churches that were being built in Panna Maria and Czestohowa. One of the oldest in Karnes City is the First Baptist Church seen above. It was used for public school classrooms during the week until school buildings were constructed. It is also one of several in Karnes City to be designated with historical markers.

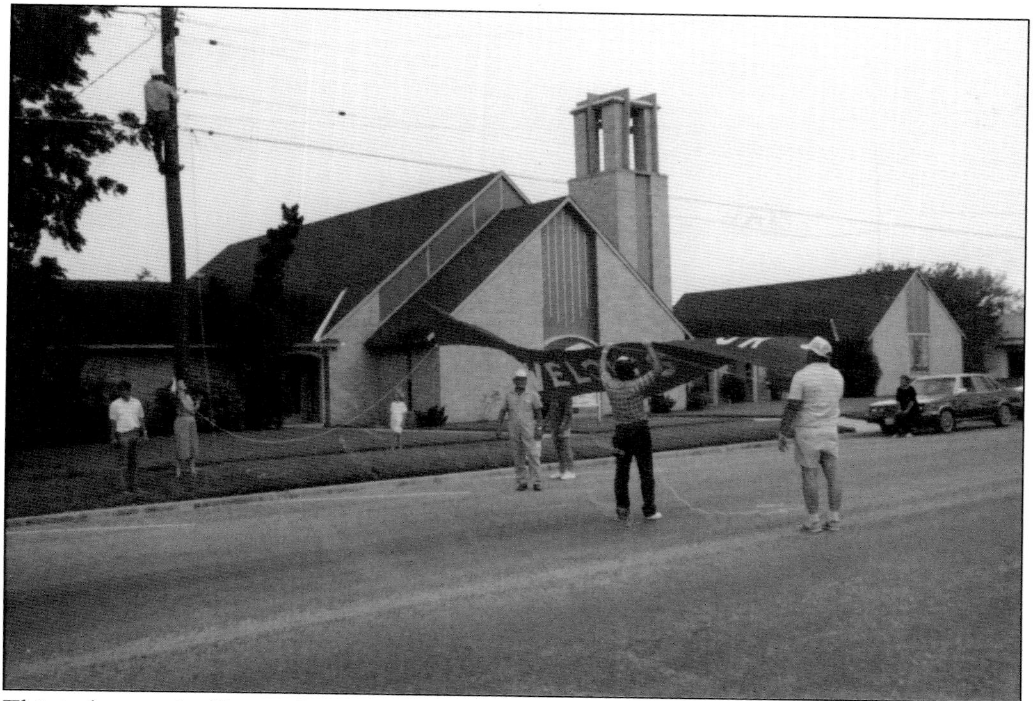

This is the way the Karnes City Baptist Church looks today. It has been enlarged and remodeled extensively through the years.

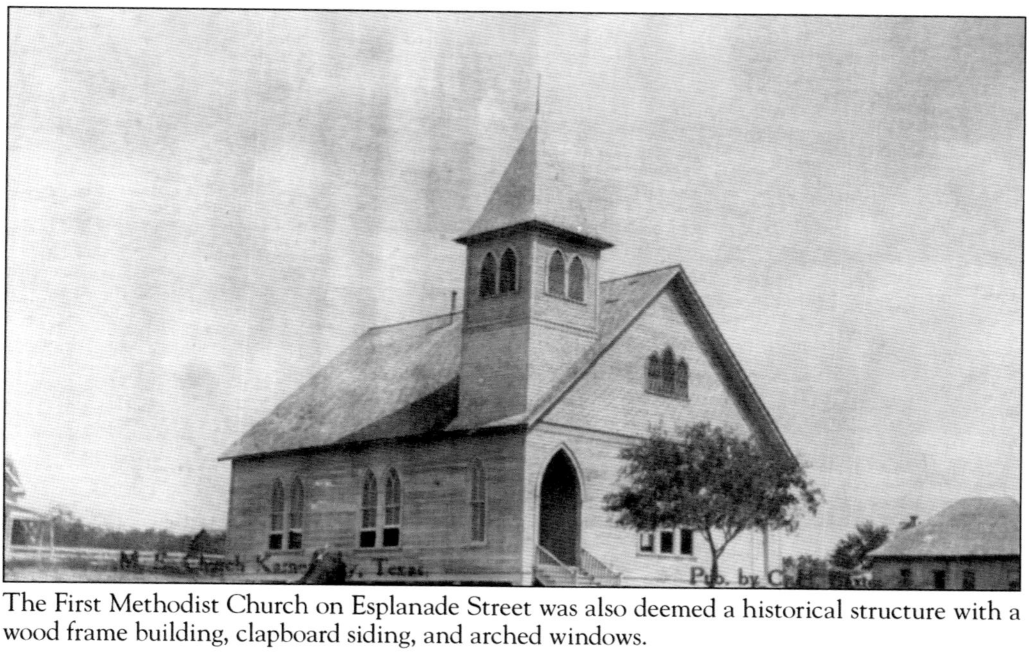

The First Methodist Church on Esplanade Street was also deemed a historical structure with a wood frame building, clapboard siding, and arched windows.

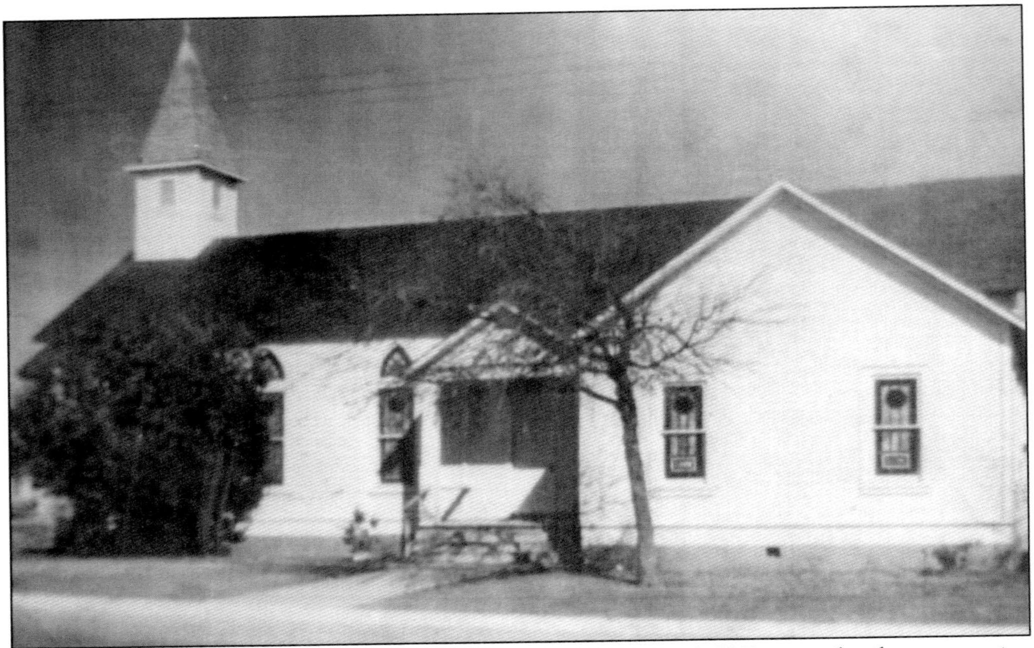

First Presbyterian Church has its marker as well. Located on Mayfield Street, it has been an active place for community life.

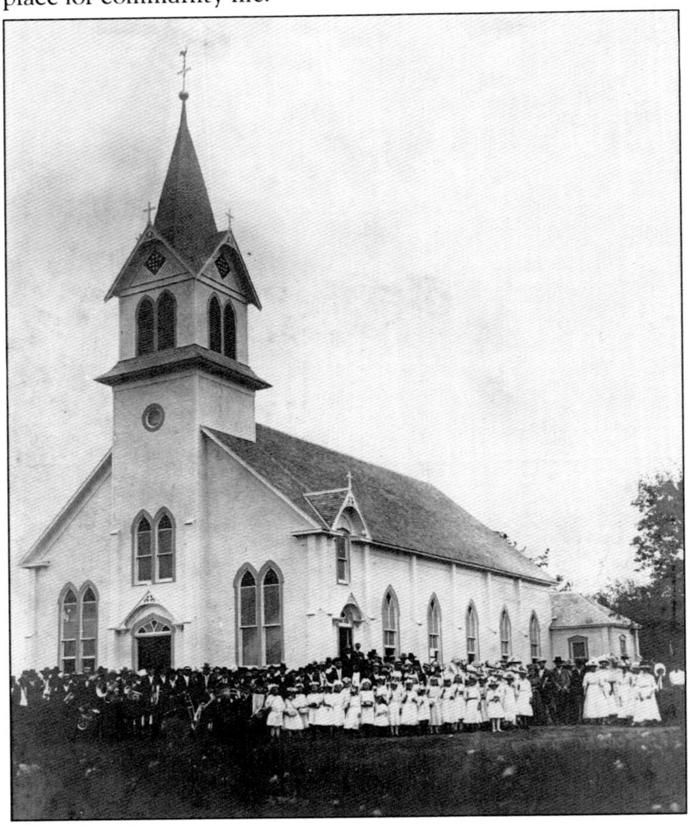

St. Paul's Lutheran Church in Karnes City is shown in a very early photograph featuring a crowd of its parishioners outside. Families of early German settlers made this church possible. (Courtesy of the Shortner-Fenner family.)

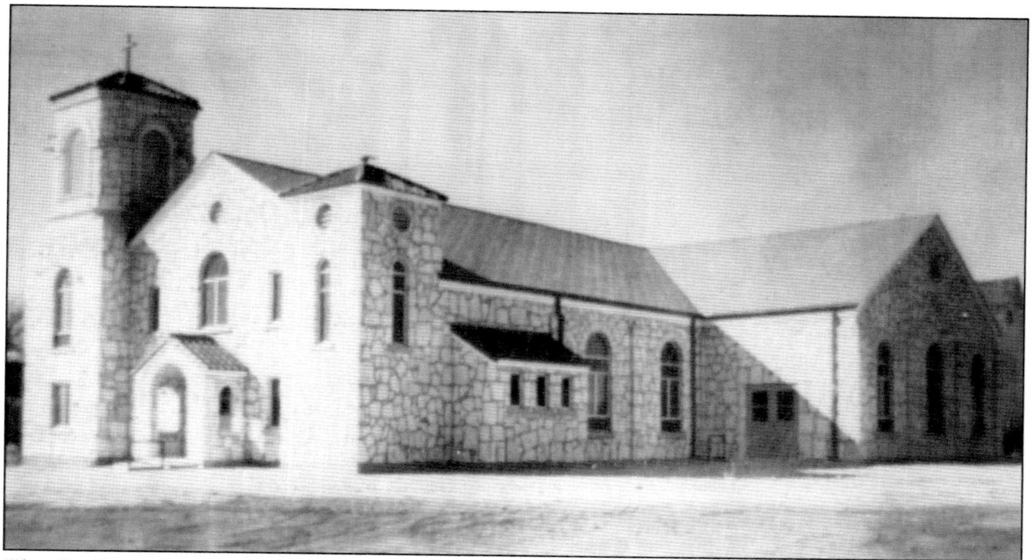

The St. Cornelius Catholic Church has been a very important part of the Karnes community, with several additions and modifications made to its building throughout the years.

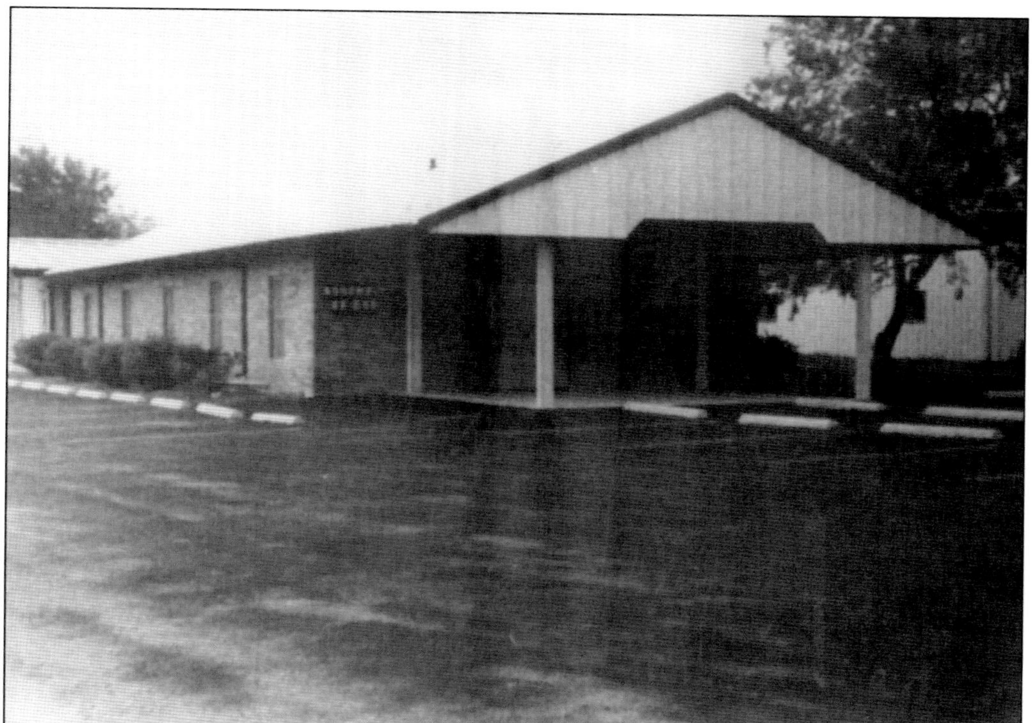

The Assembly of God Church has been a part of the Karnes City community for many years as well. The one pictured above was reconstructed to replace the original in 1961.

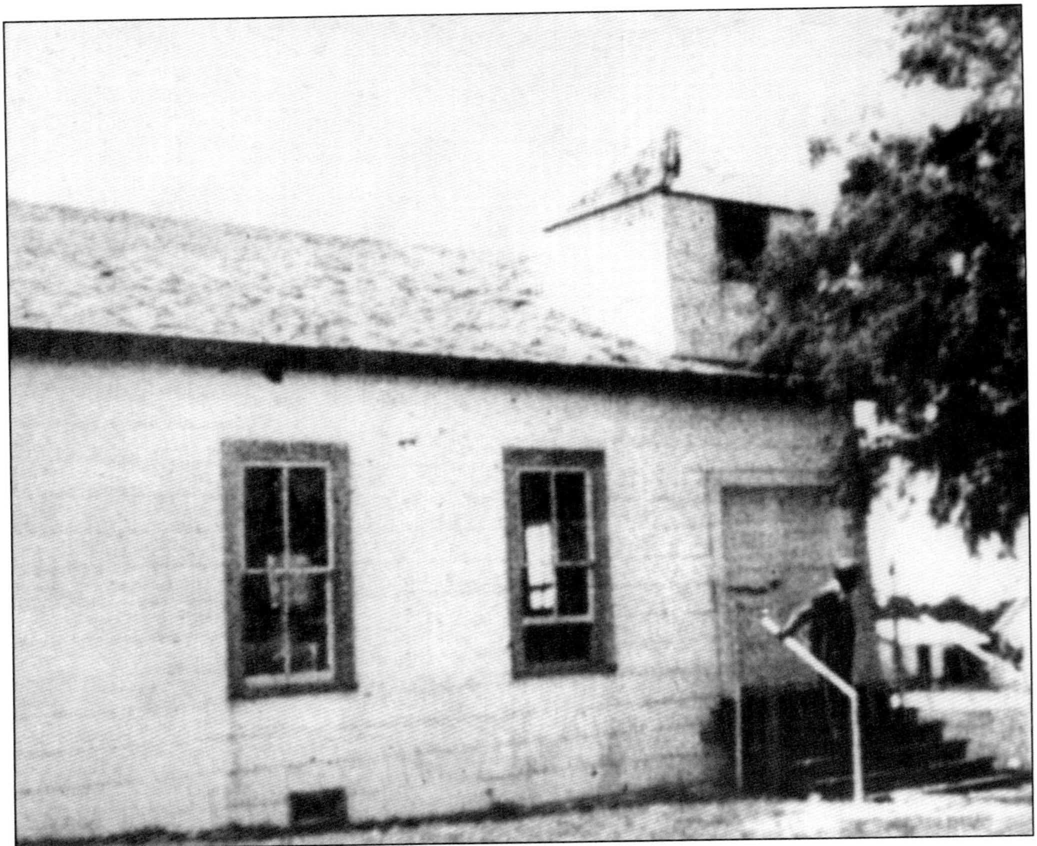

The Prospect Baptist Church located on West Buchel Street had to rebuild after the storm in 1941.

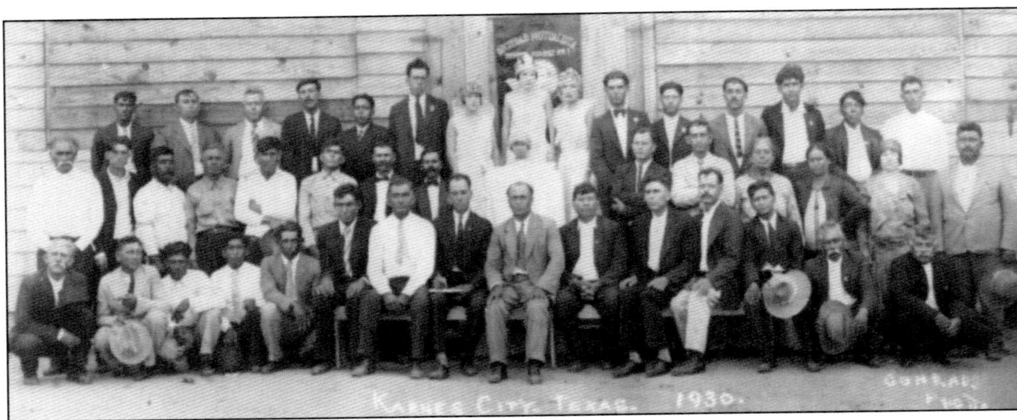

Some groups find another way to serve God than through a church. The Benito Juarez Society was established in the early 1900s. The hall was located at 410 West Buchel Street. The group has helped and assisted many in the community with such things as school supplies, clothing, utility bills, and medical bills through the years. Benefit dances are held to help those families who have had tragedies in their lives. The group in this photograph was 47 strong.

Four

The Railroads Change the Balance

The early settlers could not have imagined how much a decision made by a railroad company would impact their towns. The San Antonio and Aransas Pass Railroad, seeking a route to continue its line from San Antonio to the coast, laid out their policy and demands that a community had to meet to be included on the line. Several could not or would not concur. As a result, many of the towns in Karnes County became inconsequential or disappeared completely. A few of those left out were able to recoup, change their name, and slowly regrow as Riddleville did, and is now known as Gillette. Helena did not comply. Because of its decision, the railroad moved its line south one mile from the present location of Karnes City. They were determined to start a new town site called Kenedy, in honor of Mifflin Kenedy, an associate of the railroad. When a problem occurred with that decision, they decided to move it further south about four more miles with the establishment of present-day Kenedy, now five miles south of Karnes City. Added to the mix of new town sites was Runge, with the help of H. Runge and Company, who owned most of the land. It is now Runge. Runge was also established on the railroad line. Thus, all of these railroad station sites, including Falls City, vied to become the new county seat of Karnes County. Runge had become the largest town in the county, but a very contested election in 1894, determined Karnes City to be the new county seat as it still is today. With help of the railroads, many aspects changed these small towns. Five railroad routes were considered. Those who were on the lines in Karnes County would continue to flourish and grow with their depots halfway between San Antonio and the coast.

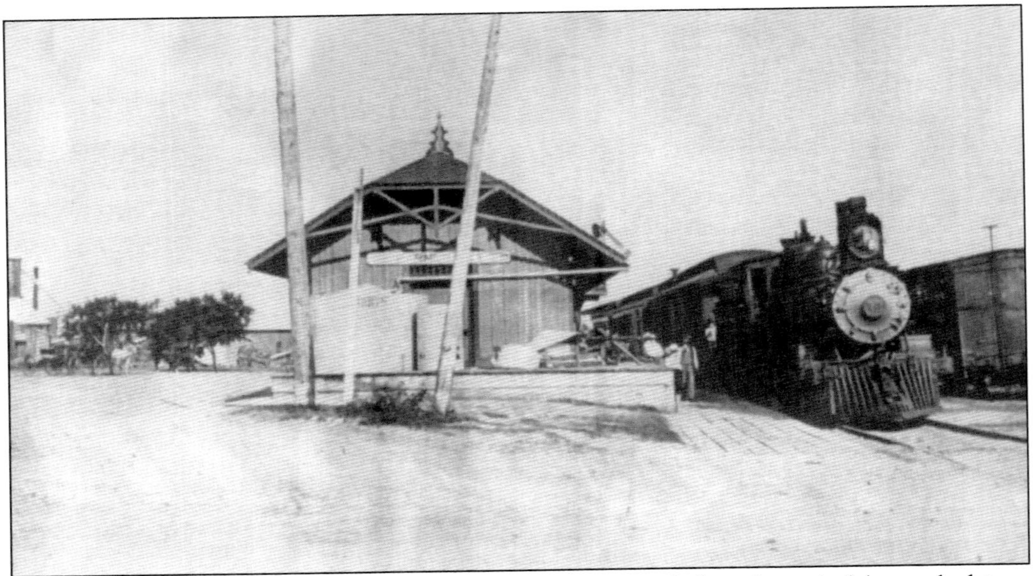

The arrival of trains and their depots changed many things, including the end of the cattle drives. Pictured is the depot that was at Karnes City.

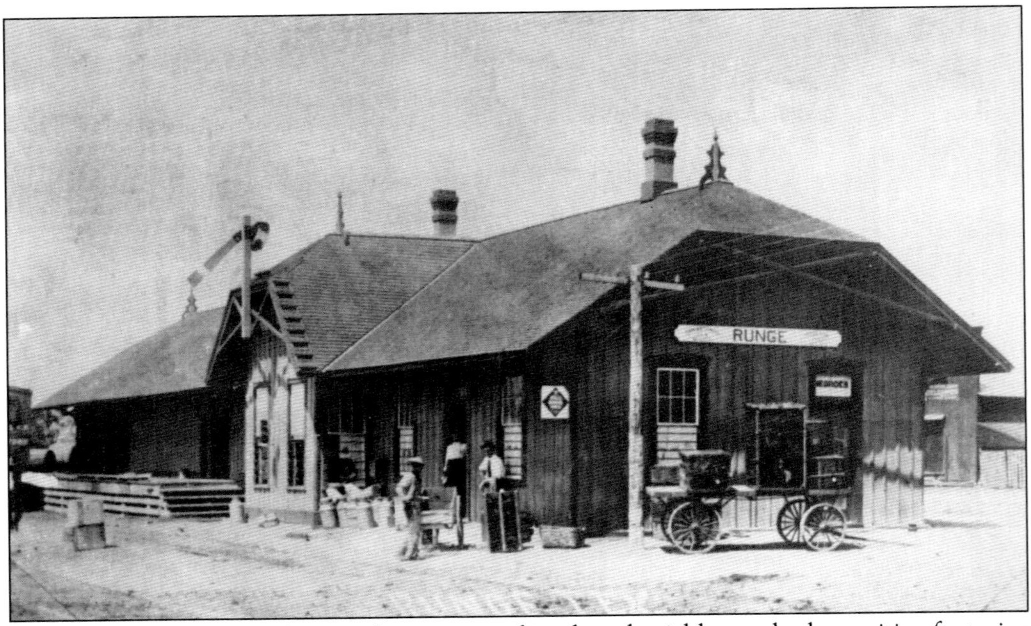

Depots did prove to be gathering places to meet friends and neighbors, whether waiting for trains that carried passengers or just the fun of seeing what was going on at the site. Note the picnic baskets, along with steamer trunks, crates, and milk cans in this picture of the Runge Depot in 1910.

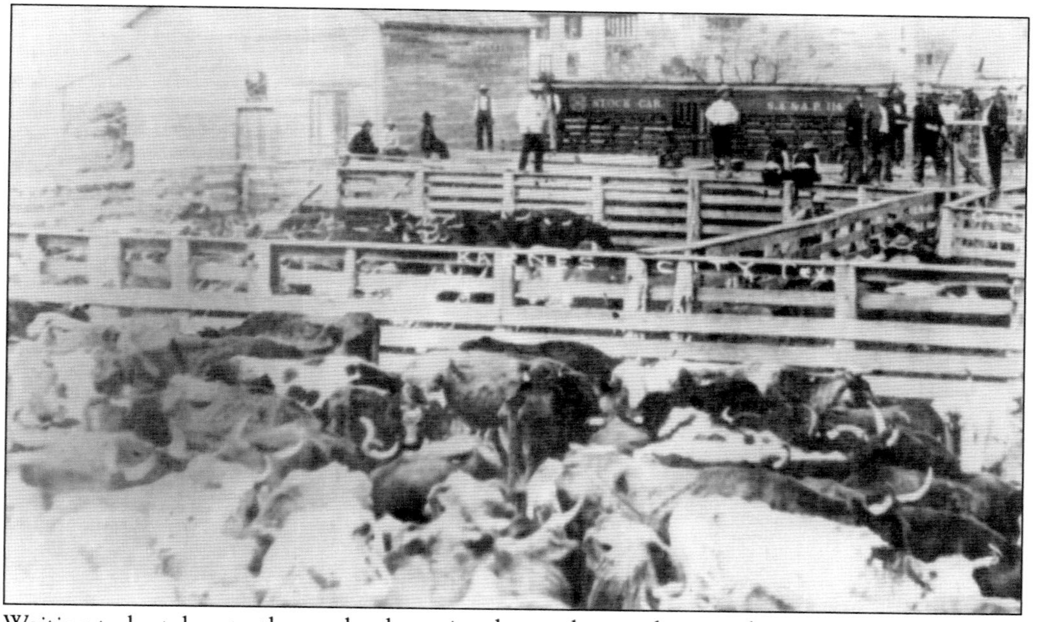

Waiting to be taken to the market by train, the cattle were kept in shipping pens close to the depot. Pictured are Dwight Nichols, Sykes Butler, Thea Butler, Andy Nichols, Marvin Butler, Toby Burris, George Campbell, and a buyer named Branch with his partner.

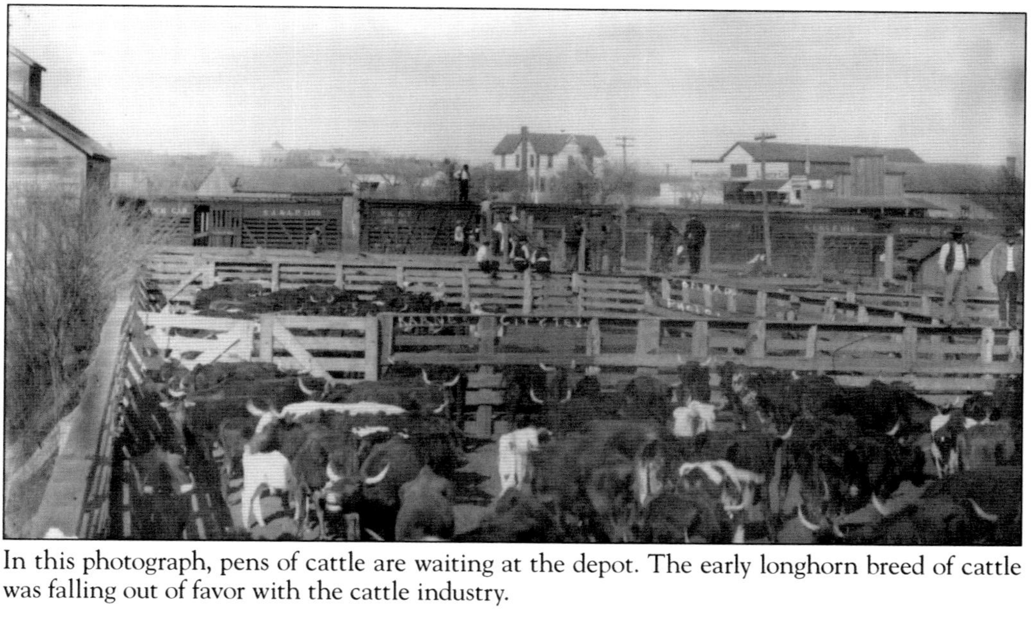

In this photograph, pens of cattle are waiting at the depot. The early longhorn breed of cattle was falling out of favor with the cattle industry.

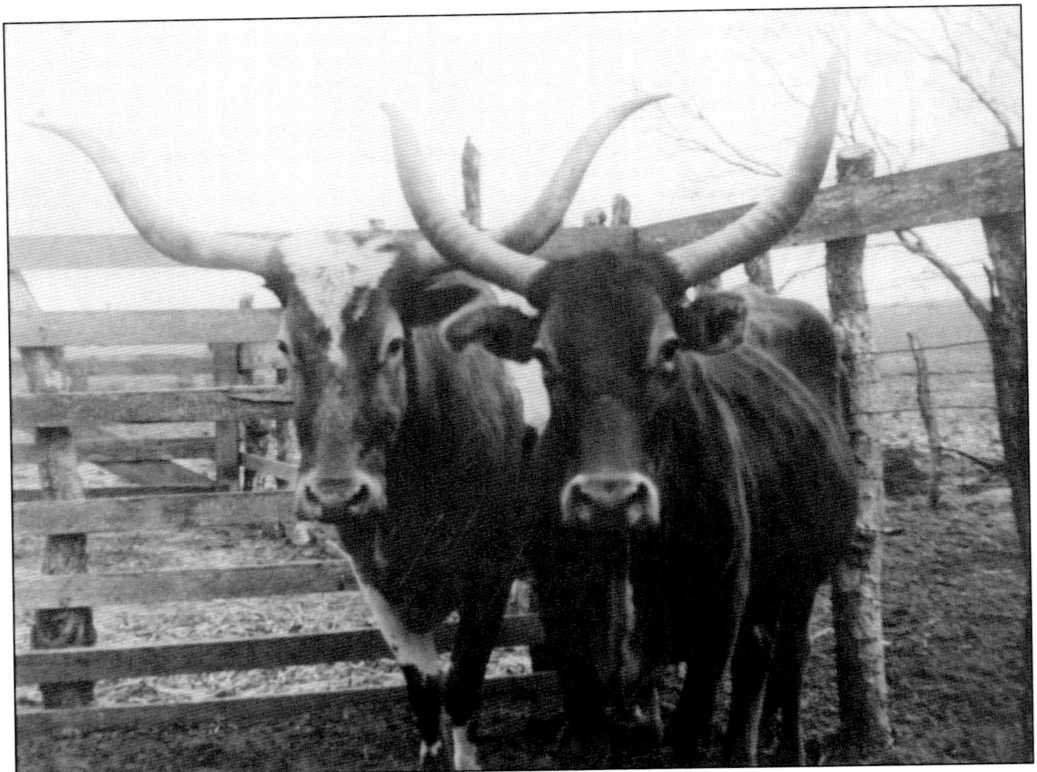

Not so with owners who just love to raise them. After all, longhorns have been in the area since the Spaniards brought them as settlers.

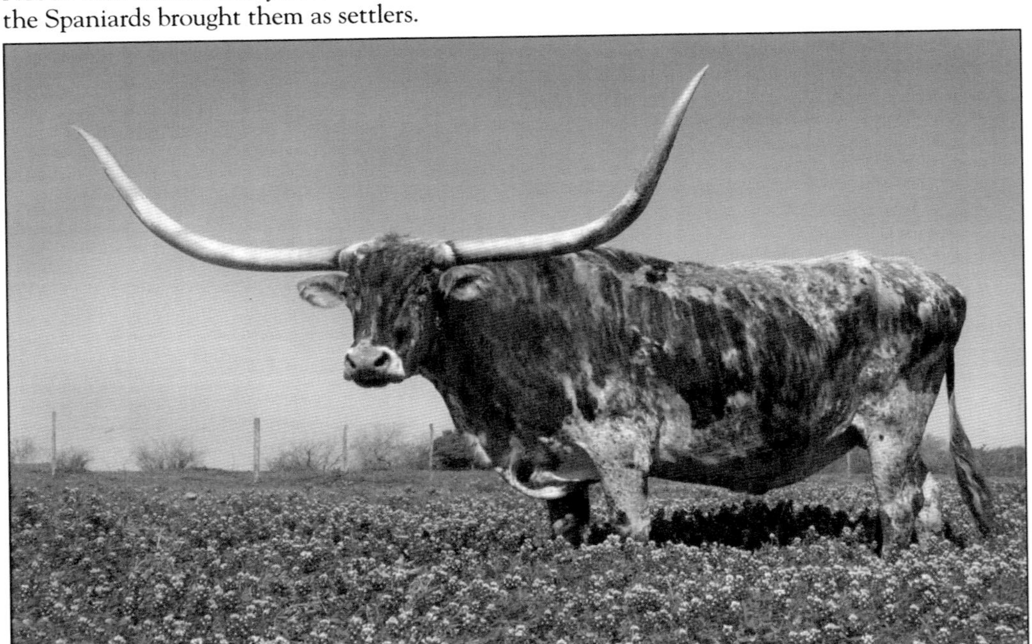

WOW is a seven-time champion with over a 10-foot horn spread, from the cattle ranch owned by Dr. Joyce Kimble and her family in Karnes City. (Courtesy of Sue Butler Carter.)

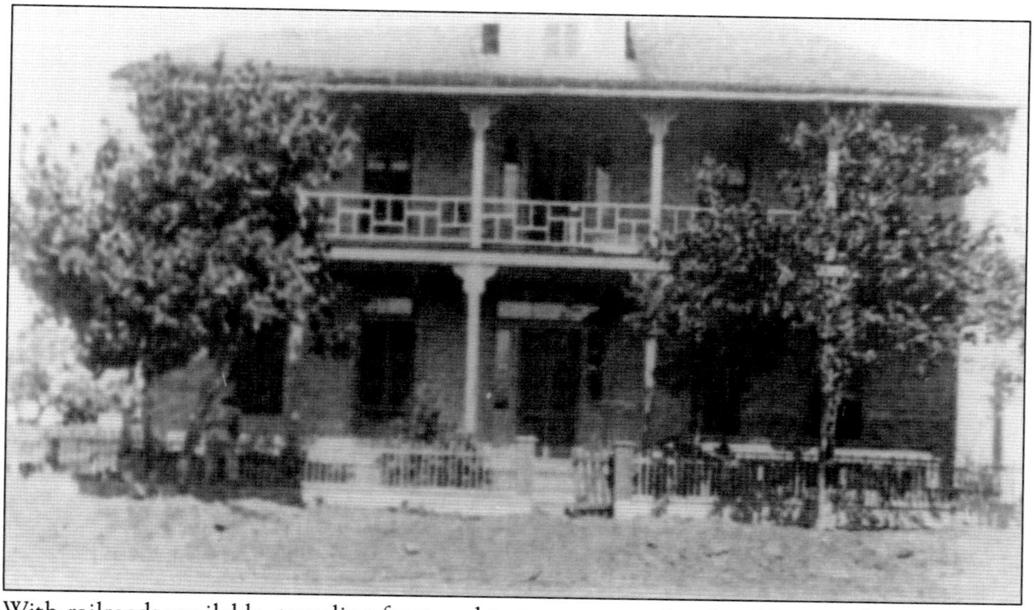

With railroads available, traveling from and to town was easier. As visitors might want to see another part of the country, a few hotels appeared to accommodate places to stay. The old Baxter Hotel was managed by Mrs. C.C. Teas. After several years, it was known as the Teas Hotel.

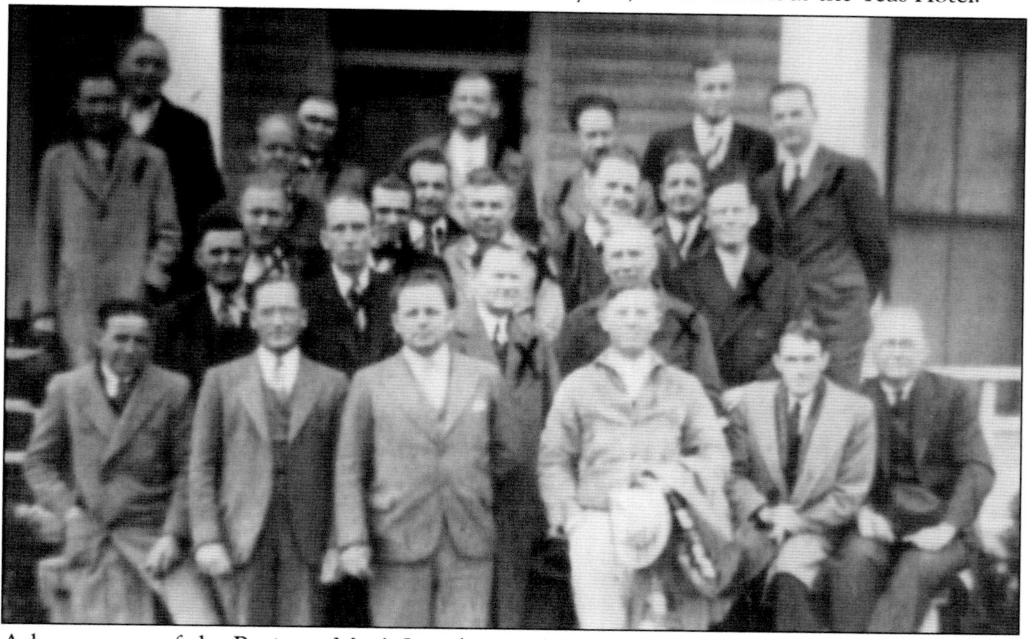

A large group of the Business Men's Luncheon Club is pictured in front of the Rohan Hotel. The members are, from left to right, (first row) Massie Stewart, A.Y. Benge, J. Ray Davis, W.B. (Bill) Fenner Sr., Dr. Shelby F. Shannon, MD, and E.A. Ludeucke; (second row) Hollis L. Smith, J. Rex Weir Sr., Sykes S. McClane, Professor Dorsey, Otto Kaiser, Tom D. Ruckman, unidentified, Rev. J.G.M. Ramsey; (third row) G.L. (Dobie) Gideon, Robert L. Barnett Jr., John H. Stamper, Dick Ruckman, W.Y. (Bill) Morris Sr., unidentified, Hy White, Herbert O. Muecke Sr., Oliver G. Abbott, unidentified, and Linard H. Menn.

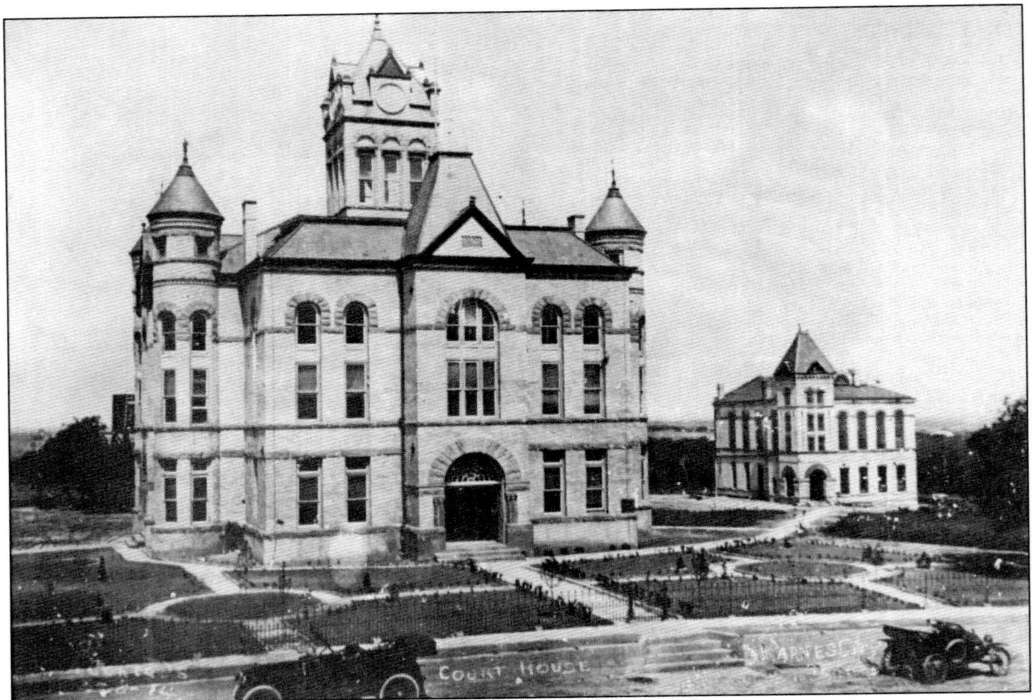

The biggest change brought about by the railroads was the loss of the county seat for Helena and the gain for Karnes City after the election. The current Karnes County Courthouse was constructed in 1894, but has been remodeled since then. There are current efforts to restore it back to its original glory.

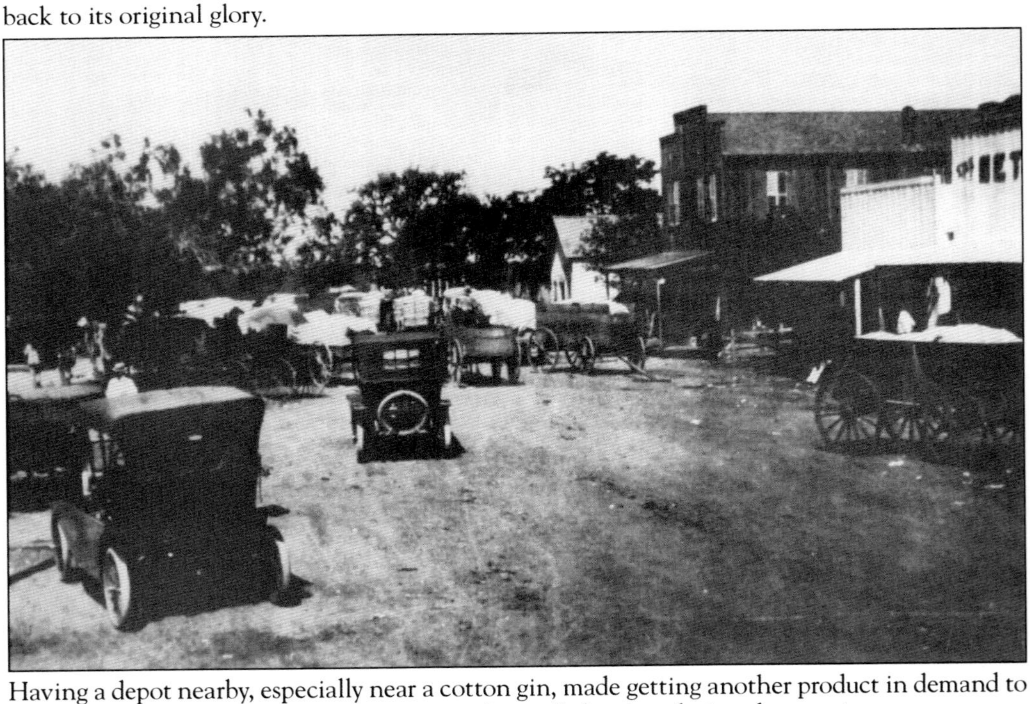

Having a depot nearby, especially near a cotton gin, made getting another product in demand to market quicker. The Gillette cotton gin was busy all the time during the growing season.

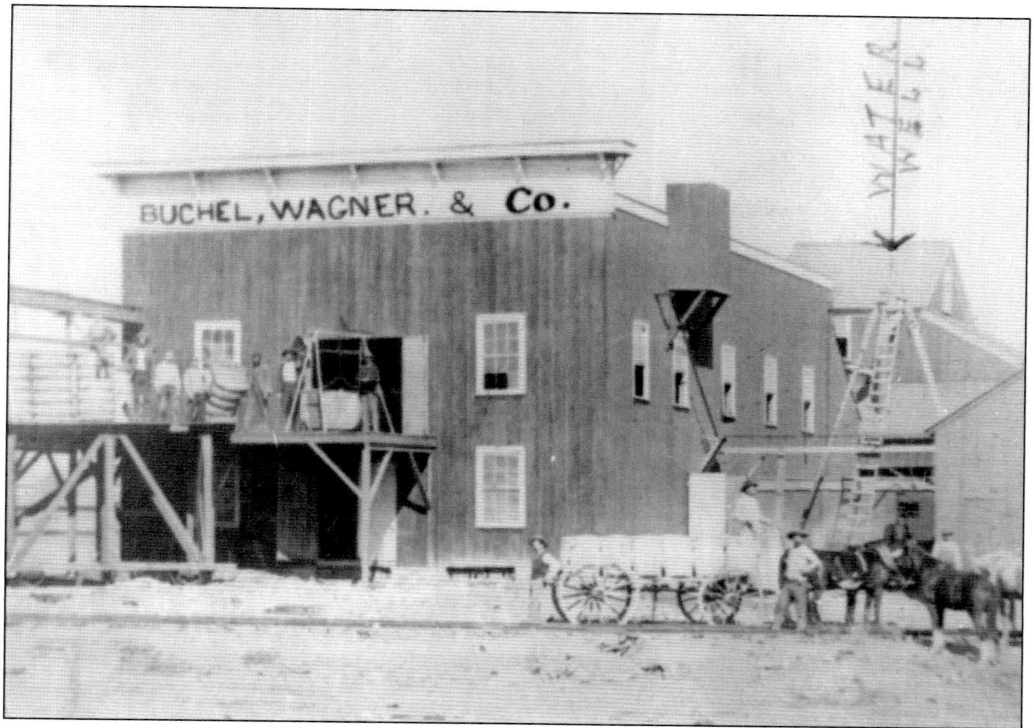

Pictured in 1898, Buchel, Wagner & Co. was said to be the first cotton gin in Karnes City. Customers included John L. Kuhnel, who is standing outside with his wagon and team.

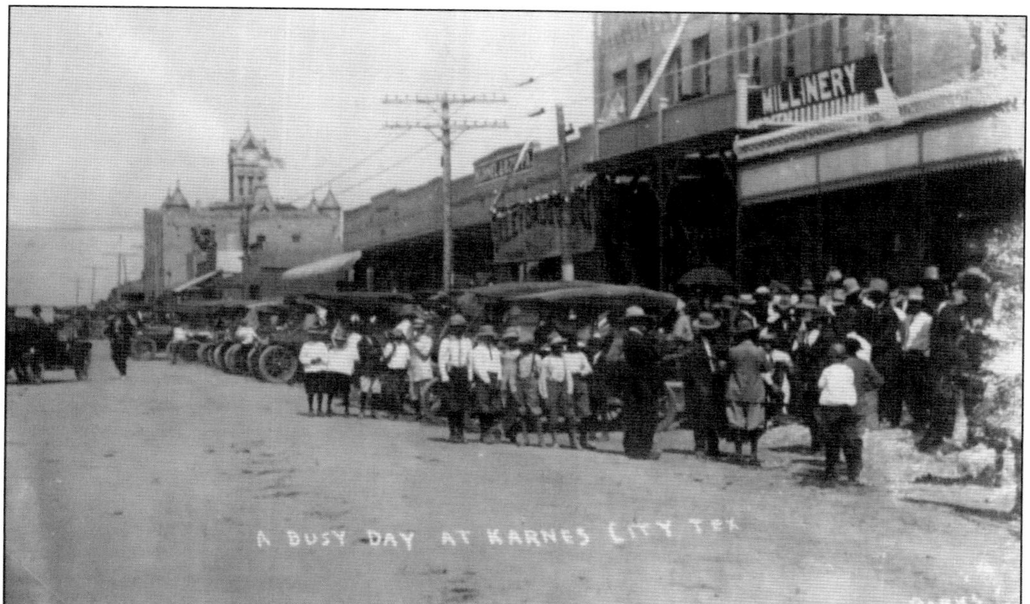

Back then, farmers and ranchers near Karnes City also came to town on Saturdays to talk about their crops, their livestock, and the latest things they heard were going on in their area, including the larger world itself.

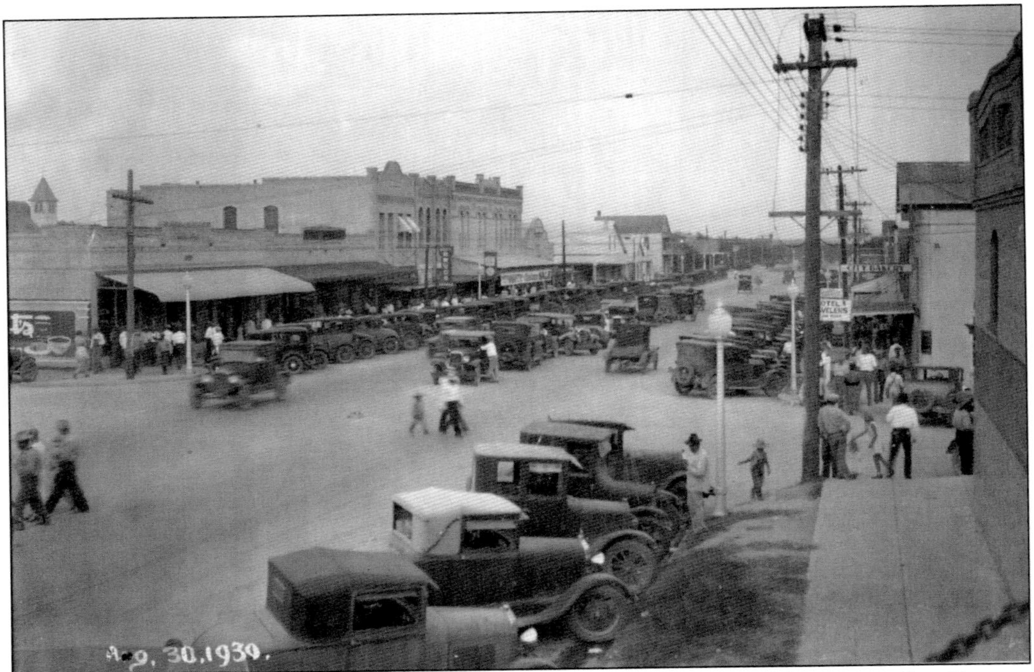

Kenedy, too, often had crowded street scenes, even when it was still known as Six-Shooter Junction. Later, it was said if you asked for a ticket to Six-Shooter Junction, they would know that you wanted to go to Kenedy.

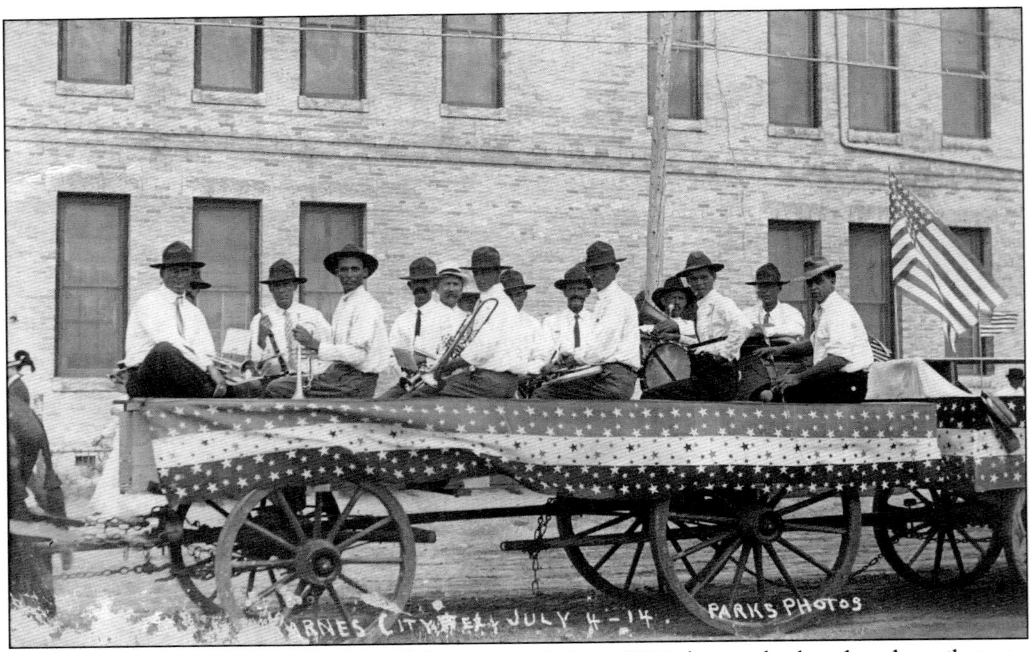

This patriotic parade float for the celebration on July 4, 1914, featured a band and a tribute to the stars and stripes.

Celebrations brought out the crowds. The days of worry and unrest were almost over.

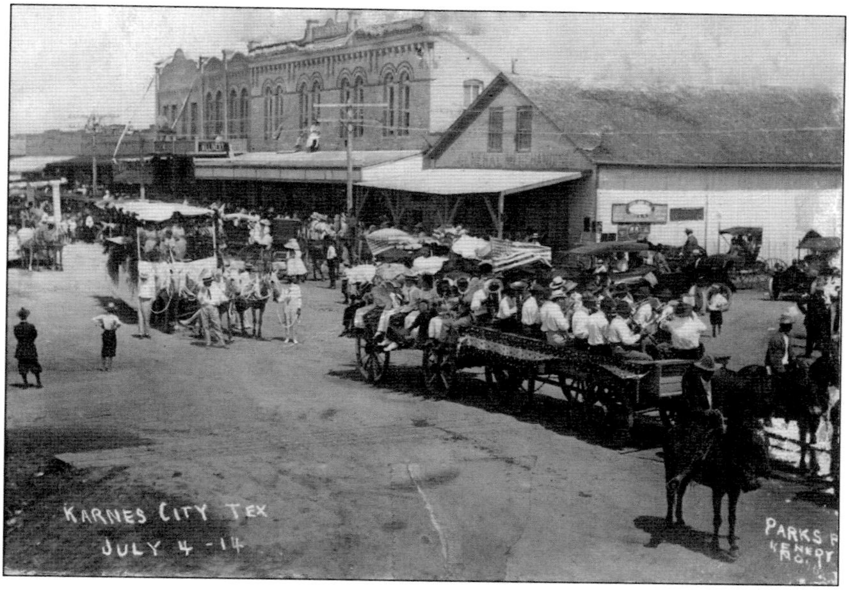

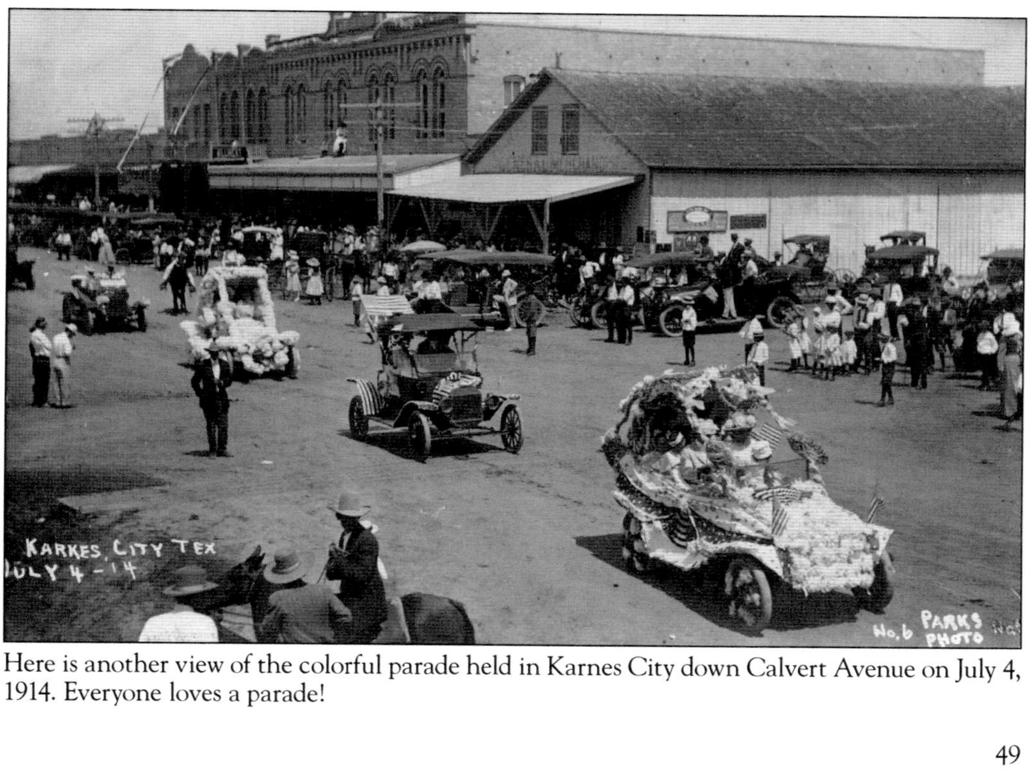

Here is another view of the colorful parade held in Karnes City down Calvert Avenue on July 4, 1914. Everyone loves a parade!

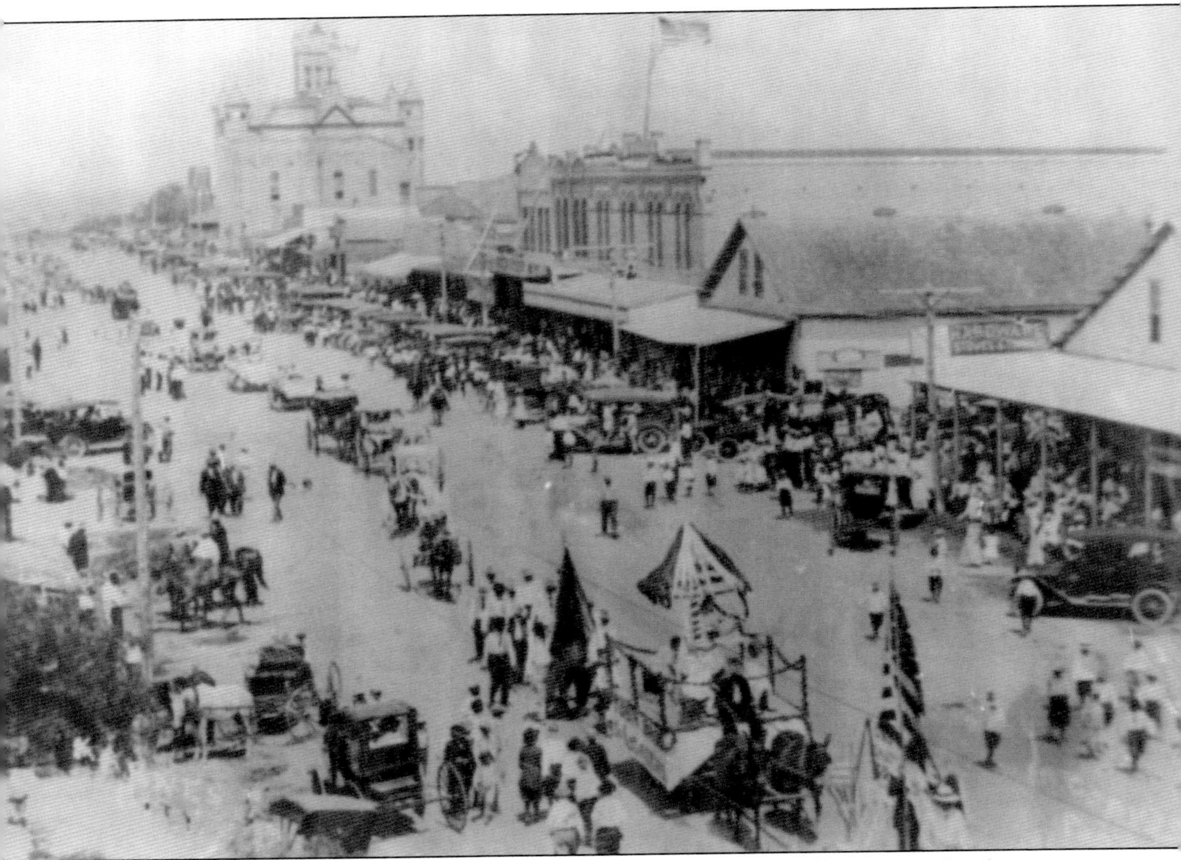

This image of the same parade on July 4, 1914, shows attendees still enjoying the day, in carts, buggies, and many on horseback.

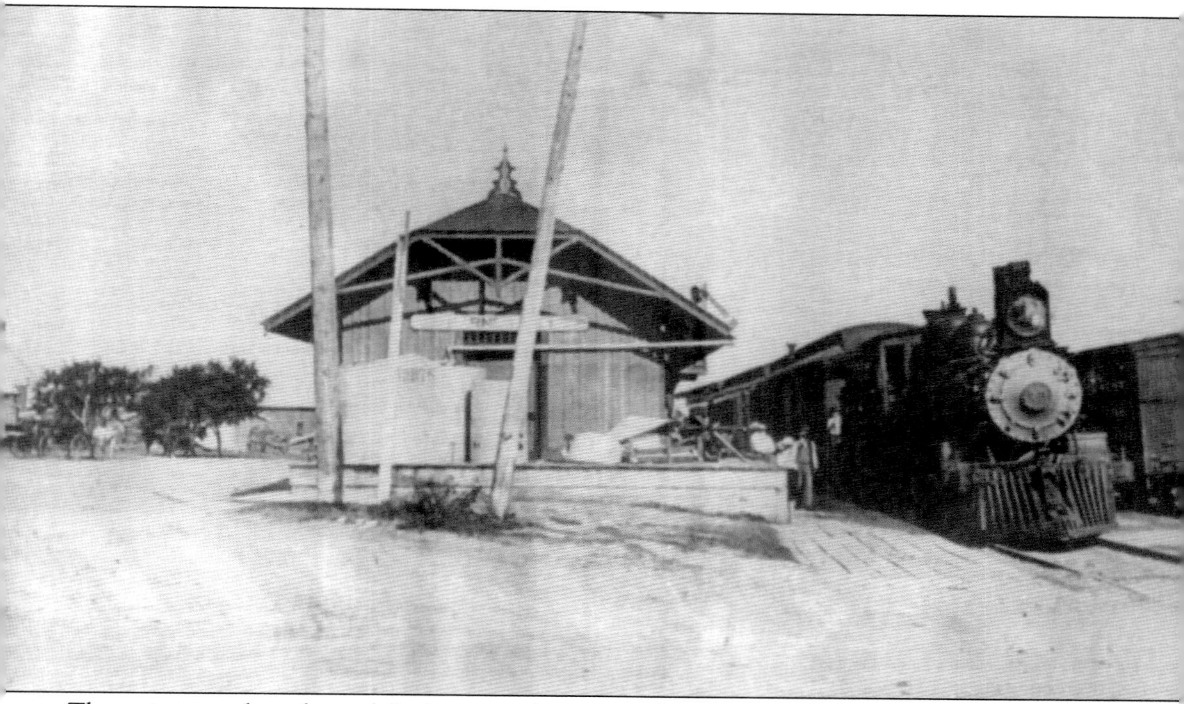

The trains were here for a while, but soon their era as the main means of transportation would be over, too.

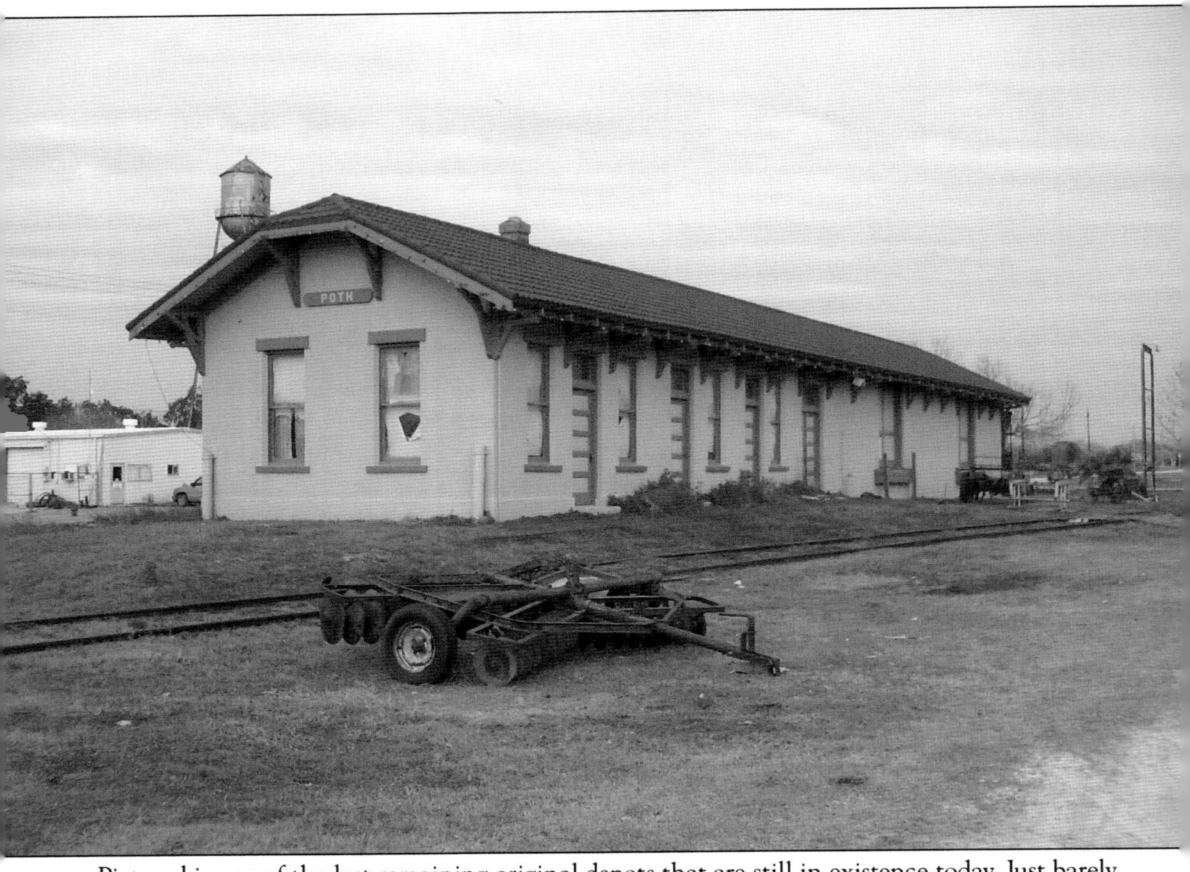

Pictured is one of the last remaining original depots that are still in existence today. Just barely over the county line in Poth, Texas, the depot is used as a museum and a reminder of the days when the railroads ruled.

Five

Famous Feuds and Outlaws

Notorious outlaws, along with gun-wielding lawmen and feuding families, were part of the scene as settlers began taming the new frontier and settling in. John Wesley Hardin was often seen in Karnes County. Later, when reconciled to his family in Gonzales County, he joined his Clements cousins who were allied with the Taylors against the Suttons in a local feud. This feud resulted in the death of John Helms, a sheriff of another nearby county. Even respected lawmen in early days were known to be prone to outlaw behavior. One in particular, a Texas Ranger and lawman in Karnes County was reputed as being violent, often shooting prisoners even after they had surrendered. Even after the election with Karnes City winning the county seat, an incident happened as several citizens went to confiscate the records and books still held by Helena. No gunfight took place, but several were carrying weapons. In those days, it was difficult to tell the good guys from the bad guys. Nearby, the Dailey brothers, David and Christopher, determined a road was needed to connect and expedite mail to newly established Bee County. They opened a general store on Helena-Goliad Road. The town became known as Daileyville, believed to be on Pleas Butler's 33 Ranch. On the west side of the San Antonio River near Woffard's Crossing, it also had a gristmill and several houses. The brothers sought and received approval for a post office in their store with Christopher as the postmaster, but soon were caught in the line of crossfire involving the Butlers and the Elders feud. Their dispute was rumored to be over whether to have saloons in the area. The Butlers voted wet and the Elders voted dry. Dr. S.G. Dailey testified that the families were destined to have difficulties and a fight was bound to happen. It ended with two men being killed, and after an inquest, all of the survivors went on with their lives. As those rough and rowdy days settled down, most communities began to shed their reputations, seeking to live in peace with one another.

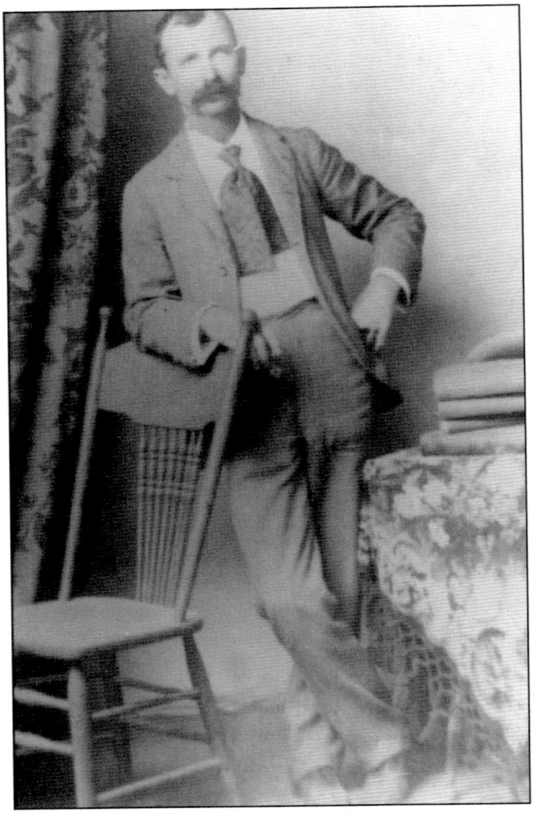

It was said that many of our small towns were notorious for attracting outlaws and at times causing feuds, especially during the Civil War. And right after that, the reputation flourished. Pictured to the left is Karnes County sheriff W.T. Morris, who served the county from 1896 to 1902. He was allegedly killed by suspected outlaw Gregorio Cortez.

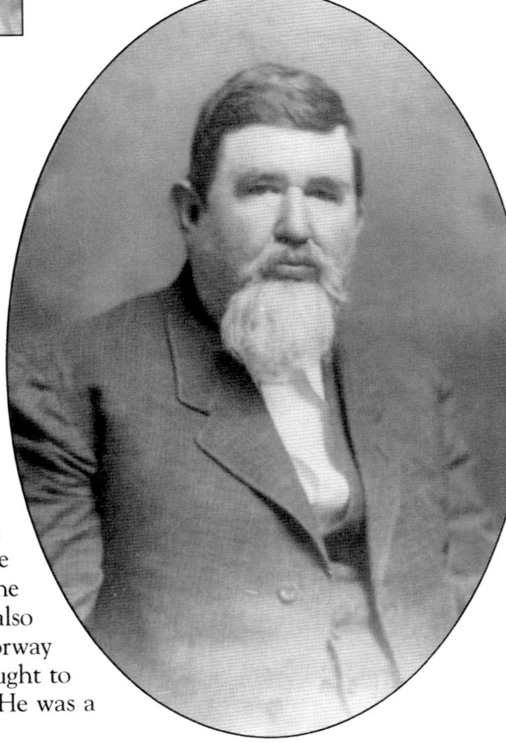

Pictured to the right is Judge Truman Phelps. Tom Ruckman reportedly said that he remembered Judge Phelps was justice of the peace in the 1920s. He also remembered that he had a small wood frame office between McClane Motor Company and the Mercantile. Tom was also said to remember seeing him sitting in the doorway of his office where he also lived. He was thought to be a surveyor and had a collection of rocks. He was a Civil War veteran.

Pictured to the right is a trio of famous lawmen in Karnes City's early years. They were known to be able to hold their own in any confrontation with known gunmen or outlaws. Hugh Kendall and John Yeary are standing, and Harper Morris is seated in front of them.

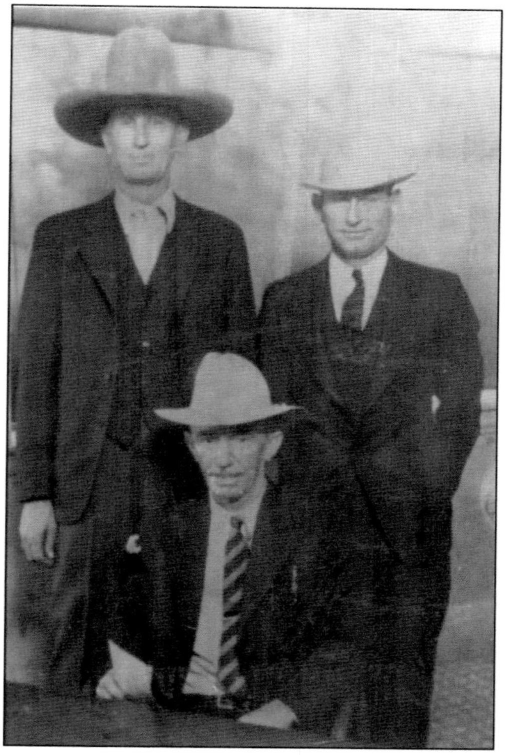

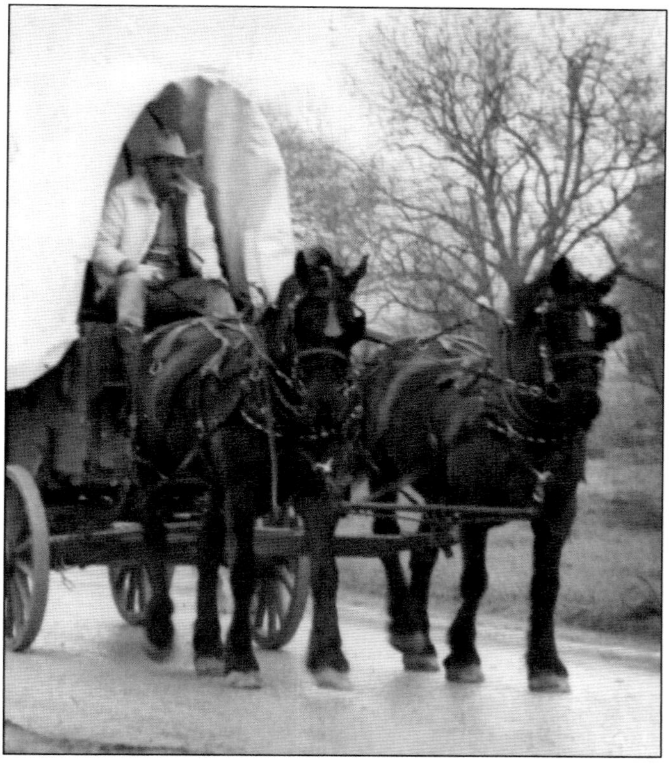

Until the county seat changed from Helena to Karnes City, many outlaws were attracted to the Ox Cart Trail and its valuable shipments. It was difficult to tell the difference between the legitimate horse-drawn carts and those waiting for an easy robbery.

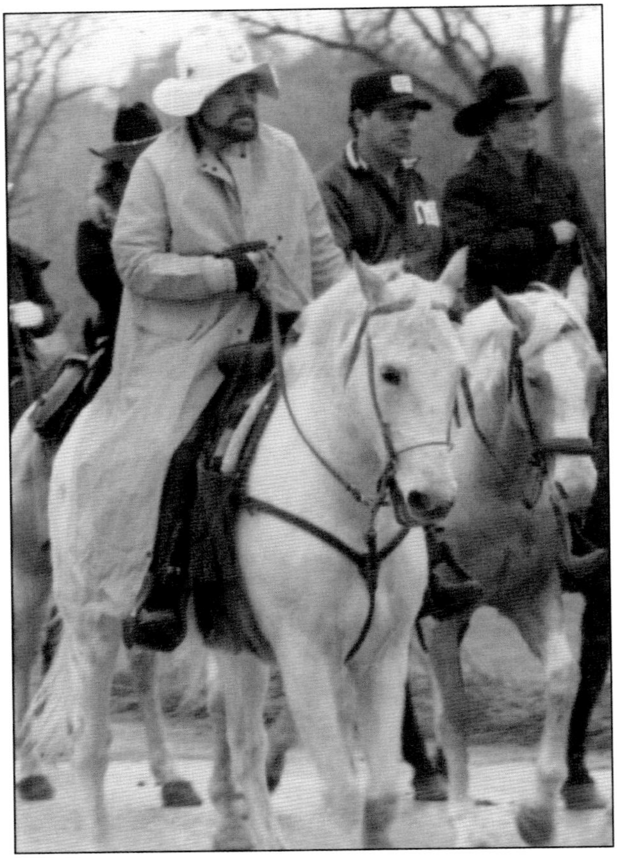

Sometimes it took a posse to escort an outlaw along those dangerous trails and through the countryside. It was reported that John Wesley Hardin came through Karnes County many times on his way to visit his relatives in Gonzales County.

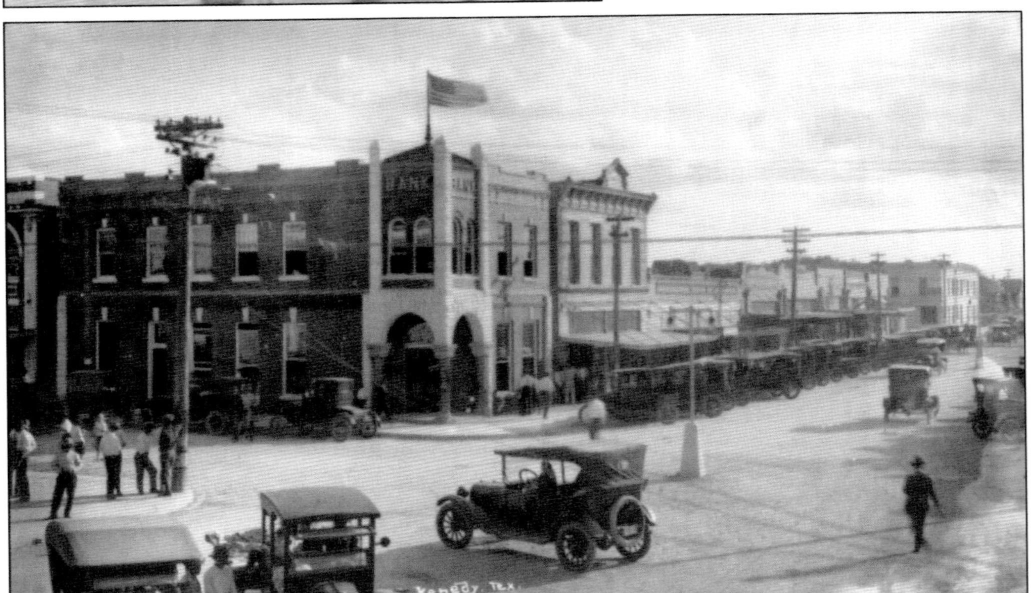

It took years before Kenedy lost its reputation as Six-Shooter Junction, due to its rough and rowdy past. But as it grew, the street began to look calm and even hospitable.

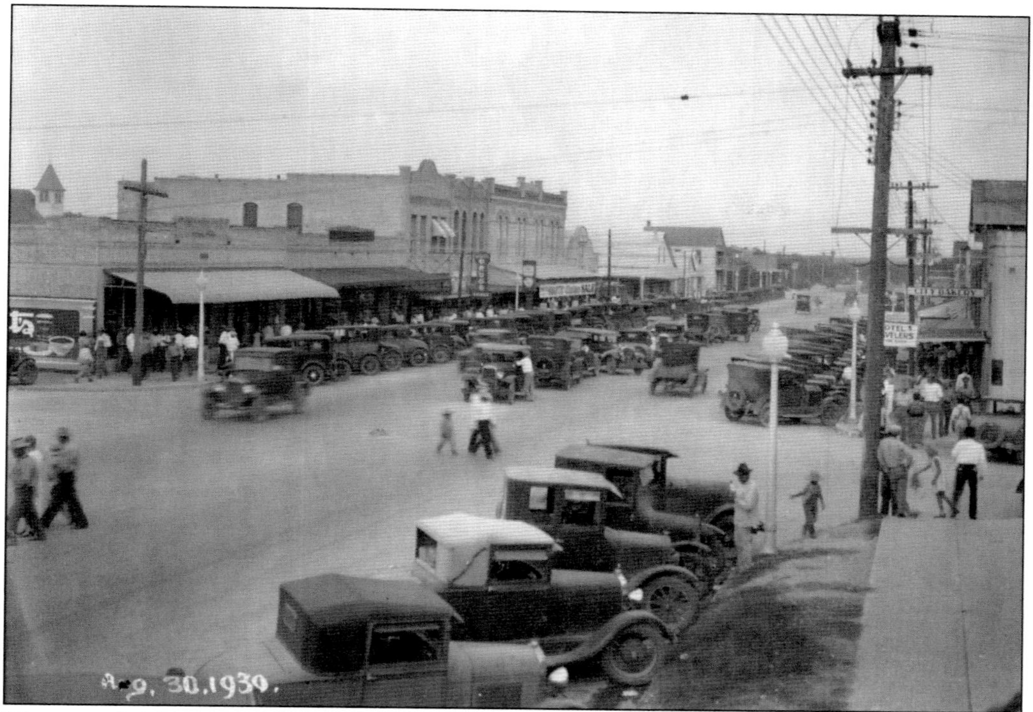

This crowded but peaceful Karnes City street scene was photographed on August 30, 1930.

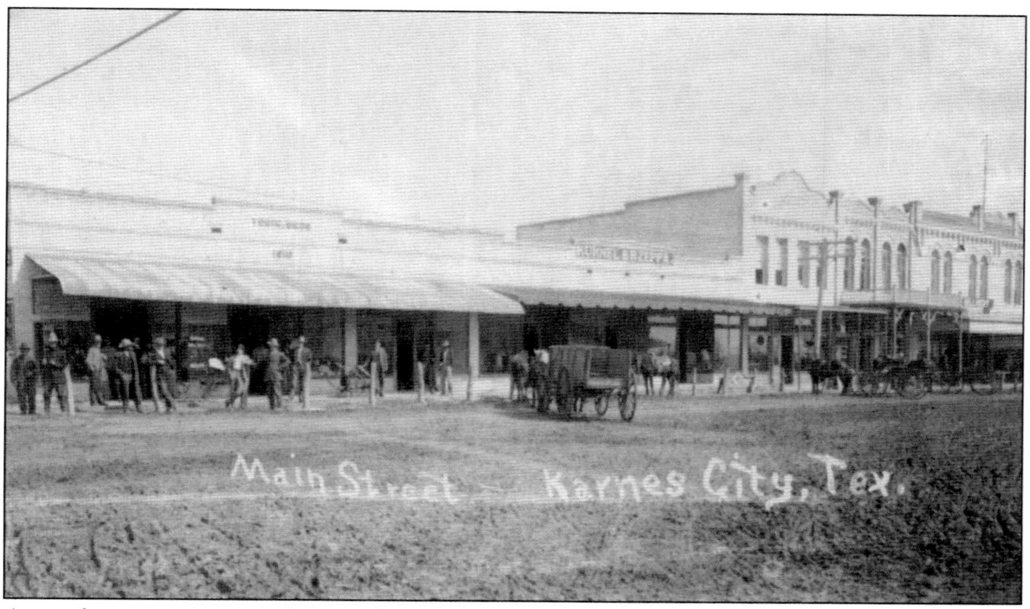

An early street scene on Calvert showing many of the buildings then in operation, including the Tobin Brothers Store, the Kuhnel and Rzeppa Store, Bailey's Drug Store, the Karnes County National Bank, and a general store.

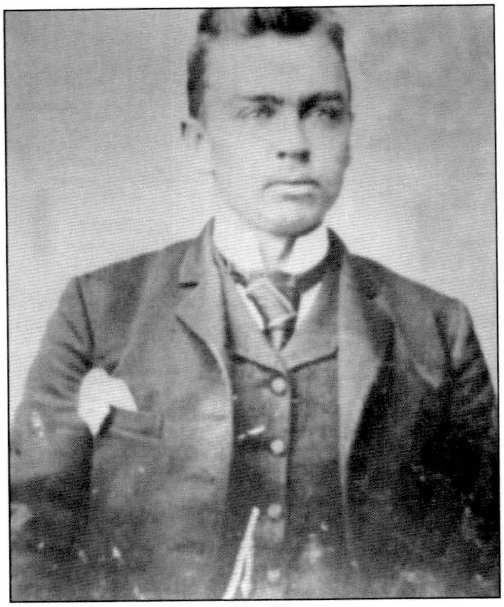

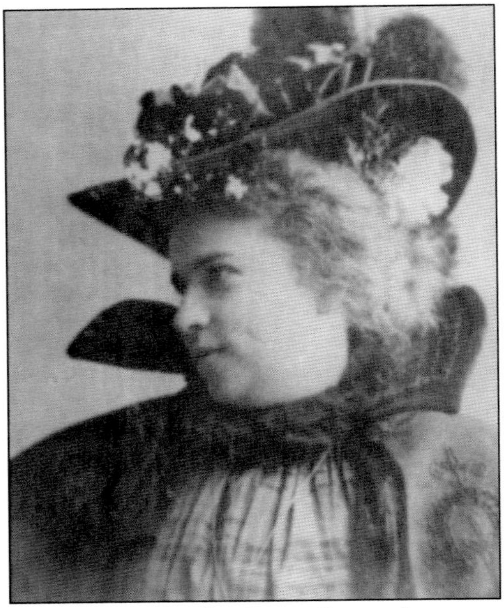

In the meantime, the larger communities were still growing, especially Karnes City with its new status. One of the first doctors to move to Karnes City was Dr. Stephen Allen King, MD, who moved here shortly after marrying Bennie Lee Makamson in Leona, Texas.

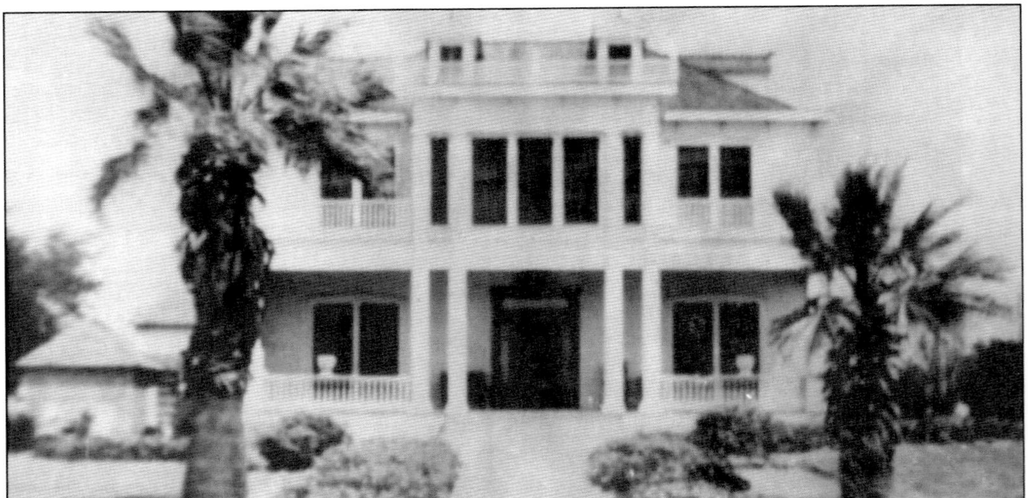

The Kings built their beautiful home, shown above, around 1940. It was said that Dr. King lined the walkway with yellow poppies, which Bennie Lee loved so much. They both died and were buried here in Karnes City. The home is now owned by Dr. Joyce Kimble and her family.

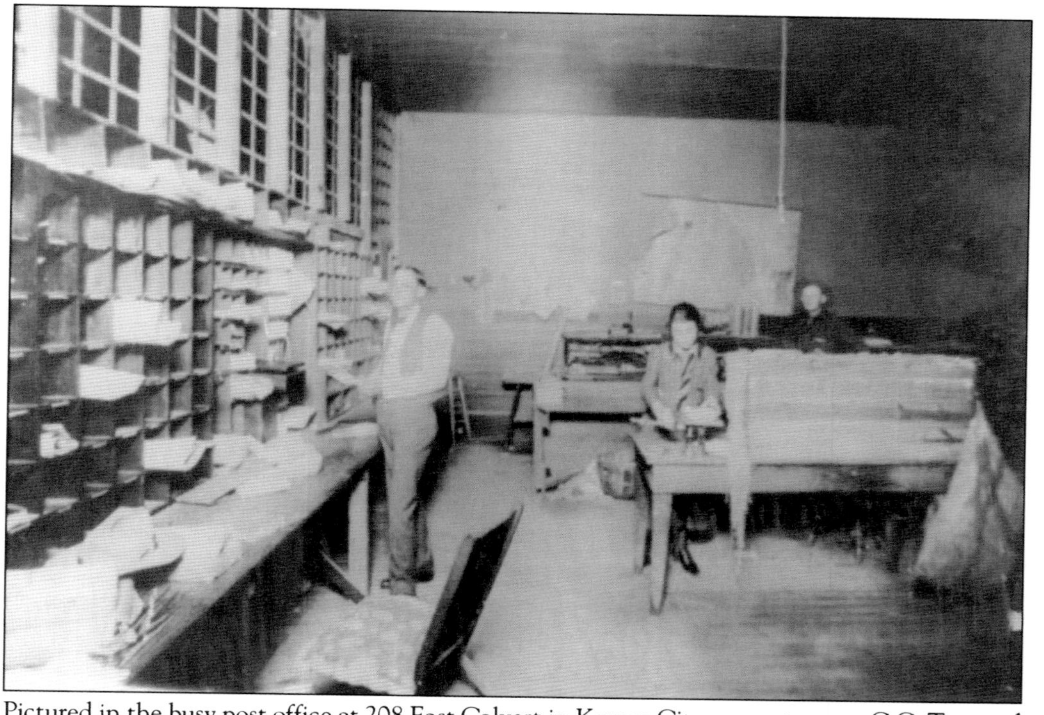

Pictured in the busy post office at 208 East Calvert in Karnes City are postmaster C.C. Teas and postal clerk Ruth Moody.

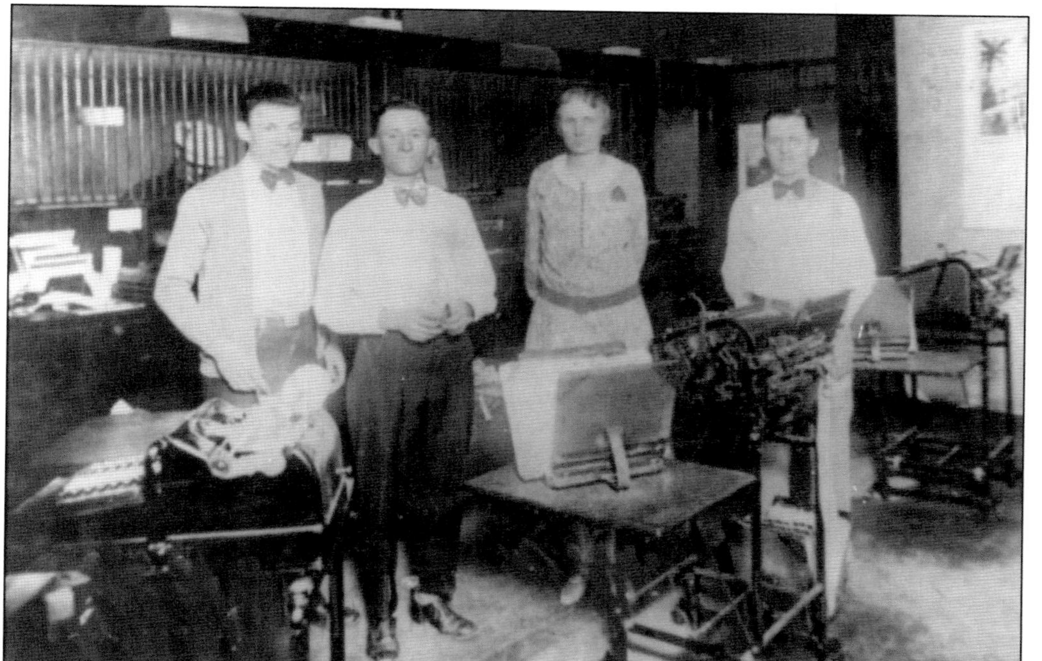

Pictured inside the Karnes County National Bank, which was first started by the Ruckman family, are, from left to right, Alvin A. Salge, Harry W. Isensee, Laura Jauer Isensee, and Joe Yeary. (Courtesy of the Sykes McClane family collection.)

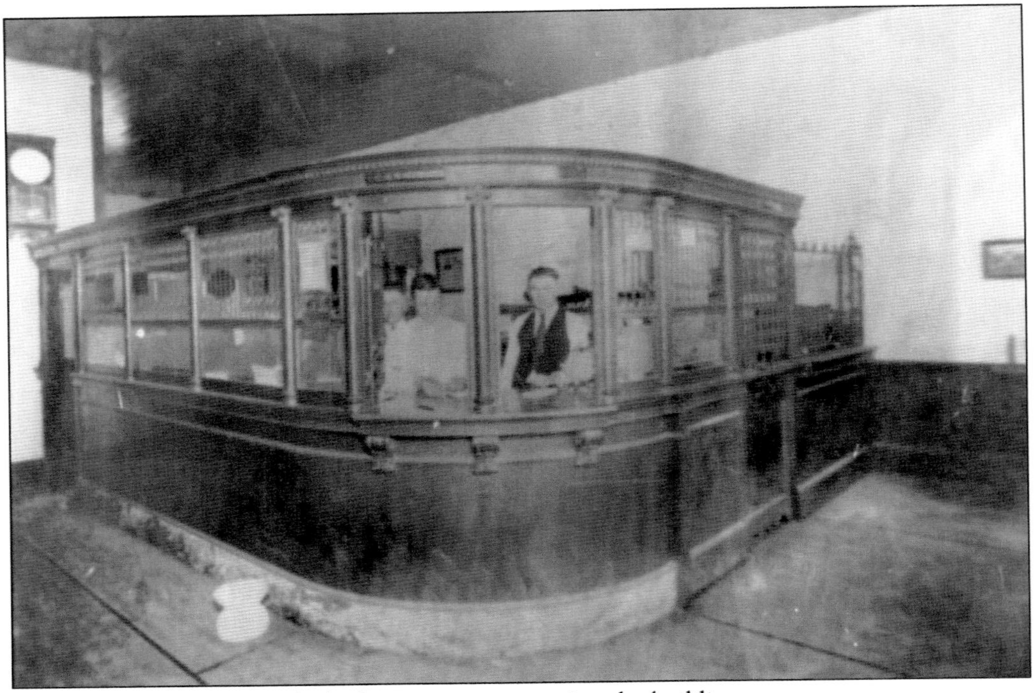

The bank is pictured as it looked to customers entering the building.

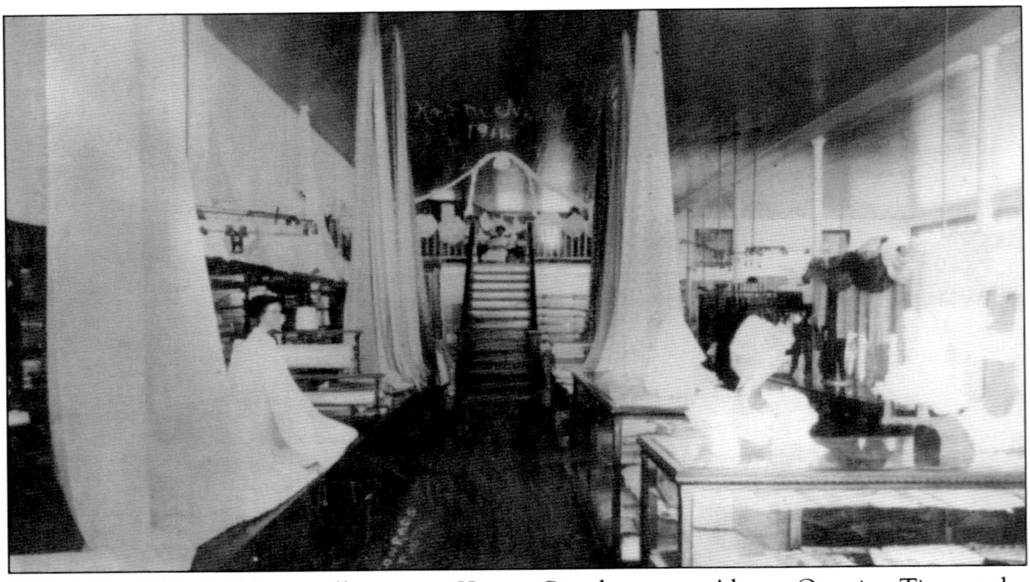

One of the oldest buildings still in use in Karnes City, known as Almost Opening Time at the Karnes Mercantile.

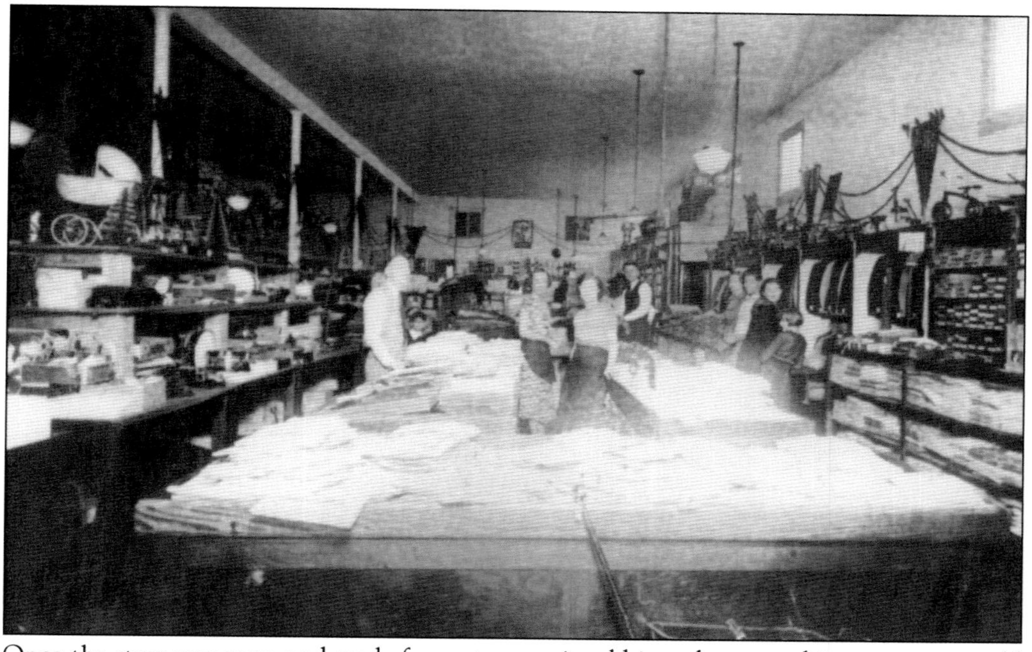

Once the store was open and ready for customers, it sold just about anything a person could ever want.

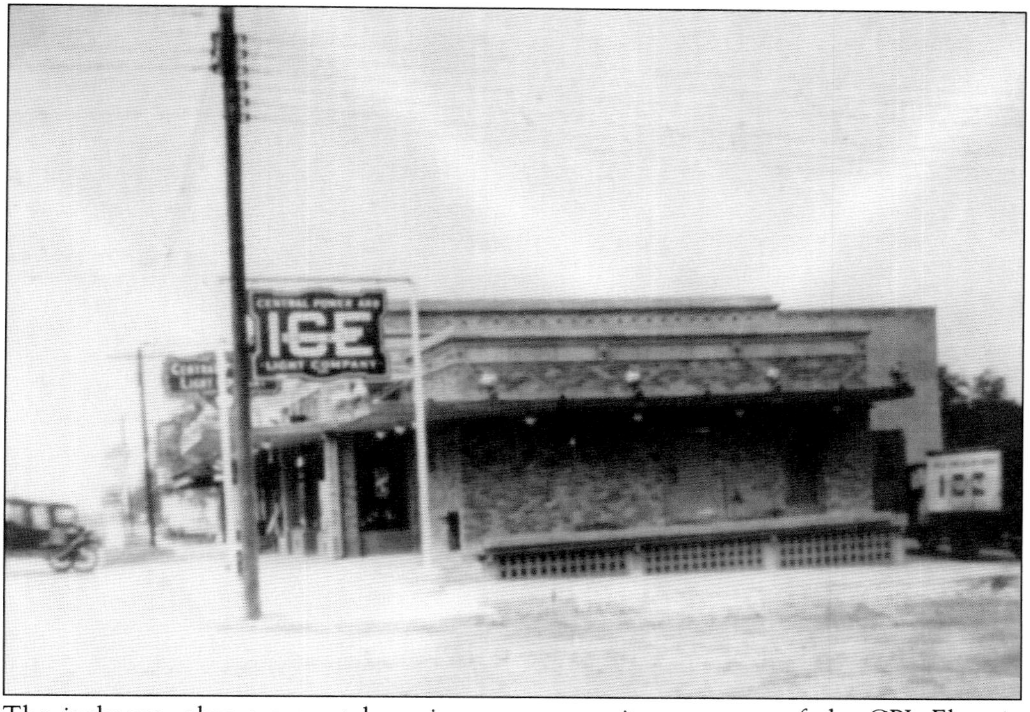

The icehouse, always a must have in any community, was part of the CPL Electric Company store.

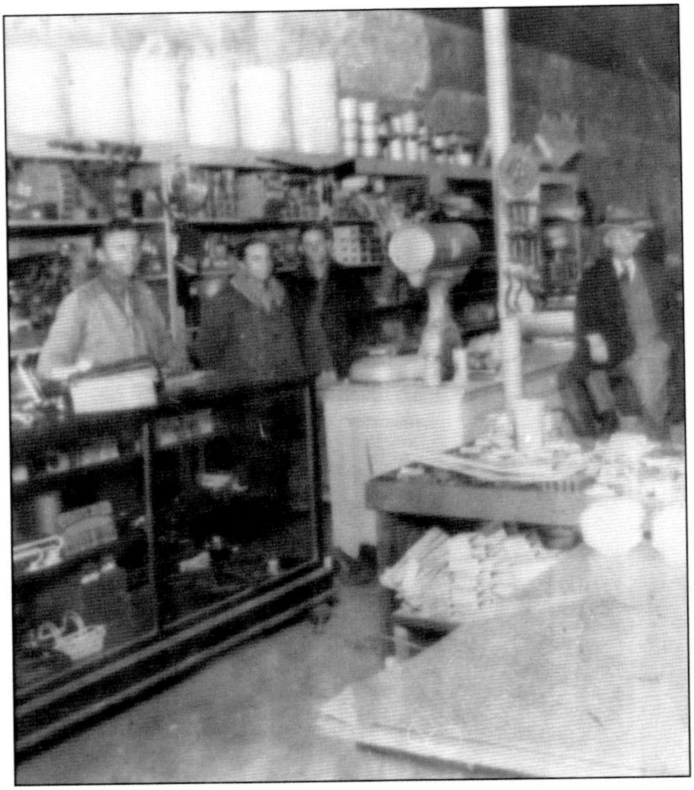

The Kuhnel family has been part of the Karnes City scene for a long time. Pictured is the early Kuhnel Hardware Store.

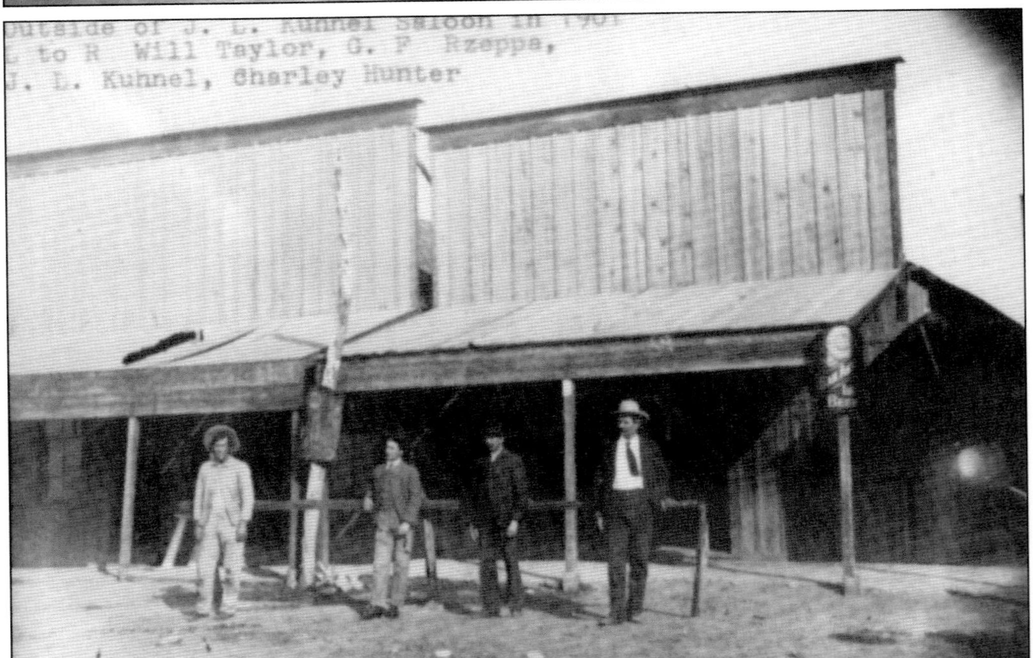

The Kuhnels also owned and operated a popular saloon. The fellows enjoying the business are, from left to right, Will Taylor, G.F. Rzeppa, J.L. Kuhnel, and Charley Hunter.

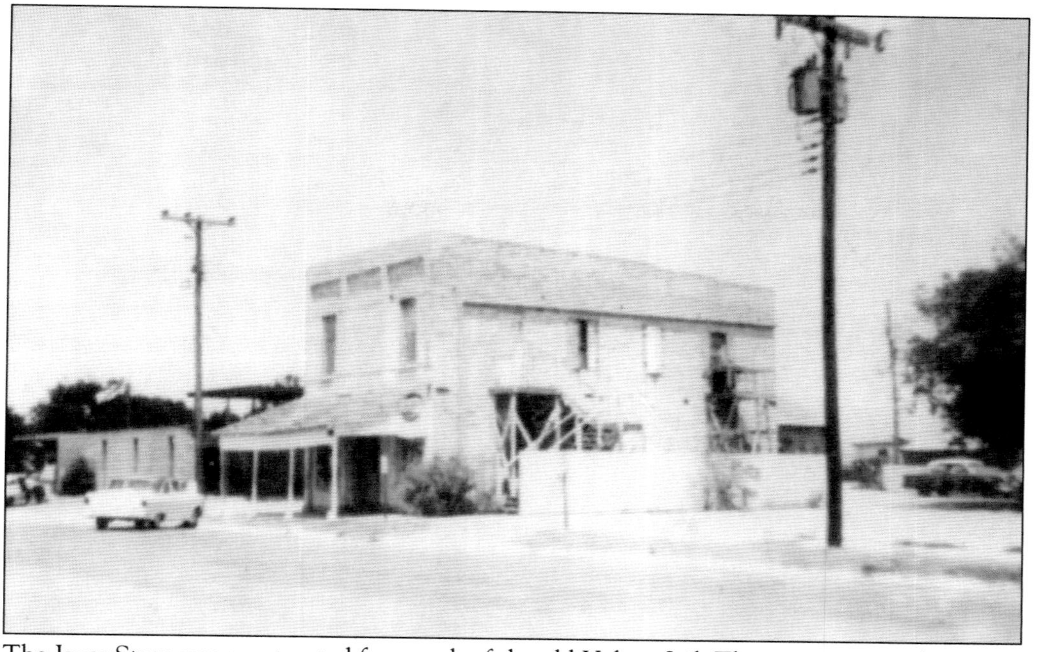

The Jauer Store was constructed from rock of the old Helena Jail. This structure was later torn down, and the rock was used as a retaining wall in front of the Karnes County National Bank. The upstairs was used for many years as a meeting hall for the Alamita Masonic Lodge No. 200.

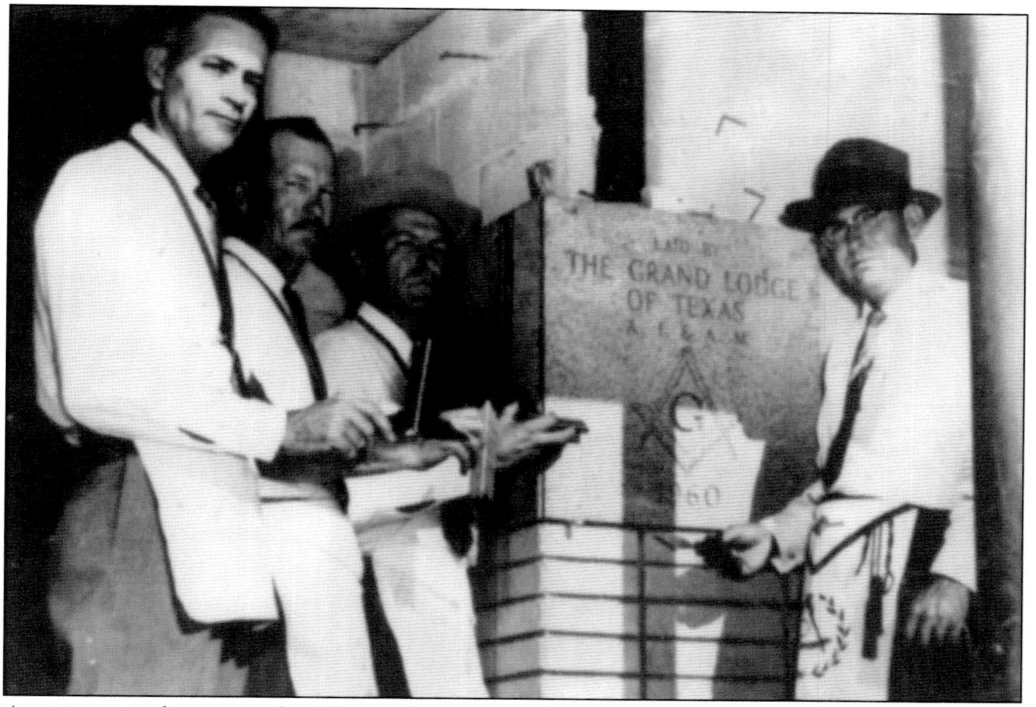

Activity stirred again at the Alamita Masonic Lodge No. 200. Shown laying a cornerstone are members James A. Stewart, J.F. Faulk, Pete Hartman, and Herbert O. Smith.

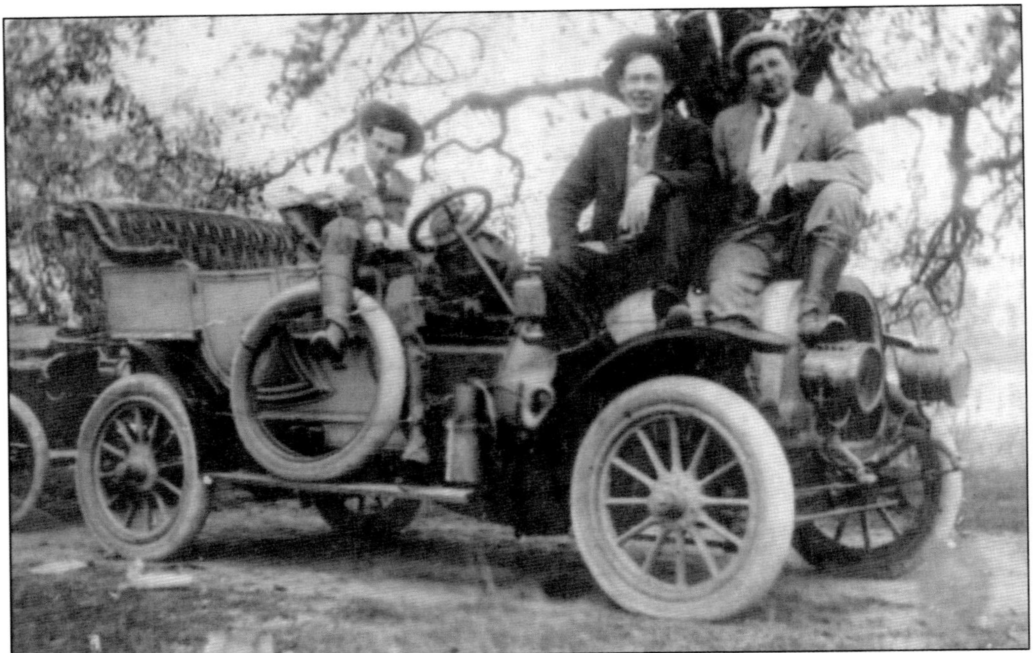

It was not long before the people who traveled the early trails and saw how much more efficient traveling on trains could be were asking for better roads. Many were already buying those newfangled motorized things called cars.

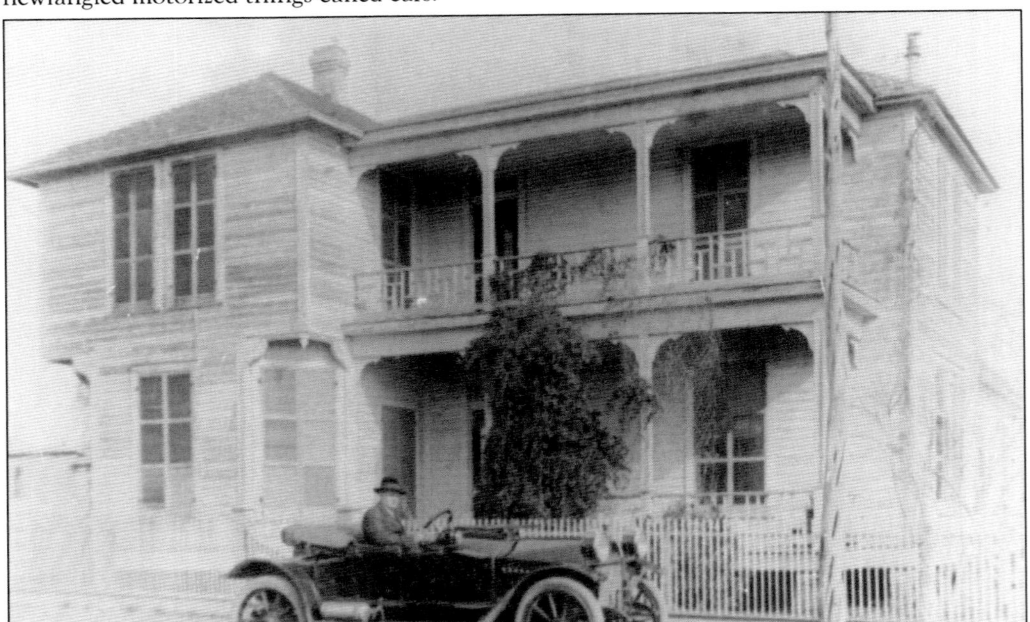

Getting to own one of those new cars could be a big deal. Plus, owners could go visit their relatives. Mrs. J.B. Pollok's nephew Albert Hackey is shown in front of the J.B. Pollok home after visiting family.

Six

Building Roads and Highways

The history of the area's early roads goes all the way back to 1540, when the first trail on Texas soil was made by Francisco de Coronado's expedition in search of the Seven Cities of Cibolo. Other trails like the Old Spanish Trail, now considered part of US Highway 90 and the El Camino Real (the King's Highway), consisted partly of the Old San Antonio Highway. Since the early days, there have been as many as five other trails in existence. Certainly, as the cattle industry began to grow, the cattle trails that were used to get the beef to the market were based on many of those well-trodden trails, but enlarged and tested by the huge herds of animals that went through the county. After the railroads took over marketing the cattle, the necessity of real roads for travelers began to be discussed. Many settlers were somewhat content to have a trail that led to home. With an awareness of how quickly travel from town to town could happen with well-maintained trails, often after the dirt roads had turned to liquid mud following heavy rains, attention was given for economic and cultural expansion among the communities. Settlers began to petition the state government for some way to finance road construction, and in the early 1880s, a system devised for counties to collect 25¢ on a $100 valuation was put into effect. In 1903, the state legislature finally authorized counties to issue bonds for public road improvement. Between 1903 and 1911, after more pressure from county governments finally led to a Bureau of Highways being enacted. Constructing roads and highways meant constructing bridges and county roads for crossing the river ways and creeks that in the past, was done the best way it could be. At last, Karnes County was growing and expanding, along with all of Texas, bringing goods and products to and from the landowners and to settlers who were here when it all began.

All of the road construction pictures in this chapter were taken by the author's father, Mason Johnson, the Texas Highway Department resident engineer for Karnes County from 1935 through 1958.

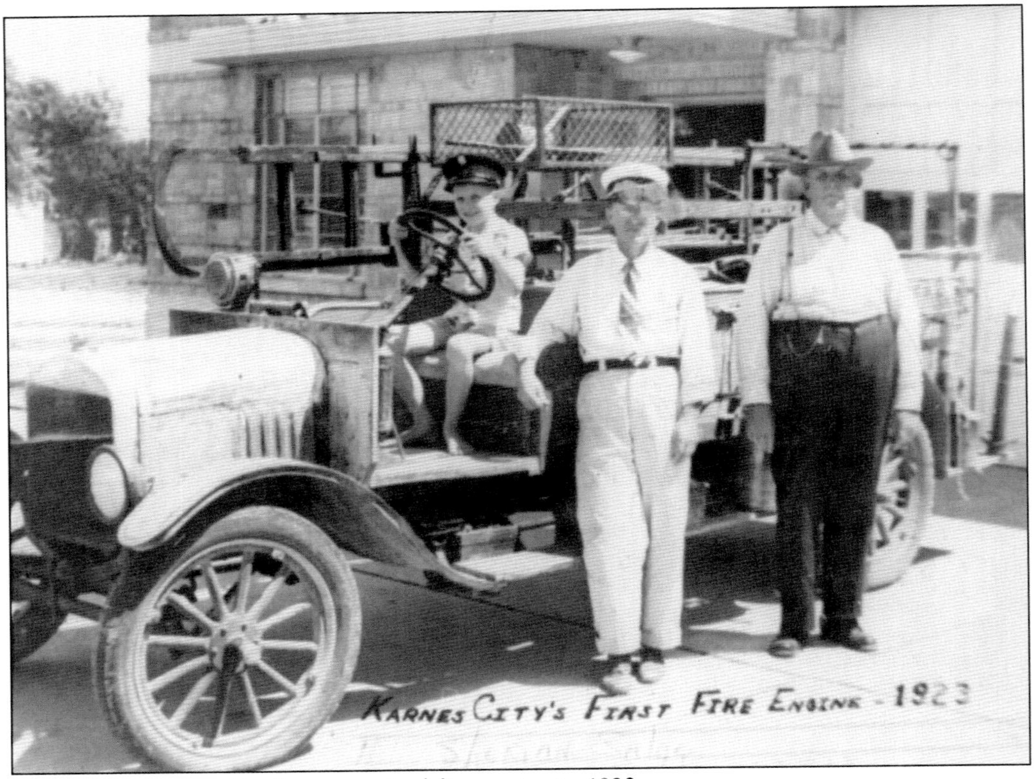

Karnes City received its first motorized fire engine in 1923.

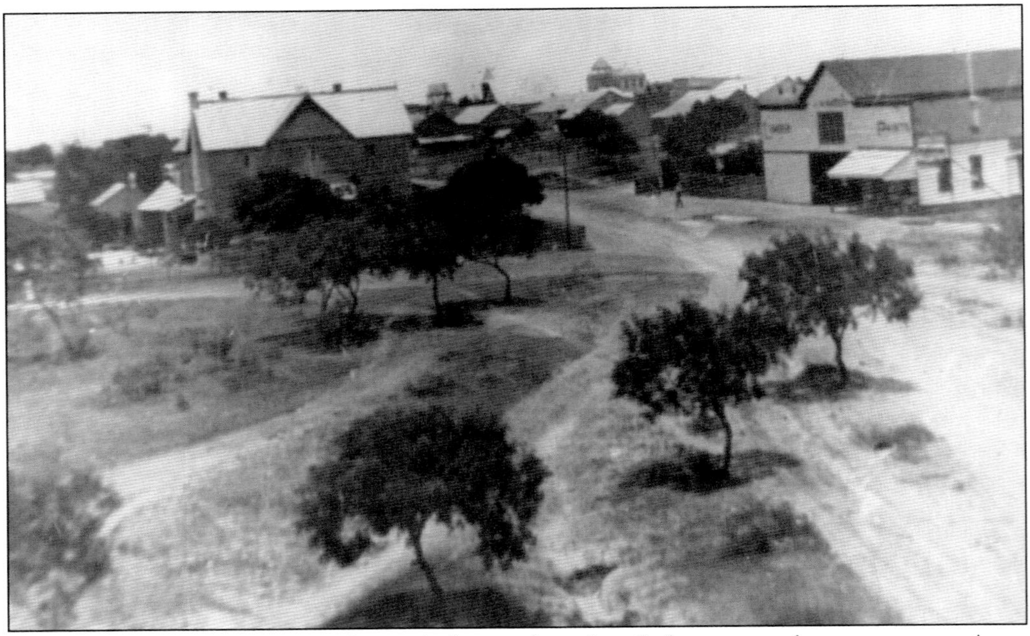
By the 1920s, adapting Karnes County's dirt roads and trails for car travel was necessary. As to these streets depicted in Kenedy, they would soon no longer be the norm.

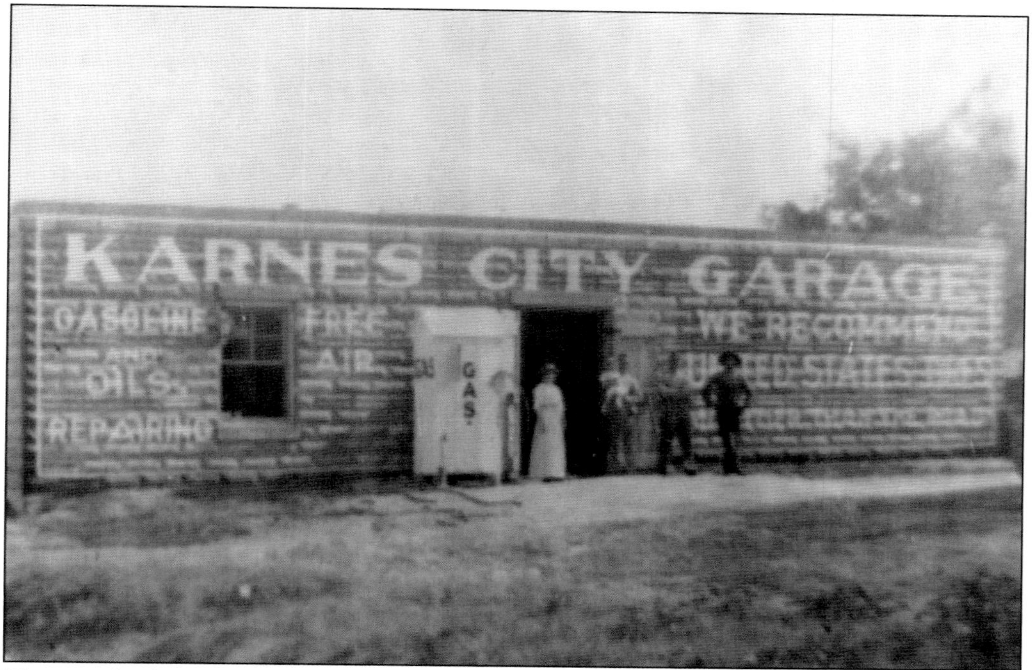

This was the first service station in Karnes City. Daisy and Albert Weir with their son stand in front of this new and different kind of business. Other shops were being added in the towns to keep the motorized wheels turning. Again, petitions to the state government were being made for road repair, including paving to stop the liquid mud that appeared in the roads after a heavy rain.

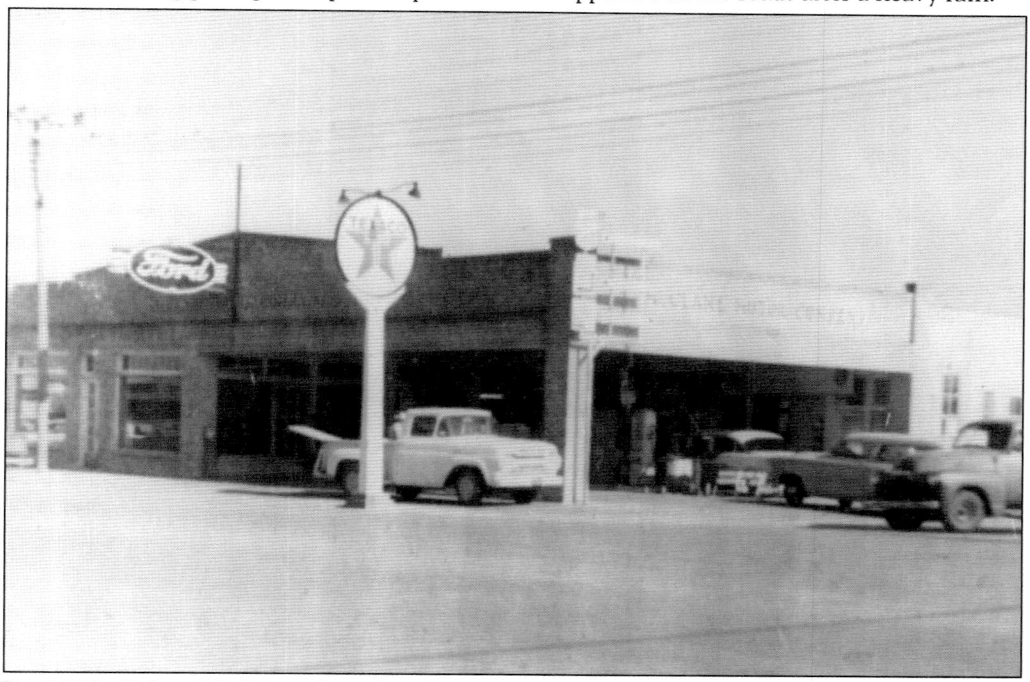

By 1930, Sykes McClane bought the motor car company pictured above from the Kauffmann Brothers.

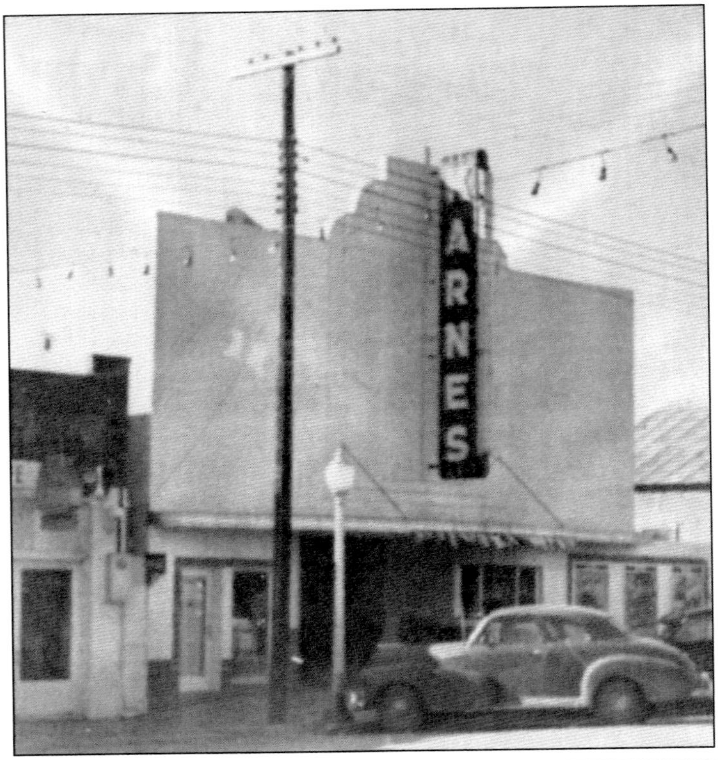

Not far down the street from McClanes, the Karnes Theater was opening its doors for customers ready to see the latest movies. It was owned by the Smason family, who had just moved to Karnes City.

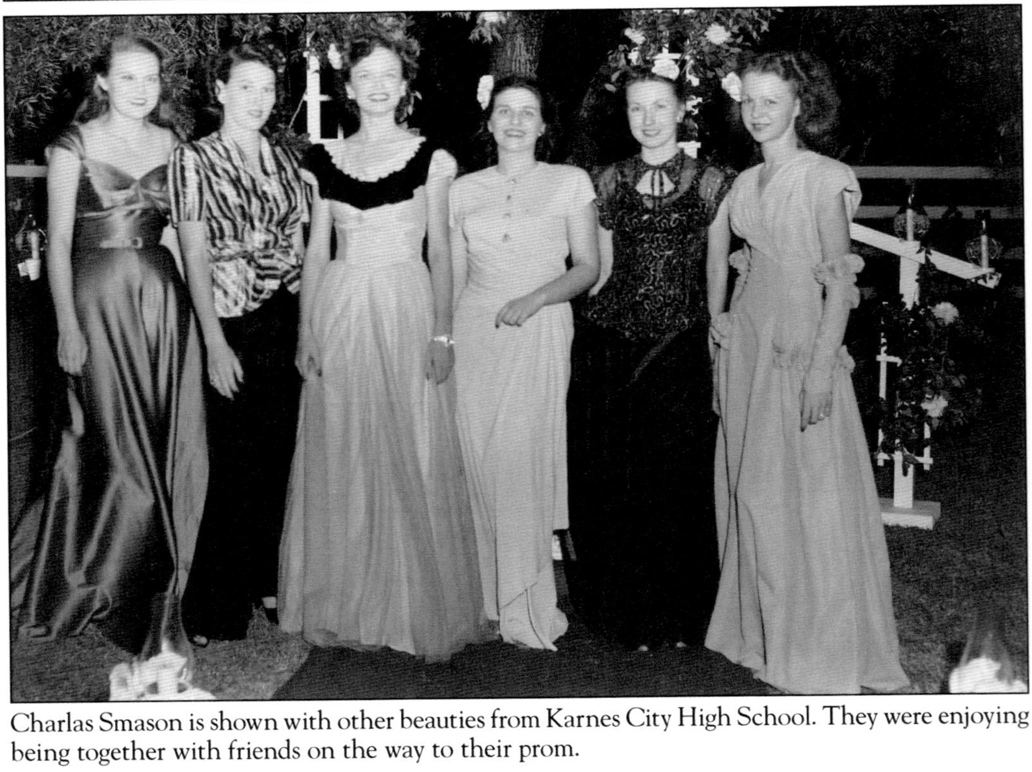

Charlas Smason is shown with other beauties from Karnes City High School. They were enjoying being together with friends on the way to their prom.

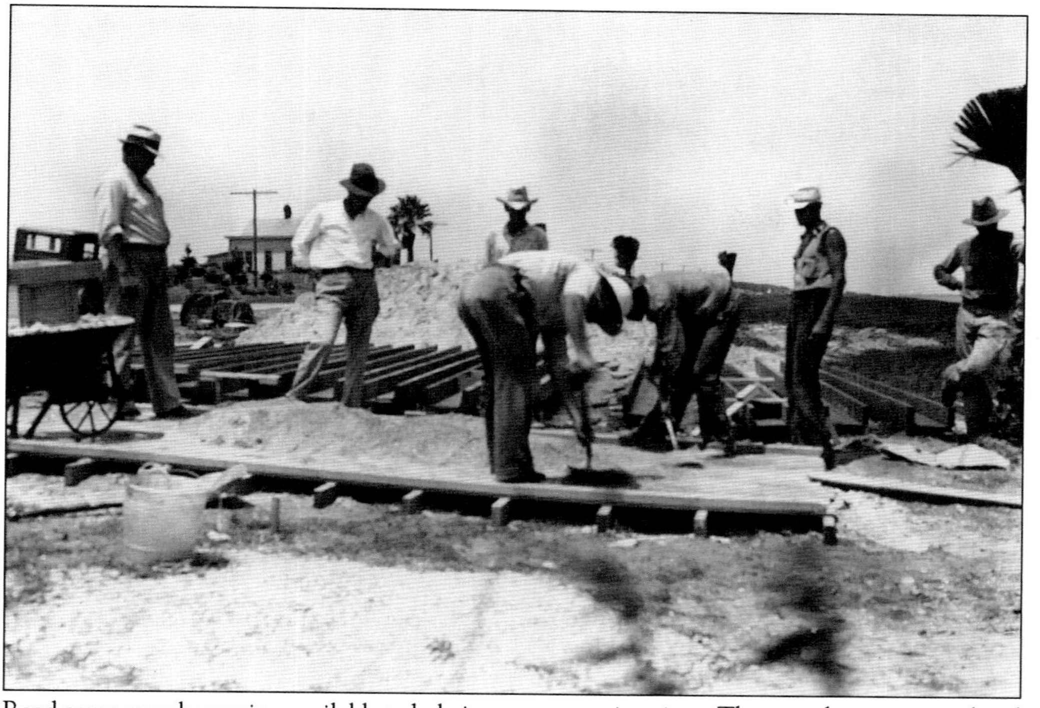

Road crews were becoming available to help in emergency situations. These workers are considered to be the first members of the highway department.

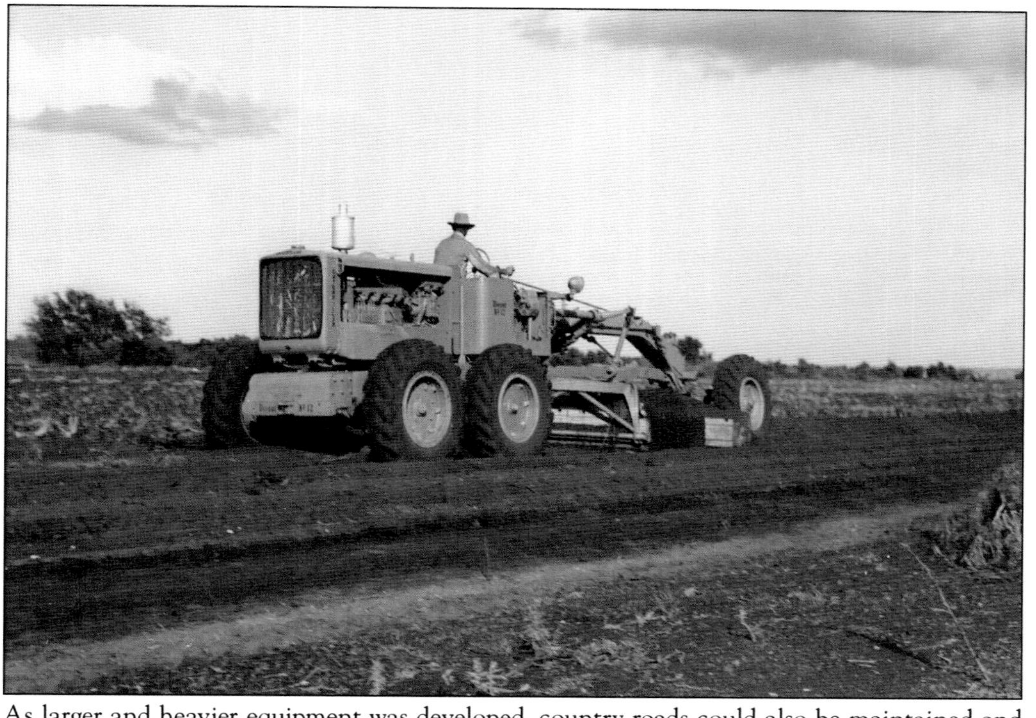

As larger and heavier equipment was developed, country roads could also be maintained and constructed for travel to and from outlying areas of the small towns.

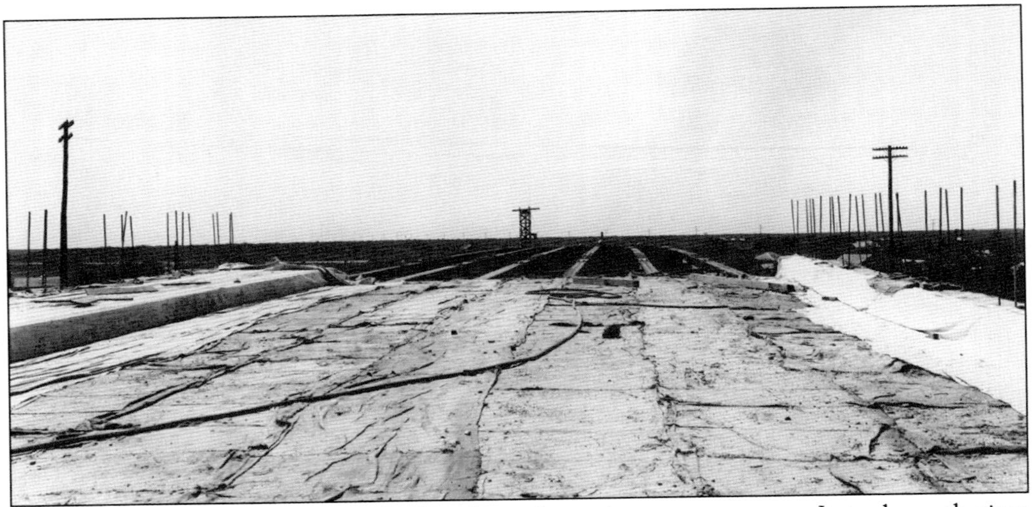

Getting roads ready for any kind of work in those days was not easy. It took much time and preparation.

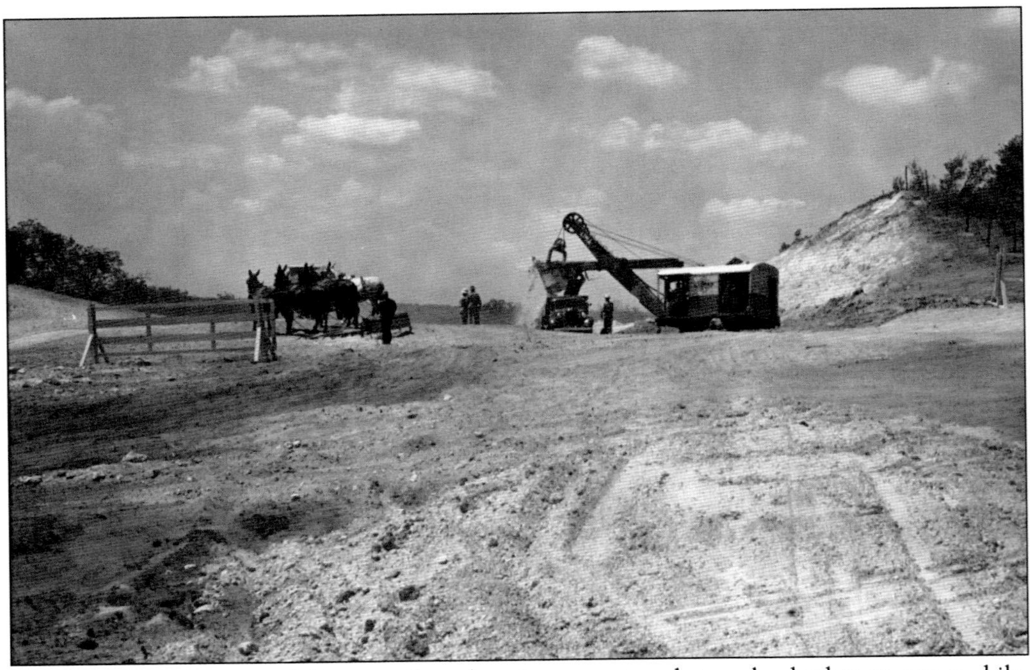

Moving a large amount of dirt contributed at times to a tough travel, whether an automobile, buggy, or a horse was used.

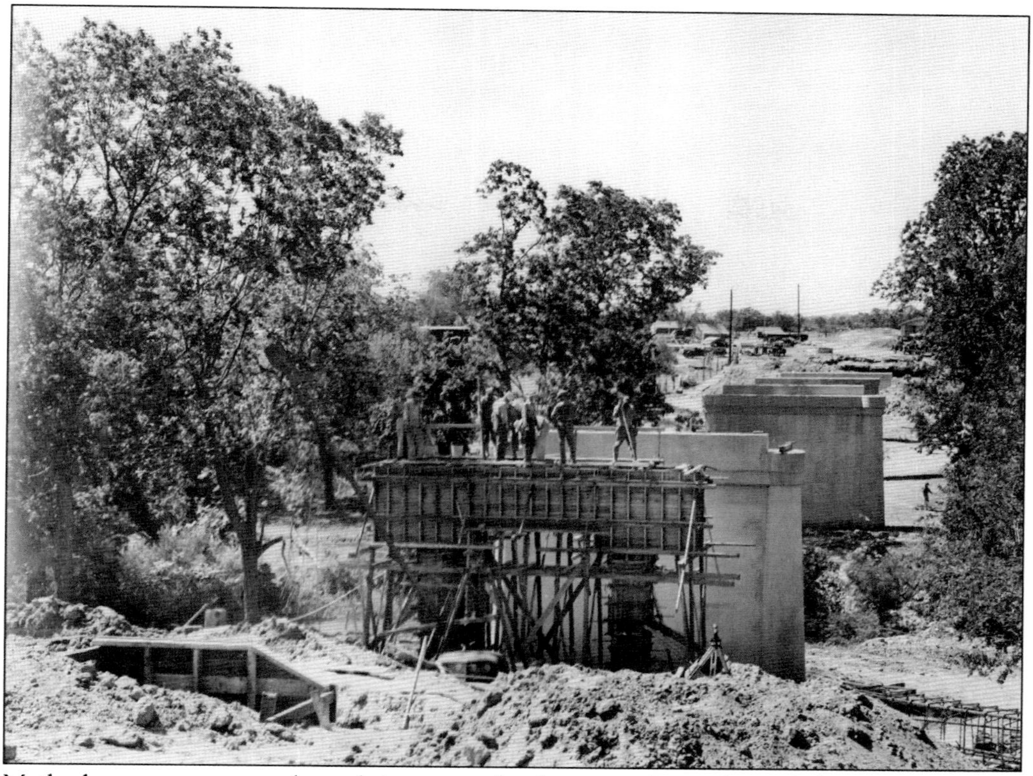

Methods to get across creeks and rivers were hard to come by in the early beginnings of road construction. It took much time, effort, and labor to find the best way to do the job.

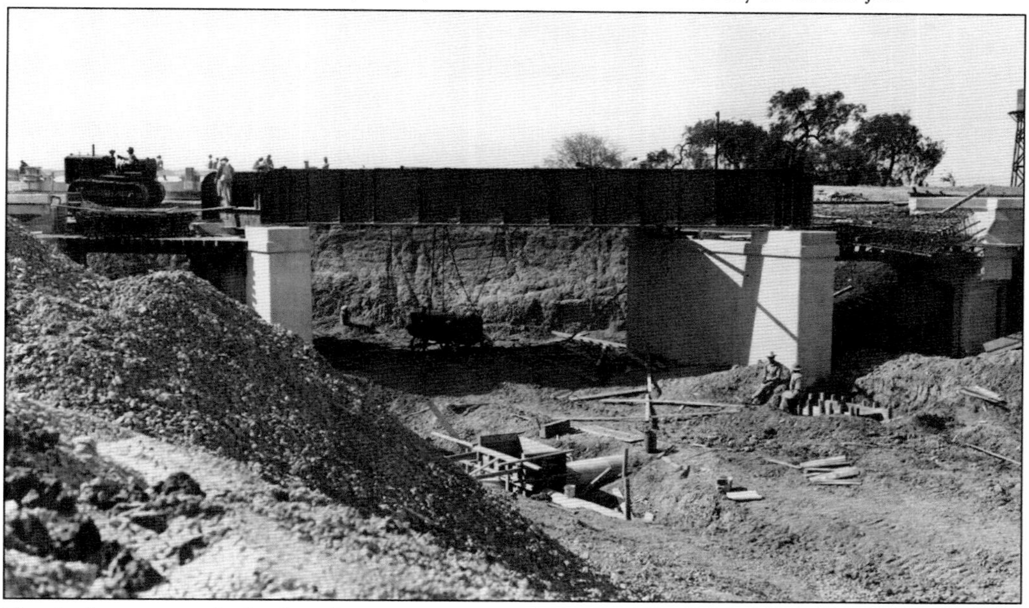

Slowly dug out riverbeds after the rainy season or during long dry spells helped construct bridges for vehicles and muscles for the men who did the work. Here, the workers below are taking a break.

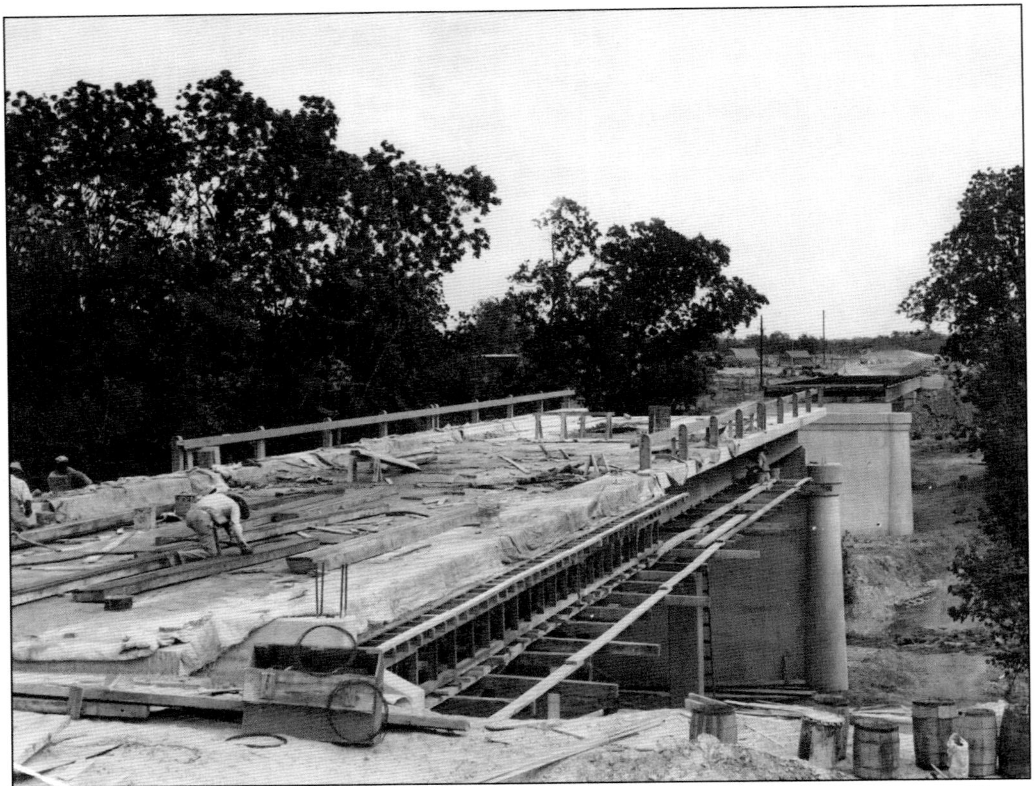

Some jobs were bigger than others. This bridge had to be constructed over the San Antonio River and Cibolo and Jacobs Creeks in 1939.

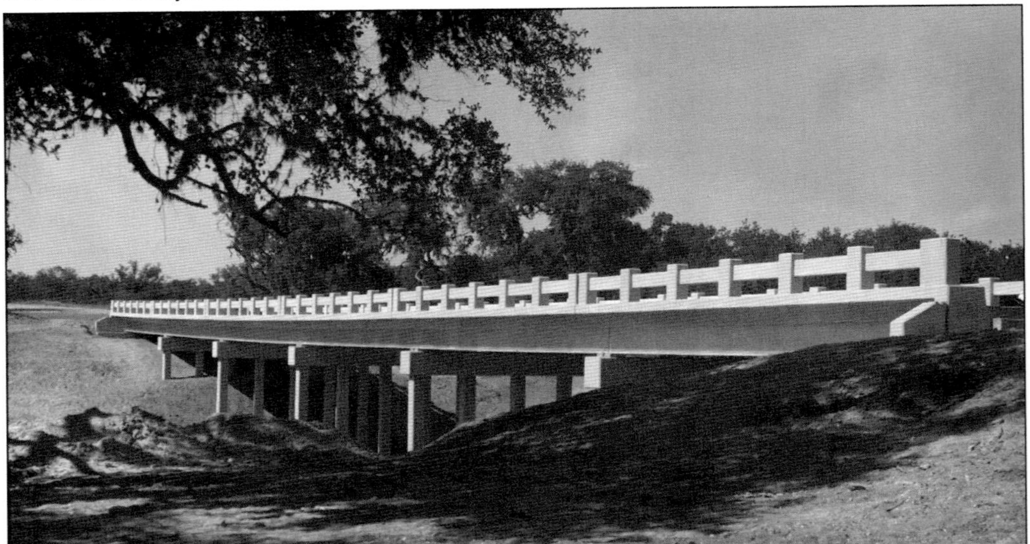

Once the bridge was completed, it made life easier for those who had to travel the roads everyday. How they managed before the bridge was completed took a lot of ingenuity, and the bridge added a measure of its own beauty to the environment.

If getting home still meant traveling country lanes, it might be a while before one could find a better way home.

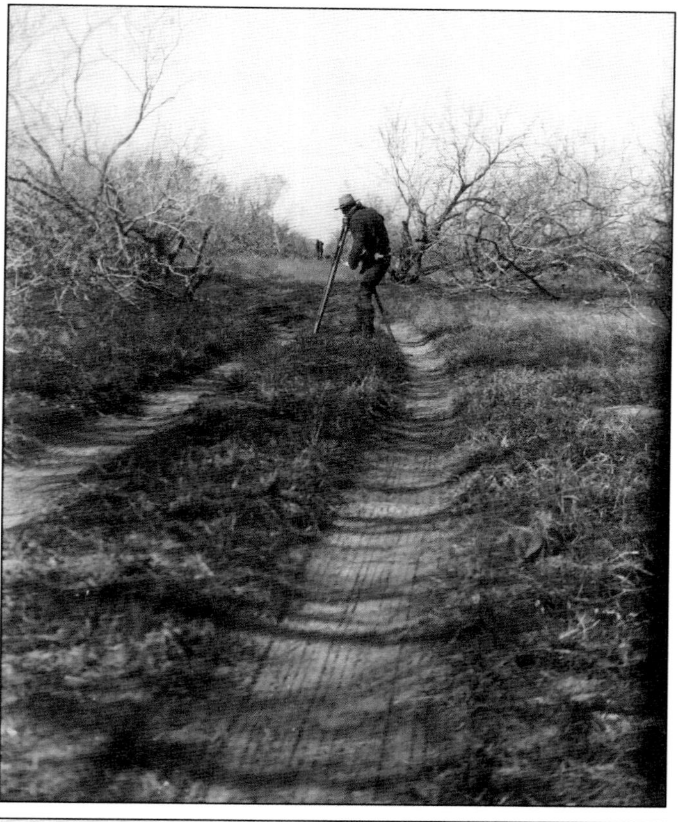

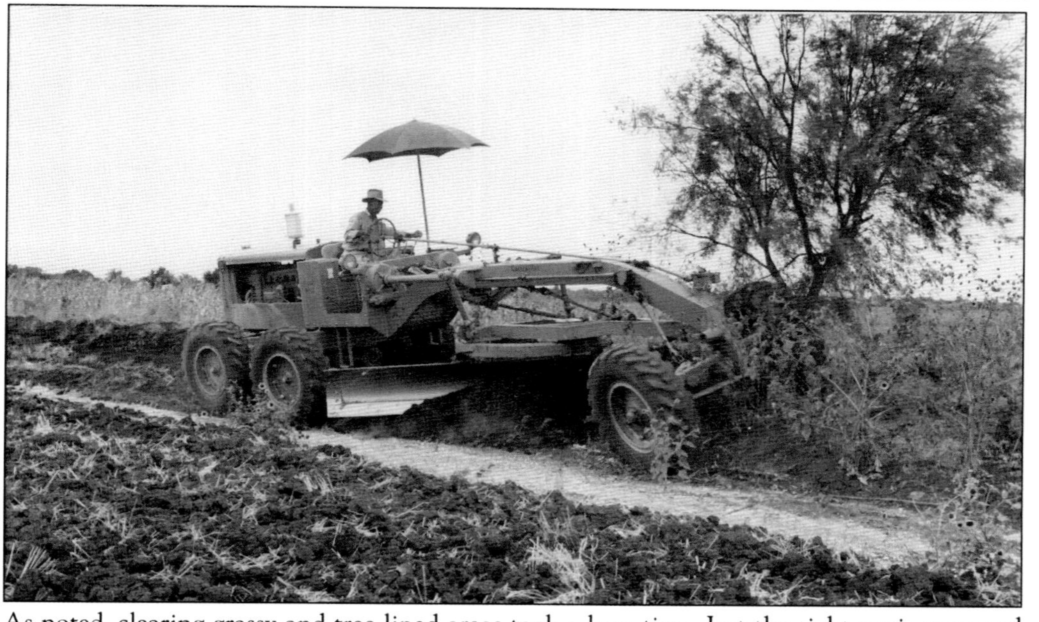

As noted, clearing grassy and tree lined areas took a long time. Just the right equipment and a person of skill to operate it helped. One of the best things about constructing the roads and highways was that it created jobs for the county.

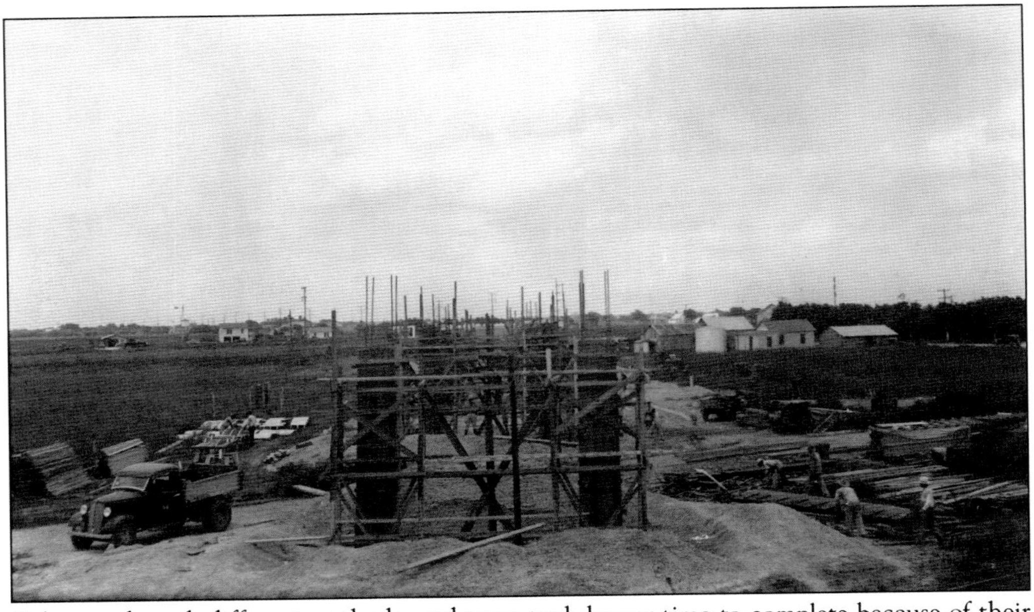

Other roads took different methods, and some took longer time to complete because of their vastness. Just surveying and scoping out the distance was quite a task.

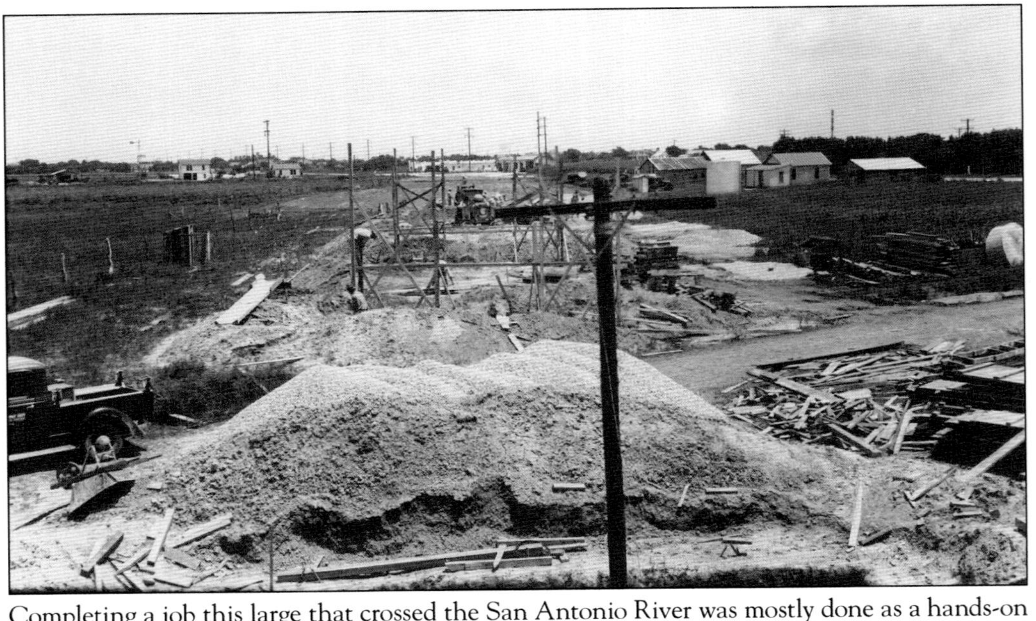

Completing a job this large that crossed the San Antonio River was mostly done as a hands-on job. The people in the dwellings across the way surely looked forward to having a substantial means of crossing the waterways.

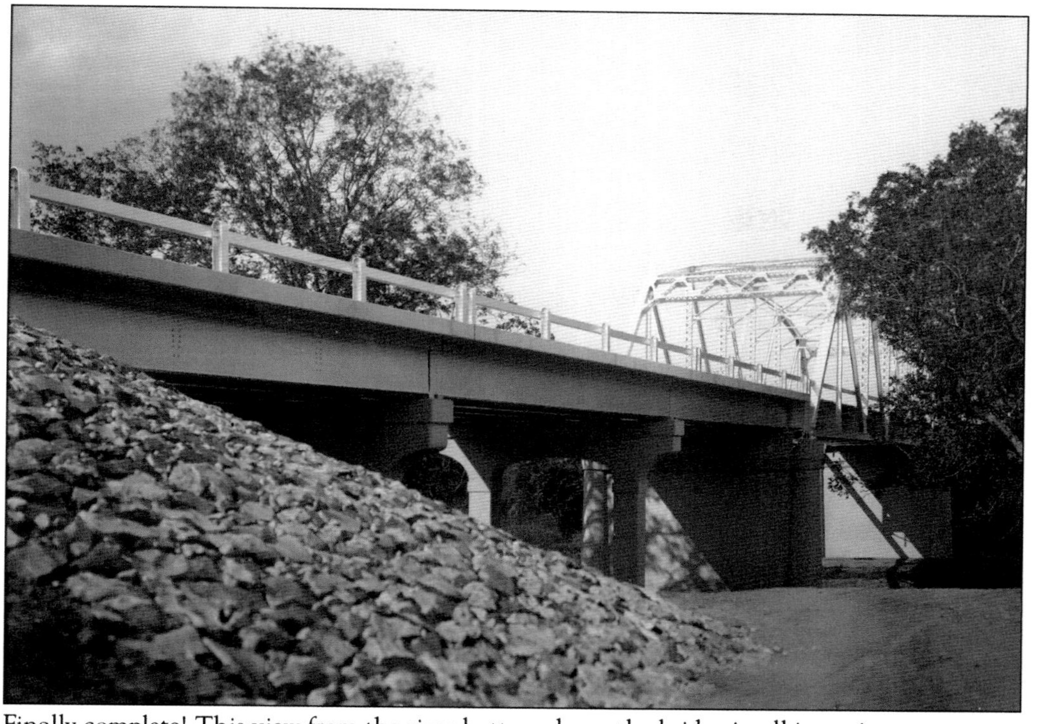

Finally complete! This view from the river bottom shows the bridge in all its majesty.

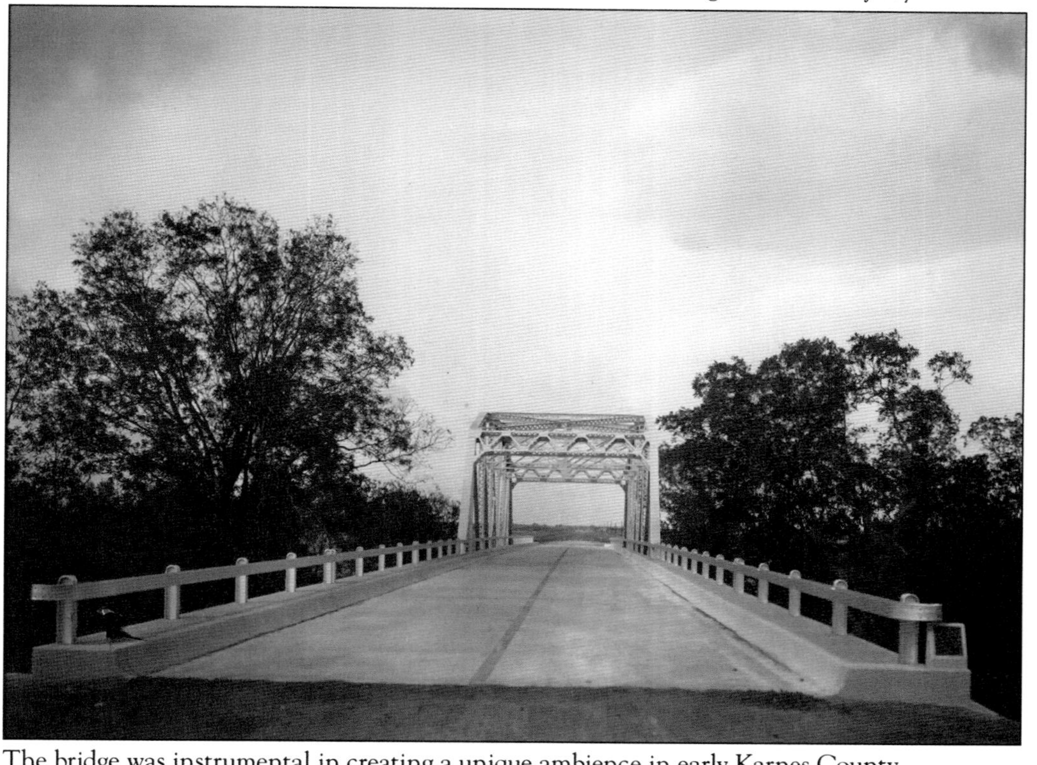

The bridge was instrumental in creating a unique ambience in early Karnes County.

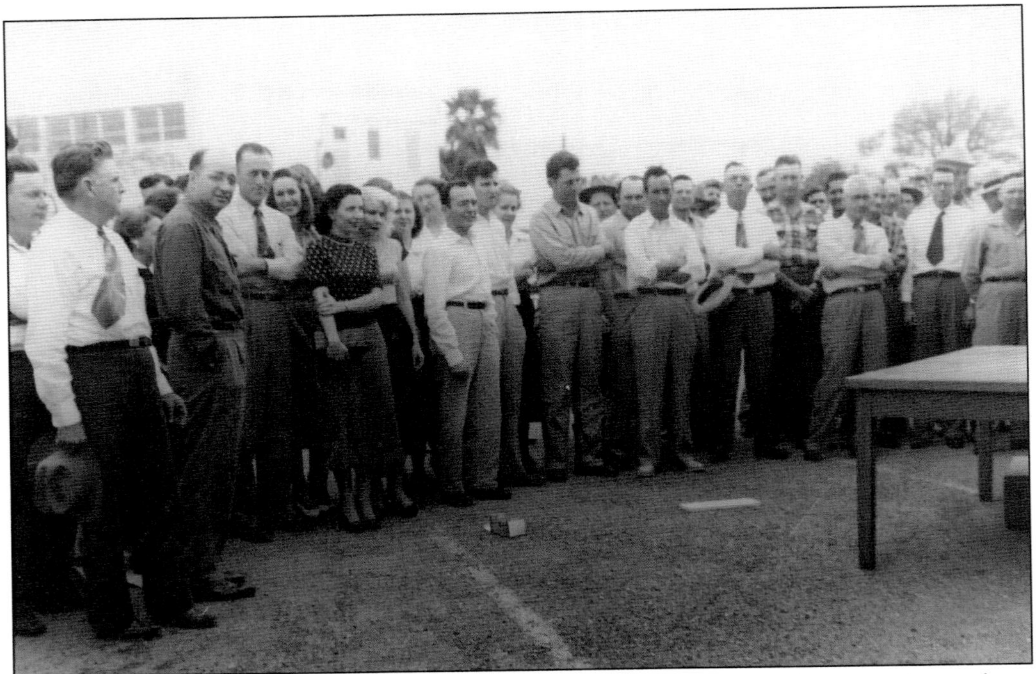

Thanking the highway department in those days meant having a party. The group shown above includes members of the department and townspeople who were happy to travel on good roads in the 1930s.

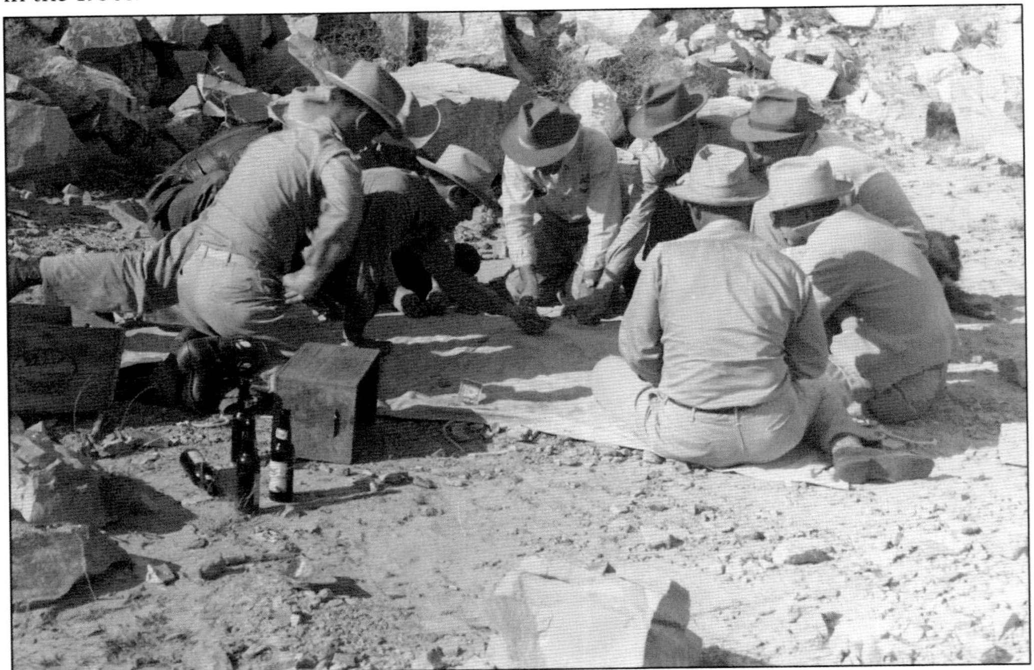

If there was a lot of rock to be moved, it was a good idea to put heads together and figure out the best way to go. On a hot day, a libation (and maybe a game of poker) provided a welcome break from a hard day's work.

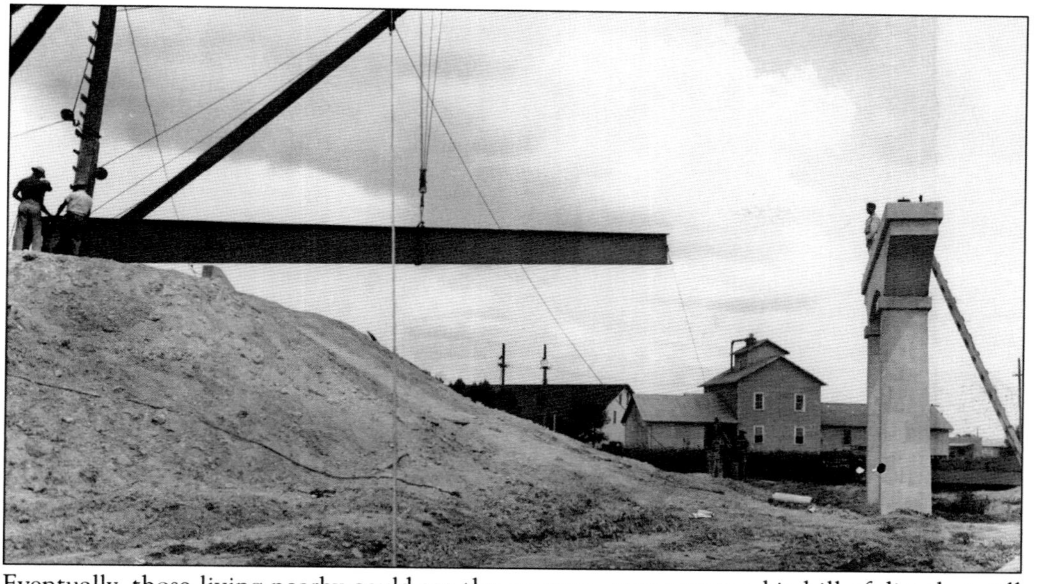

Eventually, those living nearby could see the progress, even across a big hill of dirt that still needed to be moved.

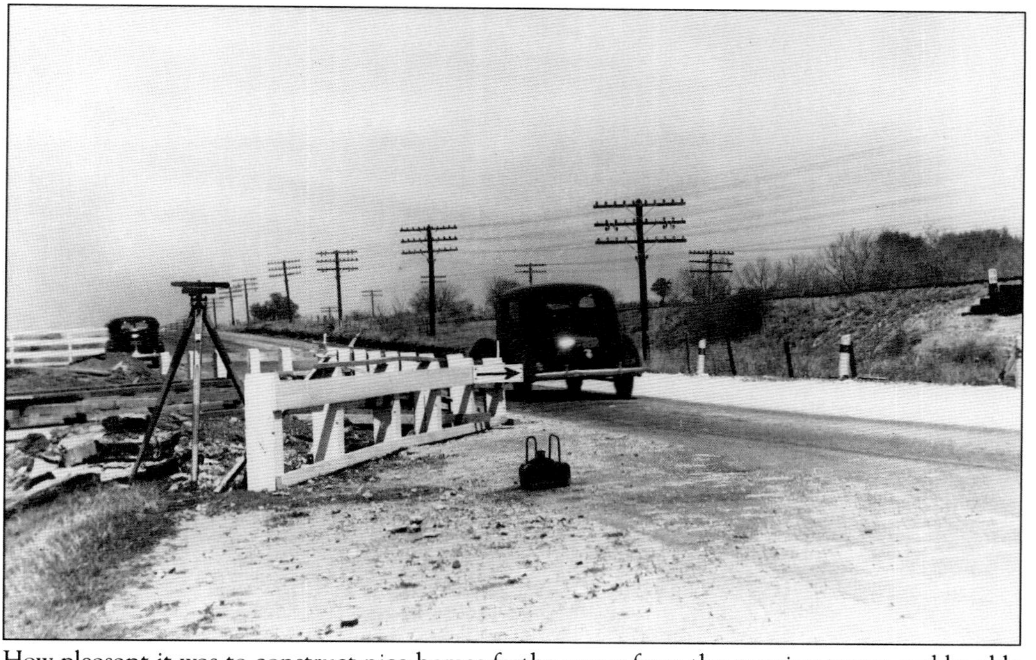

How pleasant it was to construct nice homes farther away from the growing towns and be able to get to them with little trouble.

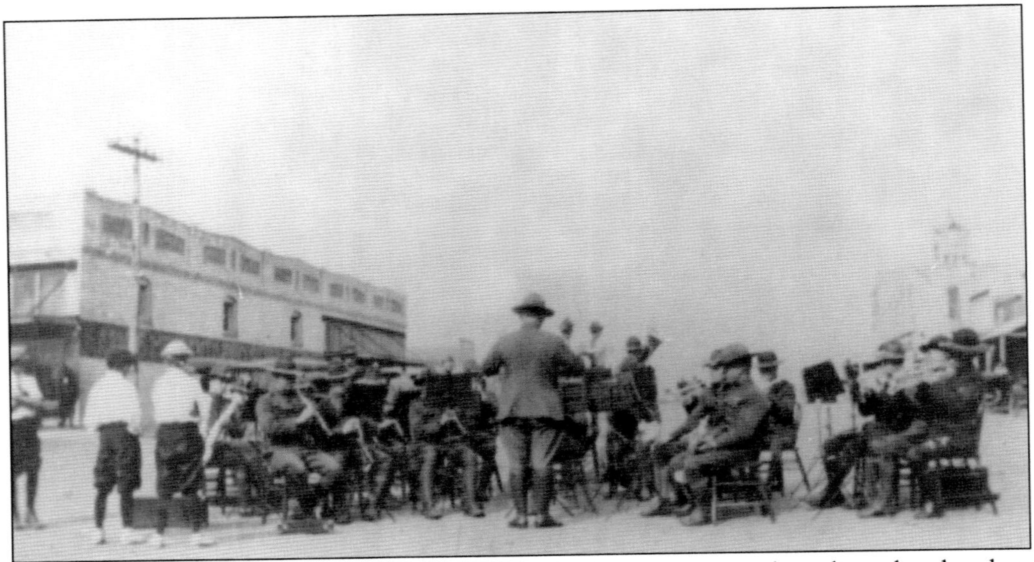

Things had been happening in town as well. World War I was over, and a military band took to the downtown streets to perform in celebration.

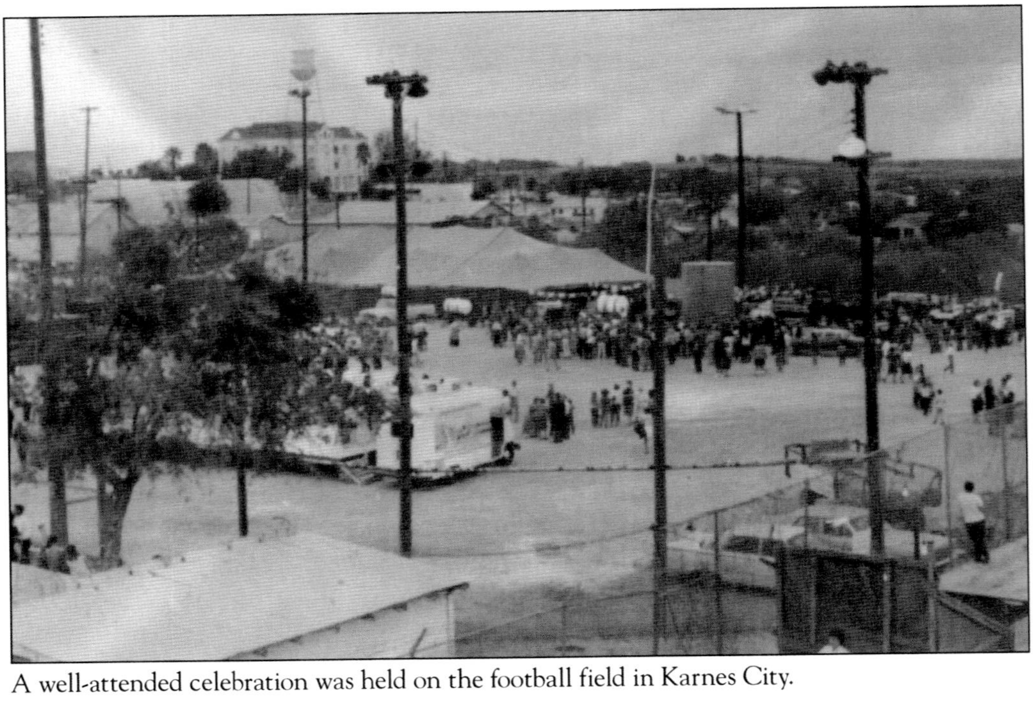

A well-attended celebration was held on the football field in Karnes City.

Seven

The Future Holds Promise

As the county roads and state highways continued to connect communities along with the farms and ranches in the area, the railroads began to lose much of the ground they once covered. Travel by car was not far behind. In place of the chaotic and unsetting presence of Indian raids and other groups trying to turn back the clock on civilization, a settling down and cumulative business growth turned into a progressive, steady rate. Most towns were building real school buildings instead of just occupying the early churches and other available structures during the week. The first larger general stores, lumberyards, machine shops, and cotton gins to aid and encourage growth in every aspect were occurring at a more and more rapid rate. Soon, every town or community had at least one doctor; some even had two. Doctor's offices expanded to provide hospital care when needed by their patients. The general well-being of the communities could then lead to times of socializing with neighbors by starting bands and developing picnic areas and playing fields for their schools and communities. Runge was one of the first towns to have an outdoor bandstand in its first park area. Some larger homes later offered rooms to rent, and one even became a hotel. This would allow outside tourists to come and stay overnight and partake in the festivities or watch the earliest horse races and rodeos. Even the cattle industry would often conduct competitions in a way for students to raise cattle and other animals through their FFA organizations; they would compete to win recognition prizes for their breeds. One family, the Kimbles of Karnes City, became famous for its longhorns, especially WOW, who has won seven Texas championships and has a longhorn spread of over 10 feet from tip to tip.

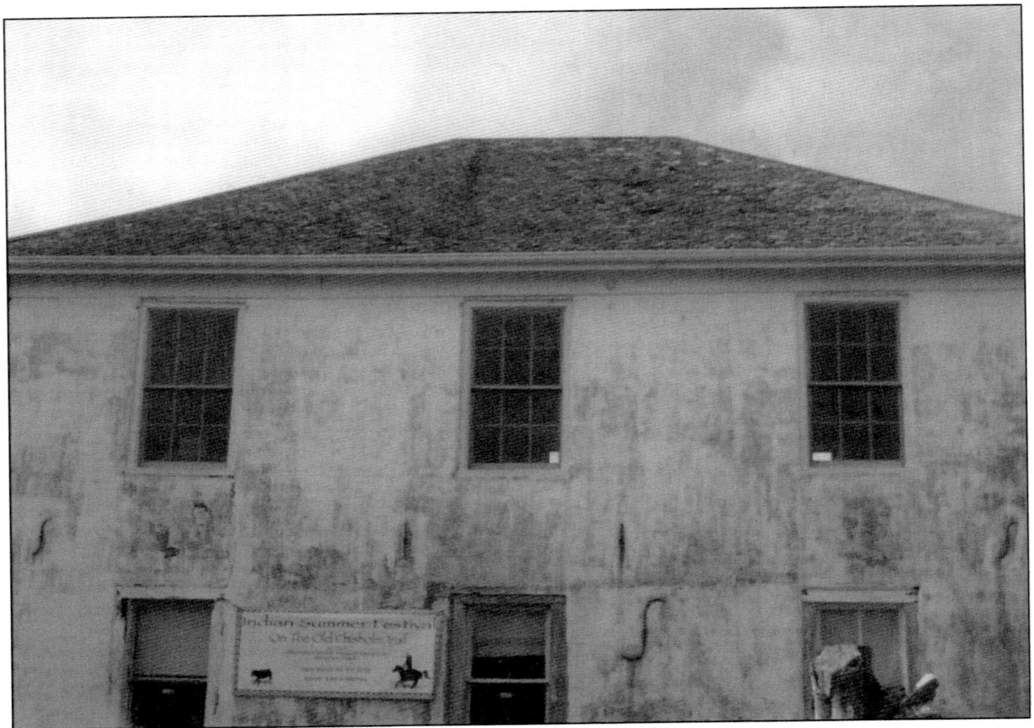

Schools had been in session almost as soon as Karnes County came into existence. Helena founders Tom Ruckman and Dr. Owings were highly educated men who prioritized the need for schools, and a school was constructed right after the first courthouse. After the county seat was moved, the first courthouse itself was used as a school.

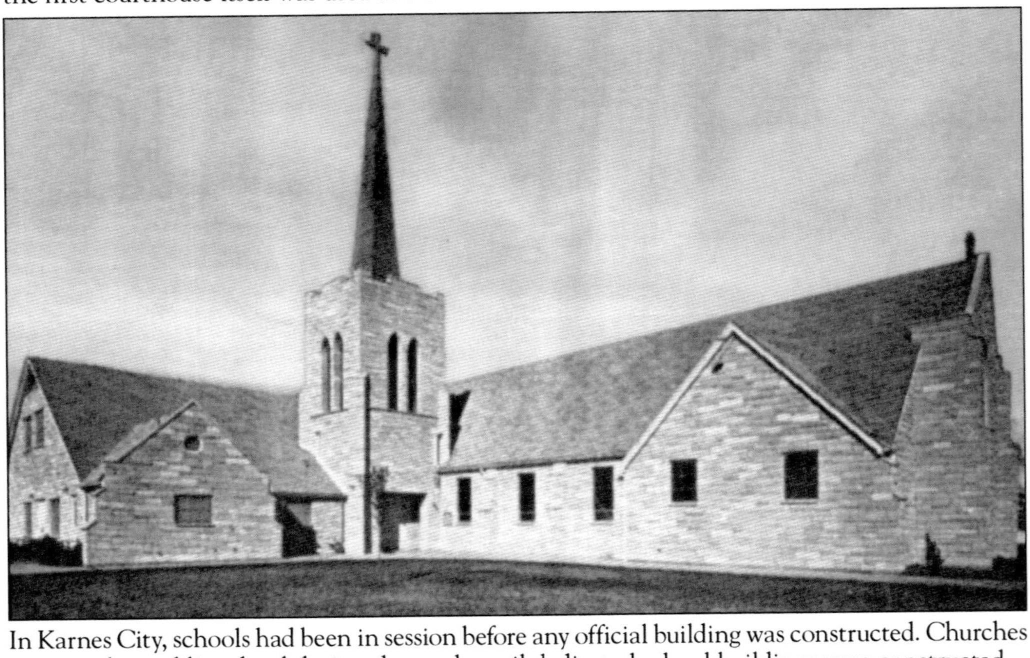

In Karnes City, schools had been in session before any official building was constructed. Churches were used as public school during the week until dedicated school buildings were constructed.

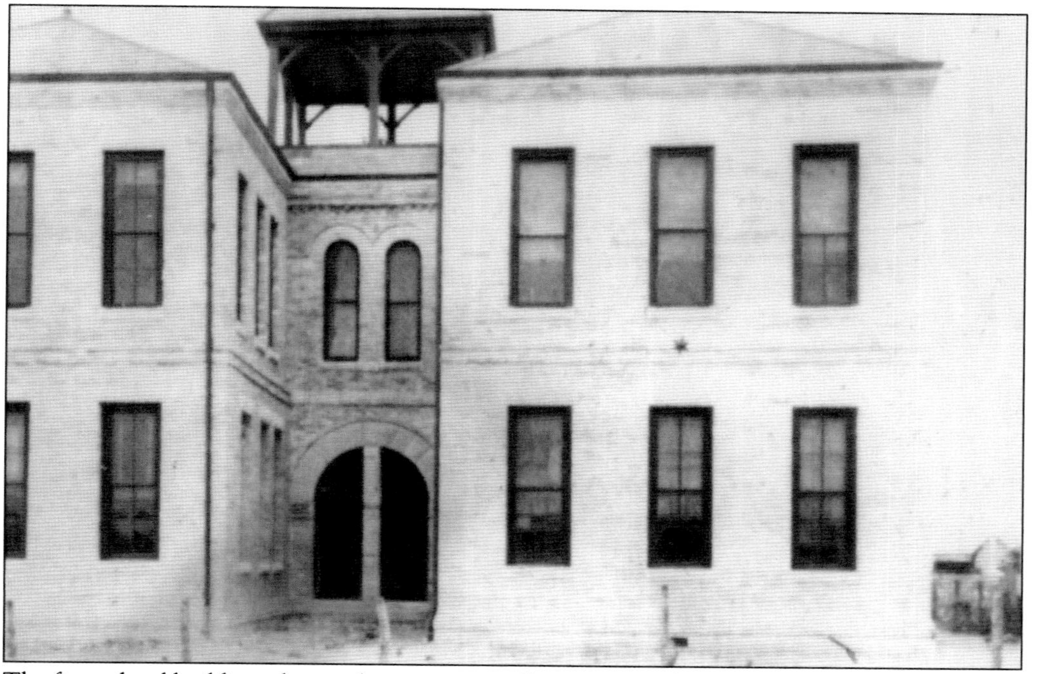

The first school building, shown above, was actually constructed in 1894. The first known official teacher was Maggie Skiles. Little is known about her and her family, but they must have been one of the earliest families to settle here.

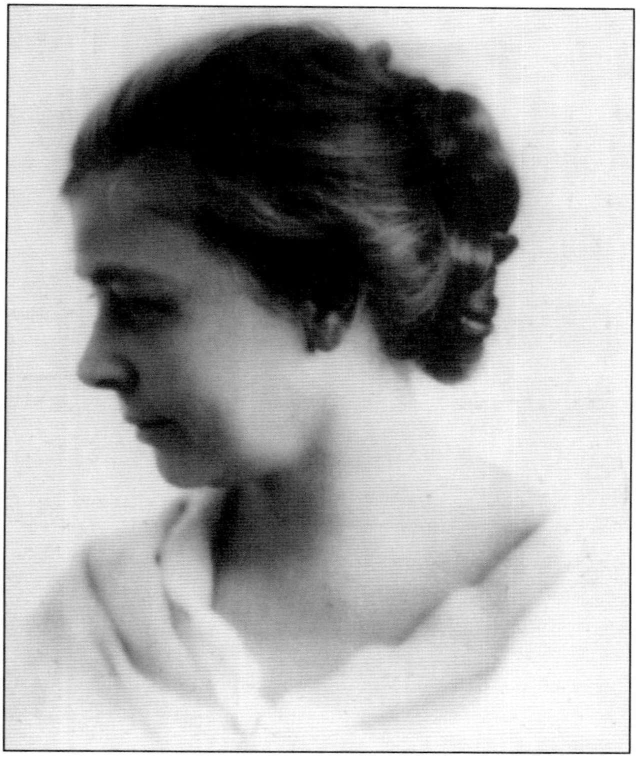

Another early schoolteacher was Lucy Baxter, known to have taught from 1918 to 1922. It was thought that she may have taught before and after those years as well.

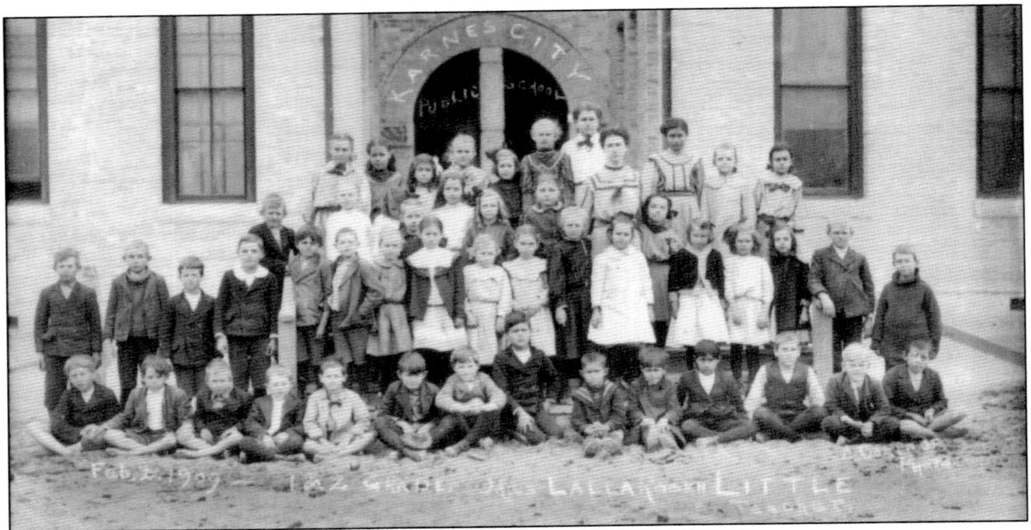

This 1909 image shows students in the first and second grades. As was the custom for those years, one teacher taught more than one grade level. The teacher of these two grades was Lalla Rookh Little.

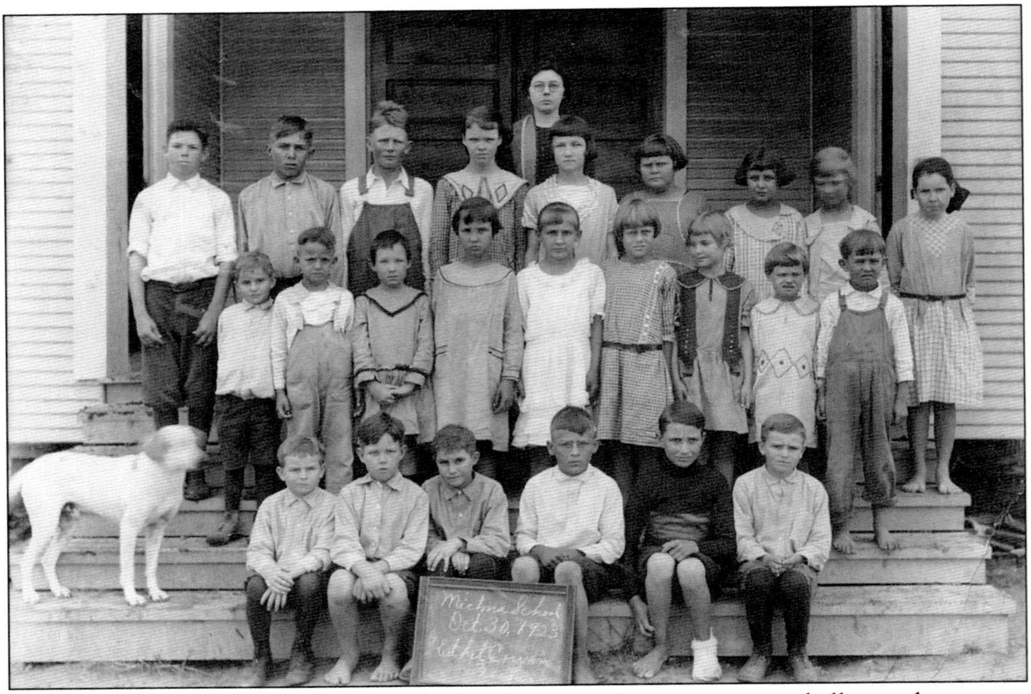

Other classes were being held and school buildings were being constructed all over the county. The Michna School was built near Kenedy in an area called Nedrick. This photograph was taken in 1923.

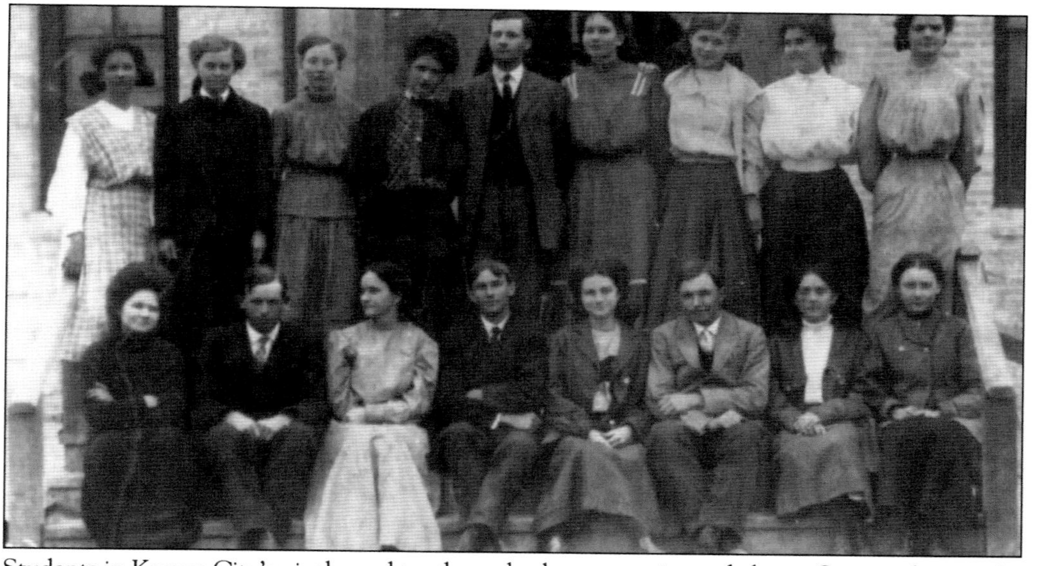

Students in Karnes City's ninth- and tenth-grade classes are pictured above. One teacher taught the students in 1909.

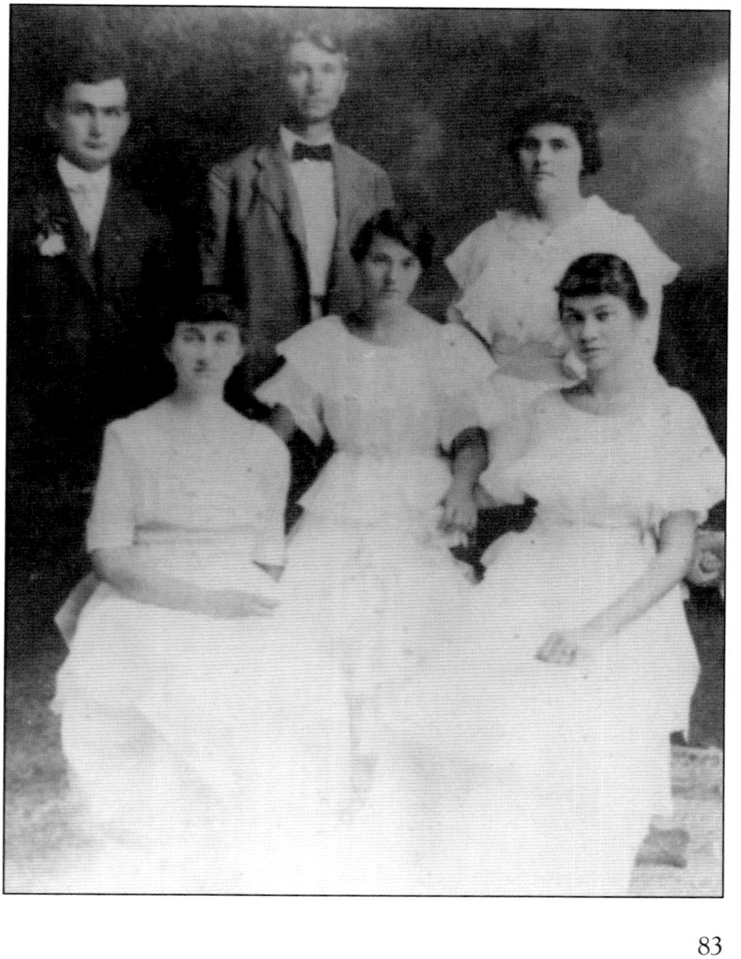

Shown are members of the 1918 graduating class in Karnes City. They are, from left to right, (first row) Frances (Franny) Yeary-Eschenberg, Erma Blakeney, and Erma Banfield; (second row) Otho Person, Superintendent W.H. Korges, and Anna Boucher.

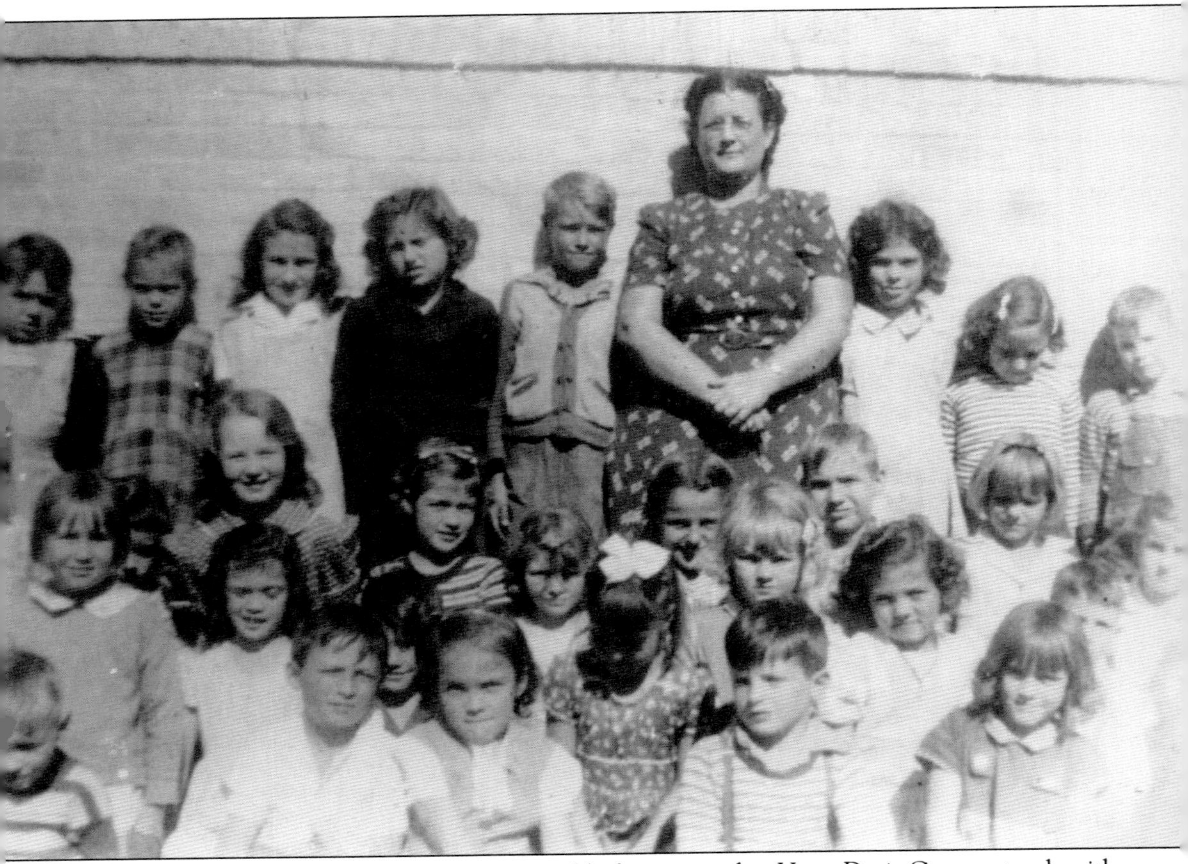

In the early 1940s, one teacher was responsible for two grades. Here, Doris Garner stands with her first- and second-grade students.

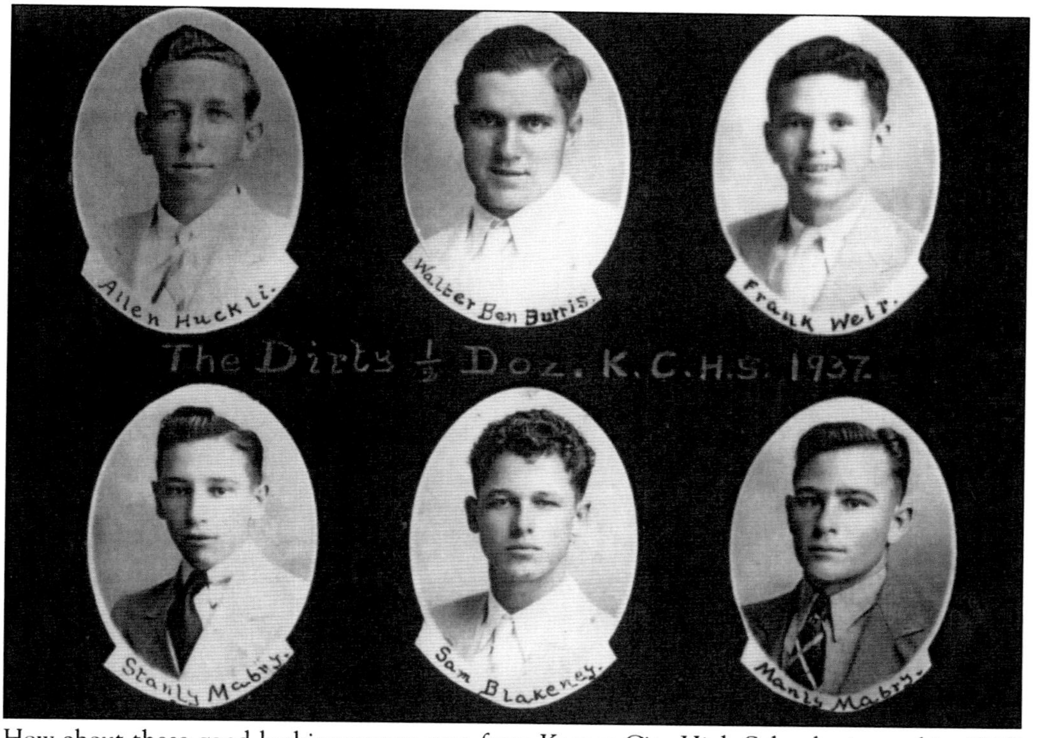

How about these good looking young men from Karnes City High School, pictured in 1937? Here they are labeled the dirty half dozen. Could that really be true? (Courtesy of the McClane family collection.)

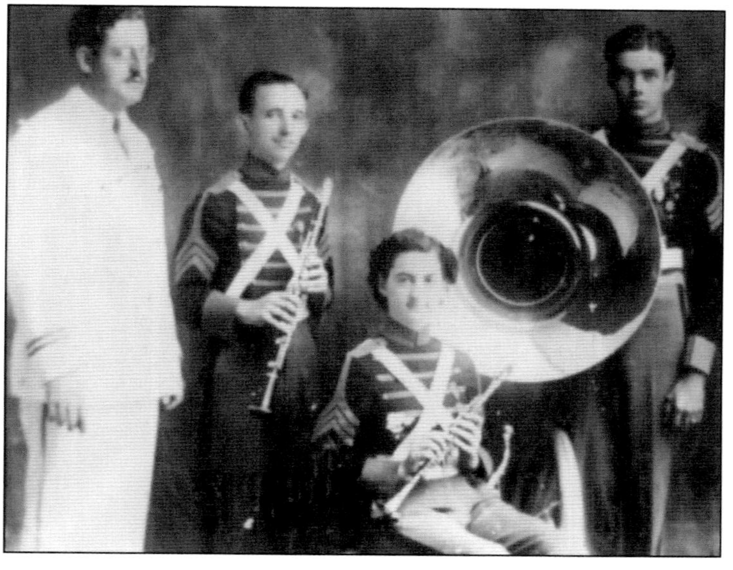

What would small towns do without their football teams and marching bands? Other activities included agricultural and future farmers clubs. Some members of the 1939 Karnes City Band are, from left to right, Mr. Shaddegg (band director), Horace Armstrong, Mary Lee Menn, and James A. Stewart.

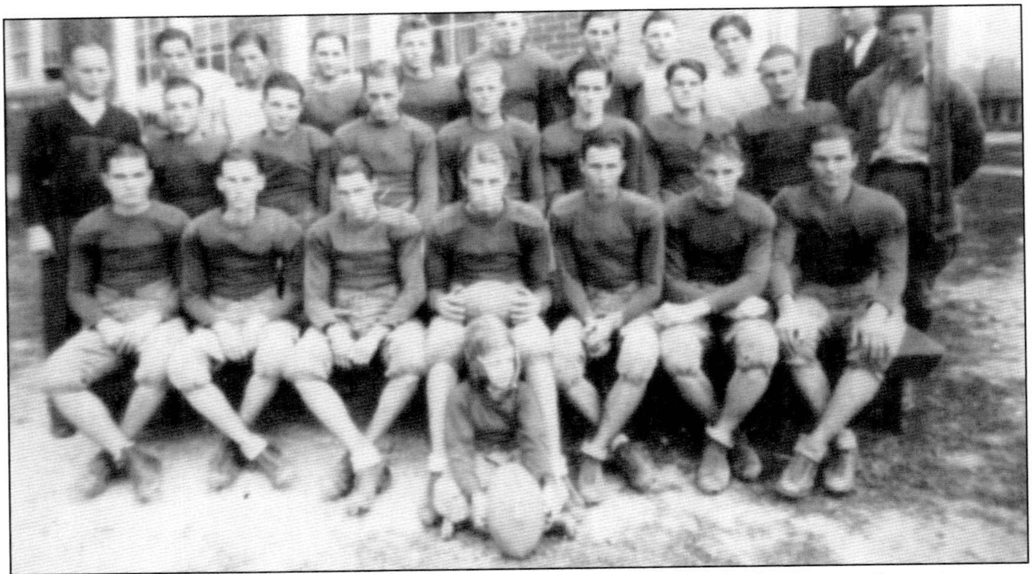

By 1930, the Karnes City football team, the Badgers, had become the bi-district champions.

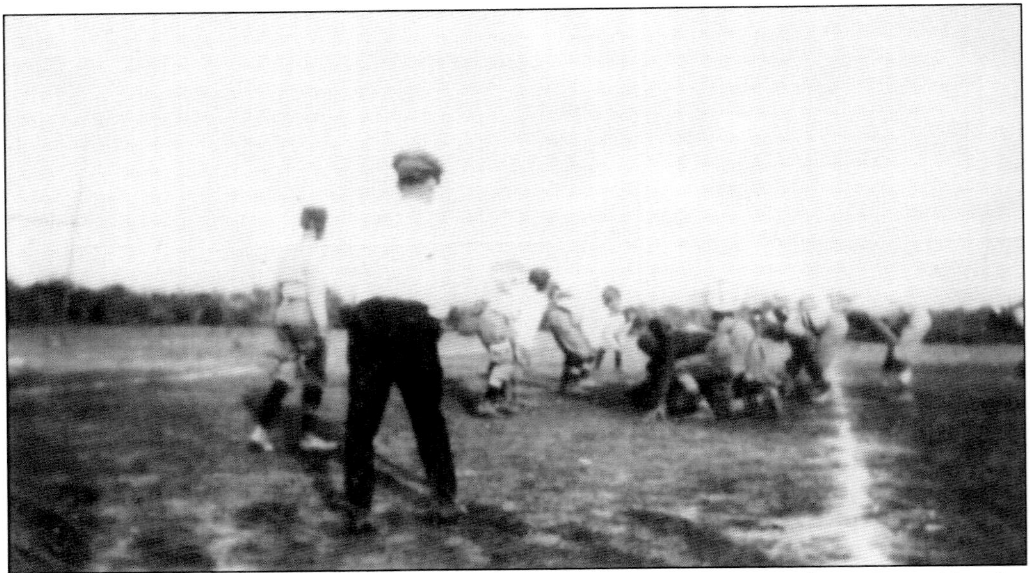

Note the old-time football uniforms in this image. The 1922 football team beat Nixon 18 to 0.

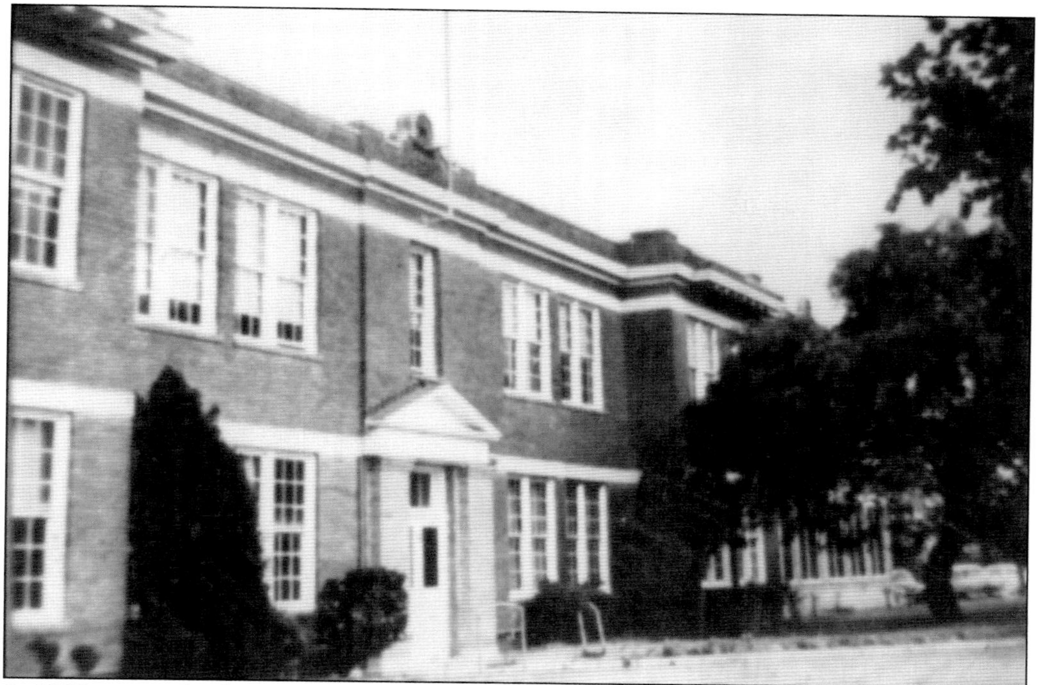

In 1925, a new school was needed and this picture shows the school as it looked at the time. Later on, several additions were made. It was replaced with another new school in 1960.

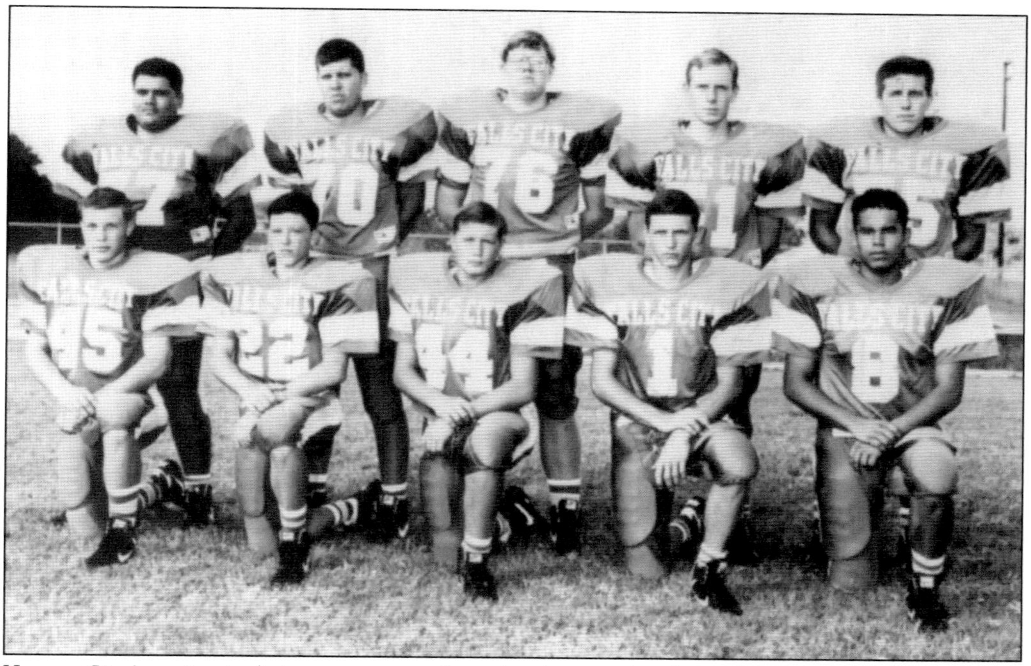

Karnes City's main rivals in sports were the other larger schools in the county, such as Kenedy, Falls City, and Runge. In 2010, Falls City won the football state championship in their league. Shown above are members of the team in earlier years.

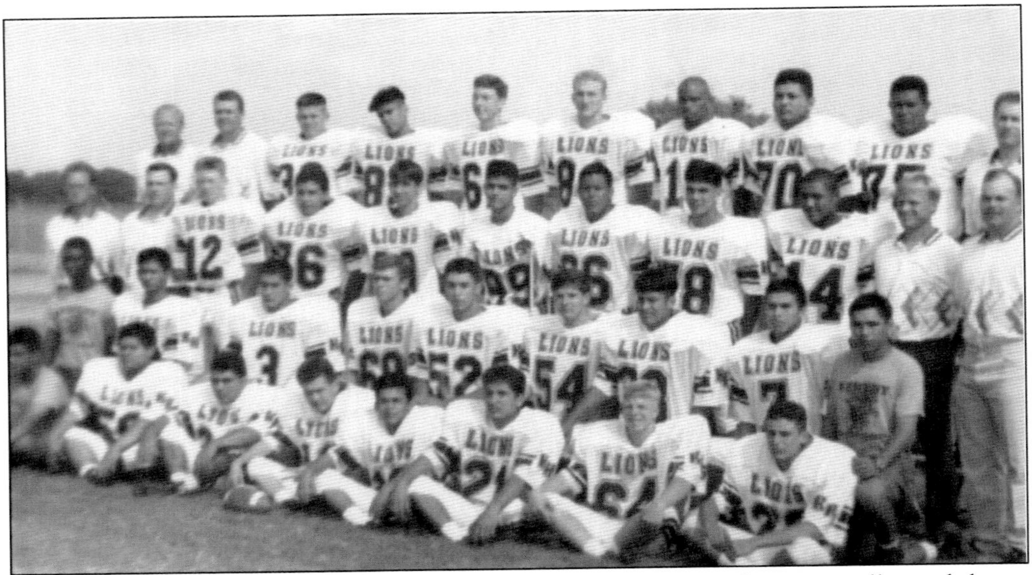

Kenedy has been the archrival of Karnes City for many years. Crowds were usually much larger when the two teams played.

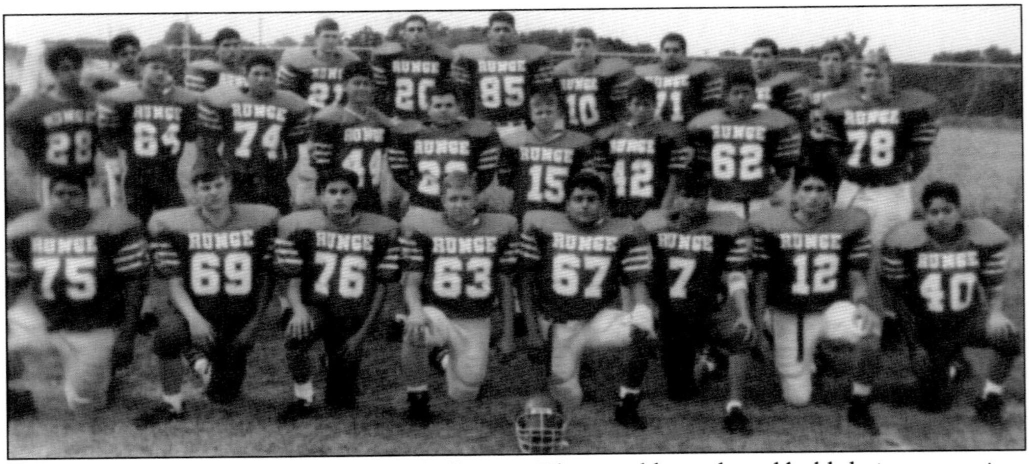

Runge always played a hard fought football game. They could match and hold their own against any of their rivals.

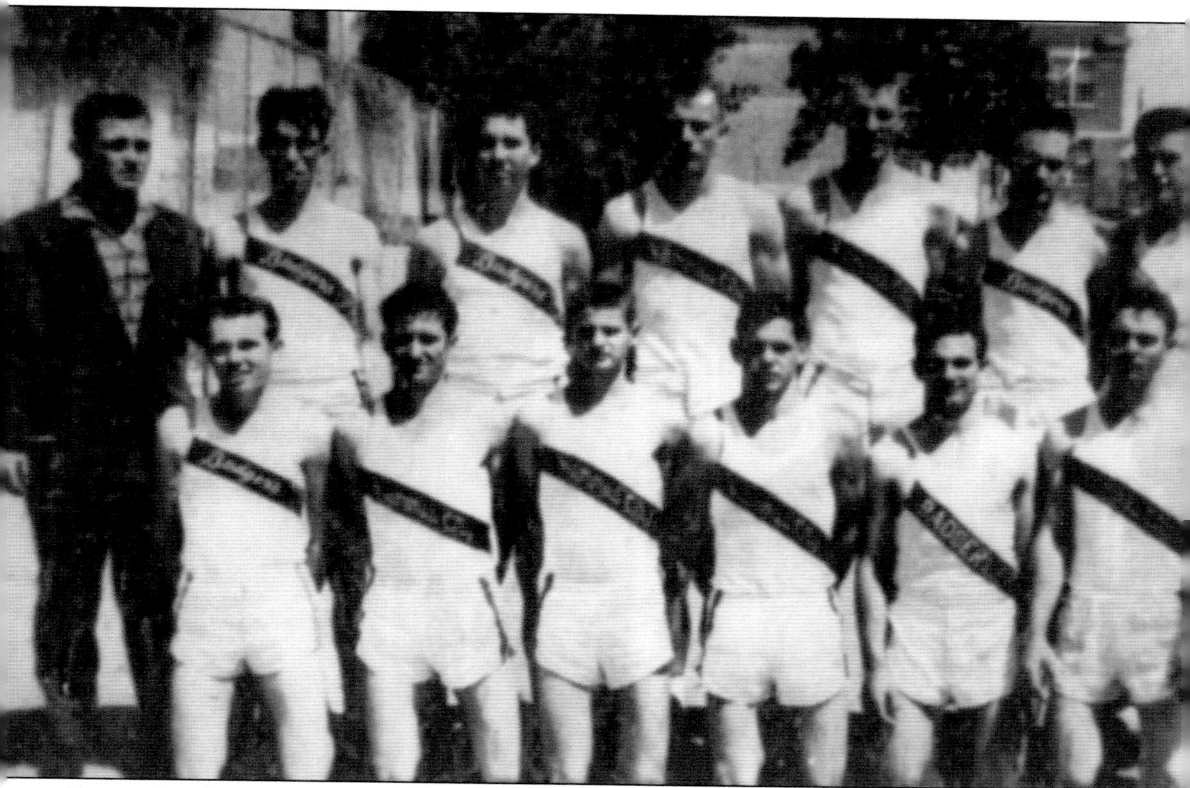

Boys and girls participated in other types of sports as well. Pictured is a 1957 Karnes City track team, coached by Campbell Hardin. They are, from left to right, (first row) D.C. Wishert, Lloyd Zimmerman, Gene Harrison, E.W. Dromgoole, Louis Bujnoch, and Joe Dragon; (second row) Alton Beuhring, Marvin Zimmerman, Leon Witte, Clarence Ahrens, Jack Sommer, and Vincent Labus.

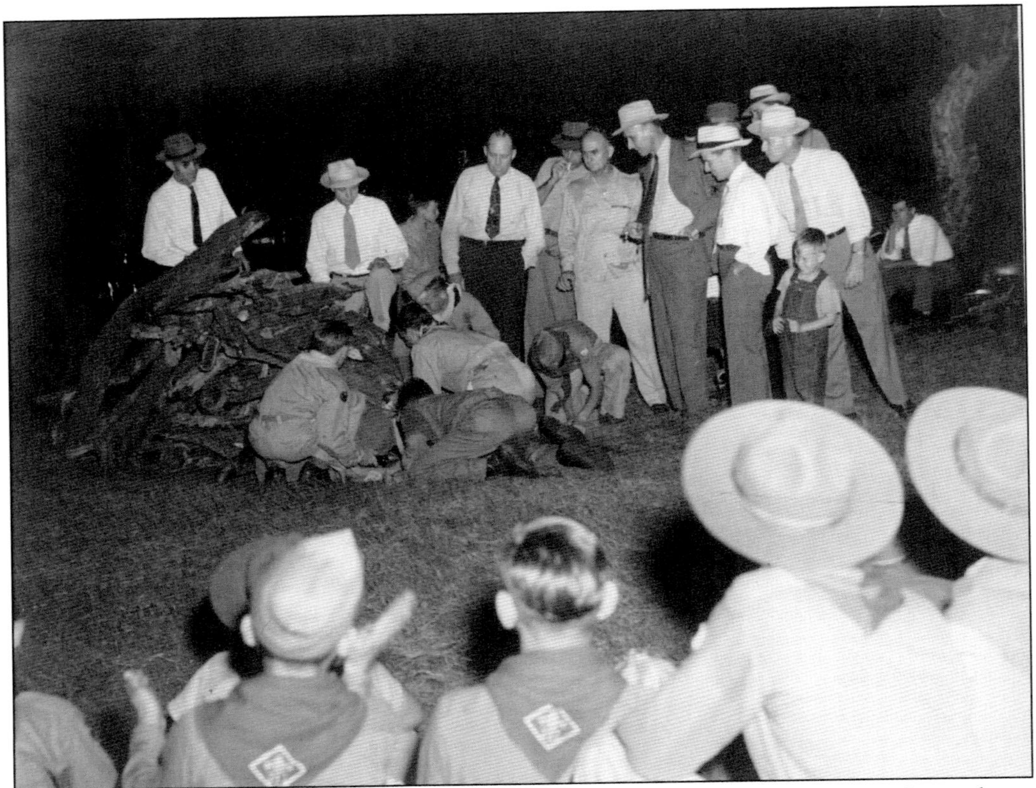

Other interests for school students included the Boy Scouts and Girl Scouts. Here, Scouts learn how to construct a proper fire.

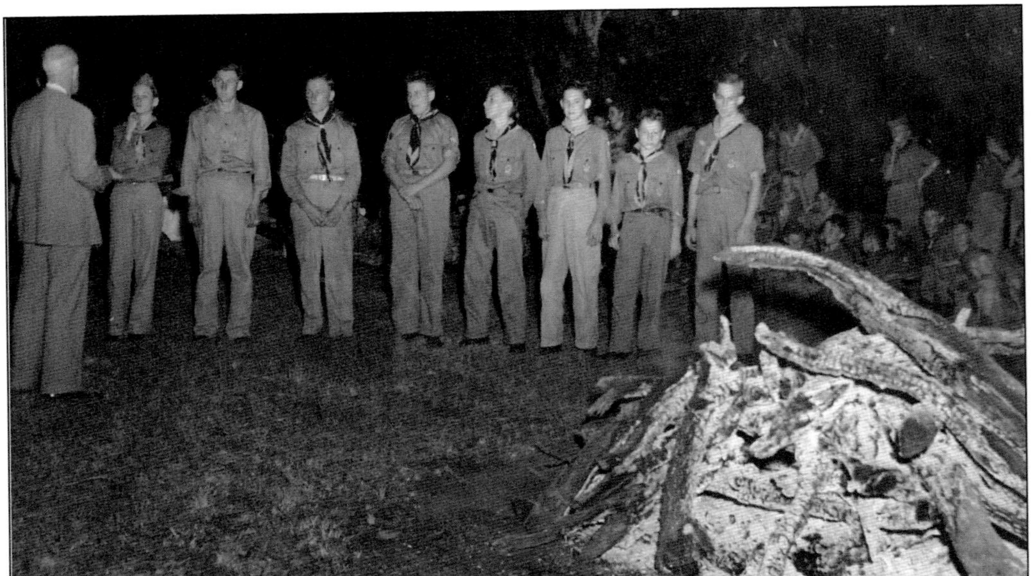

A successful fire brings a compliment from the Scoutmaster. Whatever comes next for the boys, they will be prepared.

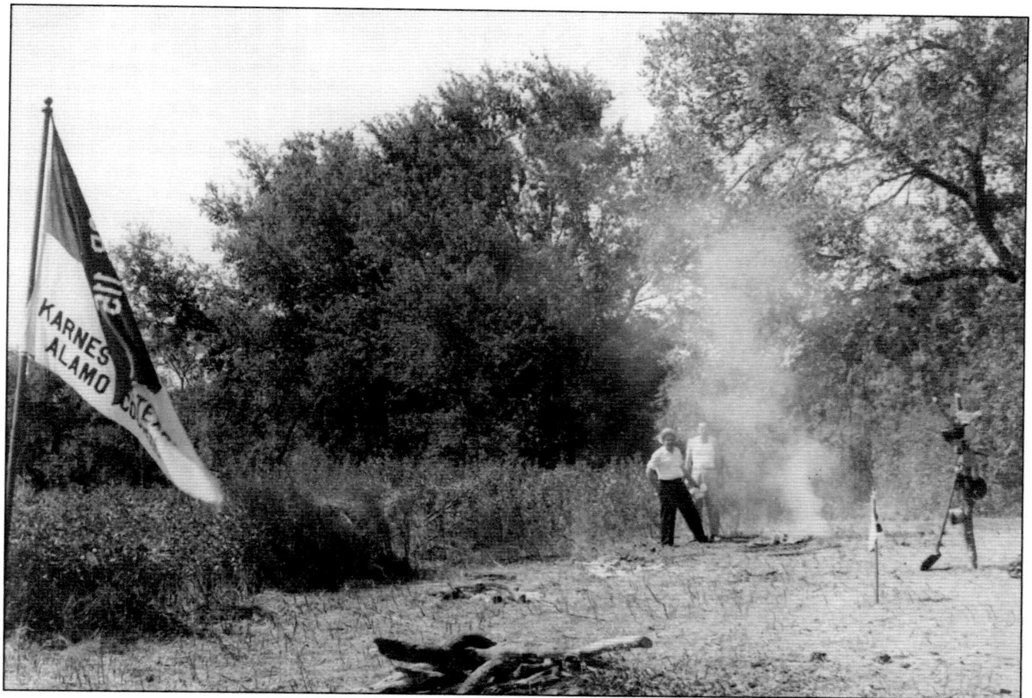

The last step is to make sure the fire is completely put out. Scouts in this area belonged to the Karnes City, Texas, Alamo Council.

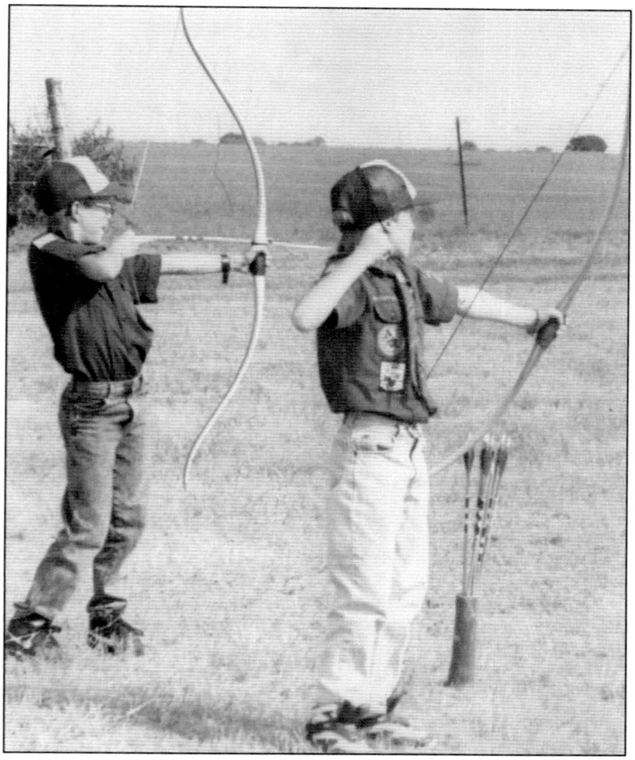

Young men enjoy learning outdoor skills. These two fellows, Brian Creswell and Austin Braudaway, get the hang of using a bow and arrow properly.

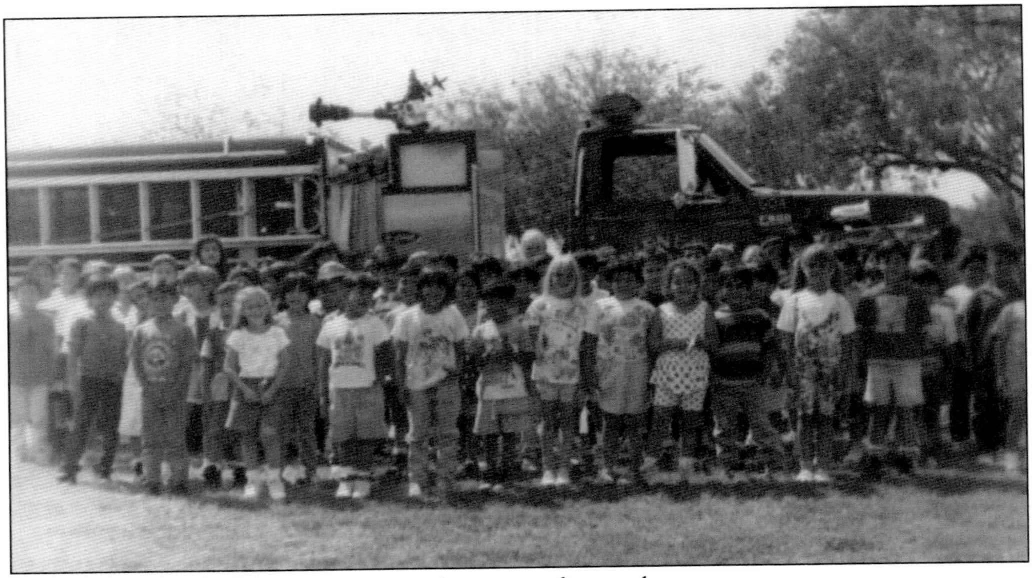

These youngsters had fun getting to explore a new fire truck.

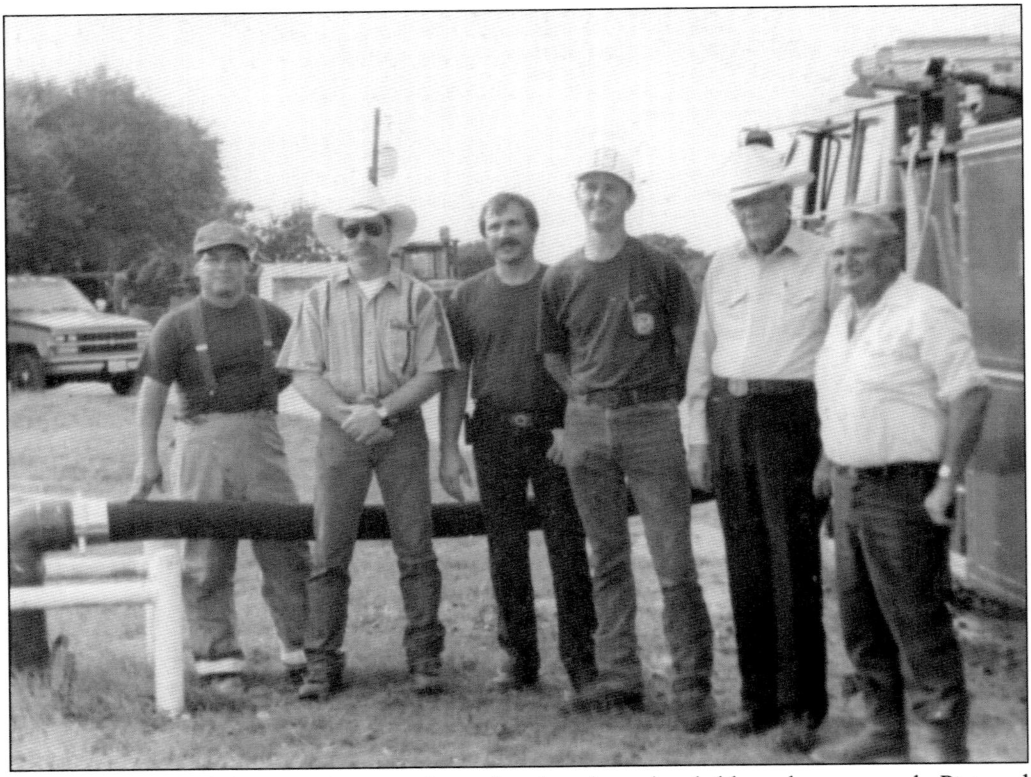

The volunteer firefighters are happy to be on hand to show the children the new truck. Pictured here are, from left to right, Jimmy Loya, Robert Gibbons Jr., Charlie Malik (fire chief), and Ronald Stolle (assistant fire chief). Also pictured are Arthur Fenner, chairman of the Soil and Water Conservation District, and landowner Scott Davidson.

Eight

Oil and Gas Rigs Dot the Future

Karnes County has always been part of the ups and downs of the petroleum industry. From boom to bust and back, oil and gas production contributed to the growth, prosperity, and reputation of the state of Texas. Its discovery can be traced all the way back to early explorers. One of the DeSoto explorers, Luis de Moscoso, was recorded seeing a substance floating on the water between Sabine Pass and High Island, off the coast of Texas in 1543. The explorers noticed an asphalt-like characteristic to this crude form of oil. They began to use it to caulk their vessels and saw the Indians using it for medicinal purposes. Early settlers remarked of sulfur-smelling areas that seemed to seep up through the ground. After the Civil War, a growing interest in turning some of this early crude into kerosene grew and expanded. It was the discovery at Spindletop in Texas that brought in the gusher age, and soon more areas of the state were claiming substantial finds, including Karnes County. Most were ranchers and farmers who quite often found crude instead of water, as they were drilling to water their fields. There was another mineral discovery, which happened to be uranium, in Falls City, part of our county off Highway 181. The petroleum and uranium industry brought a lot of interest to investors in our land and property. The profits proved to be a real boon to school districts, while adding more to the folklore as well as the public revenue. Other industries needed to produce, refine, and transport the oil and gas, which grew as well. After years of over 70 to 100 million barrels of oil a year that was being produced in Texas, there began a decline in the industry. Several fields were shut down in the 1930s. After World War II began, petroleum markets were curtailed by price controls and rationing to reserve what might be needed for war use. But, as usually happened after a shortage, new discoveries were made and a petroleum boom began again.

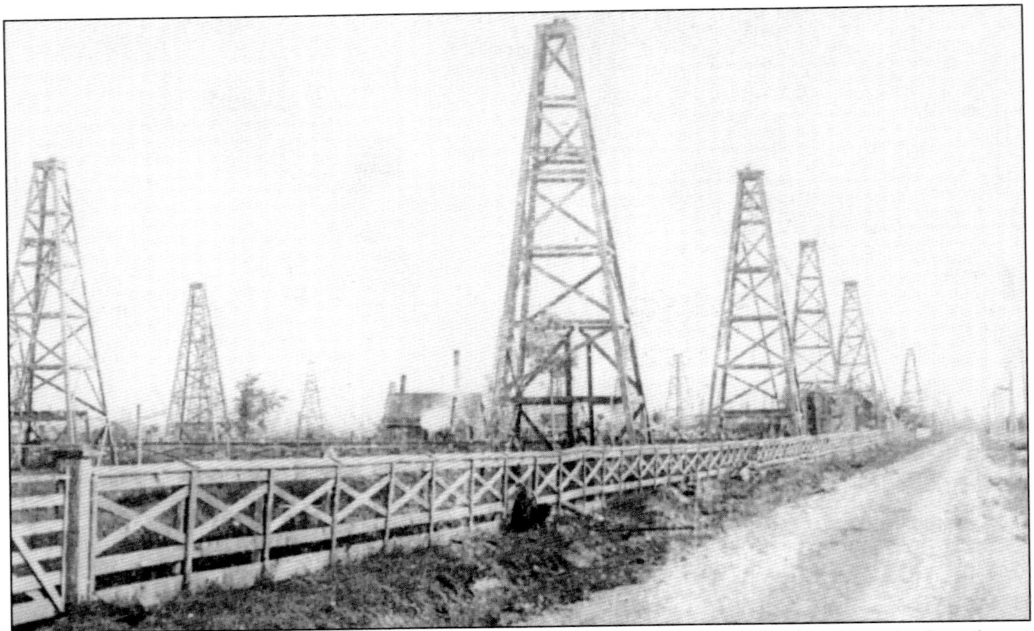

Karnes County has experienced the ups and downs of discovering the booms of oil and gas. Having gone through the process of drilling for the petroleum products in the 1950s and 1960s, most people are familiar with seeing them dotting the landscape.

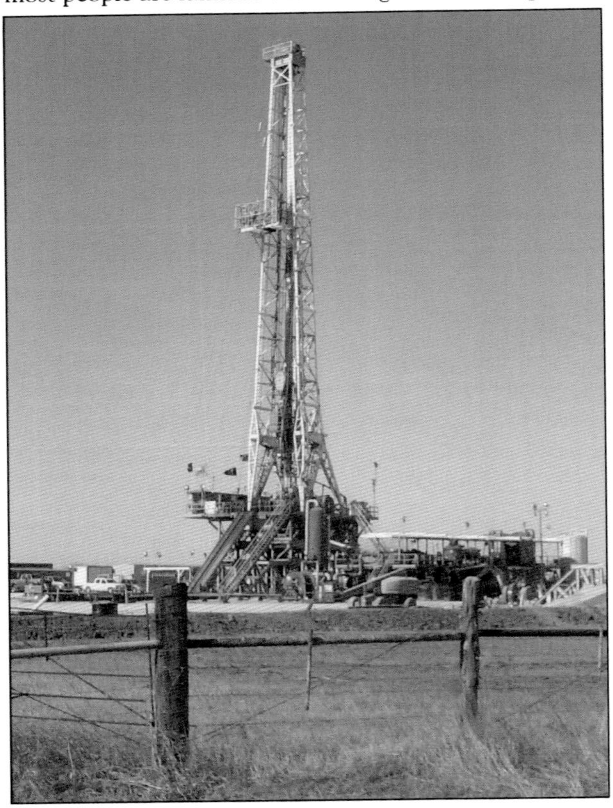

At this time, it is reported that Karnes County is the hottest site for the discovery of the huge Eagle-Ford shale deposit of oil and gas. The much bigger and taller rigs seem to prove it, which are everywhere, just like the one pictured to the left sitting next to a busy highway.

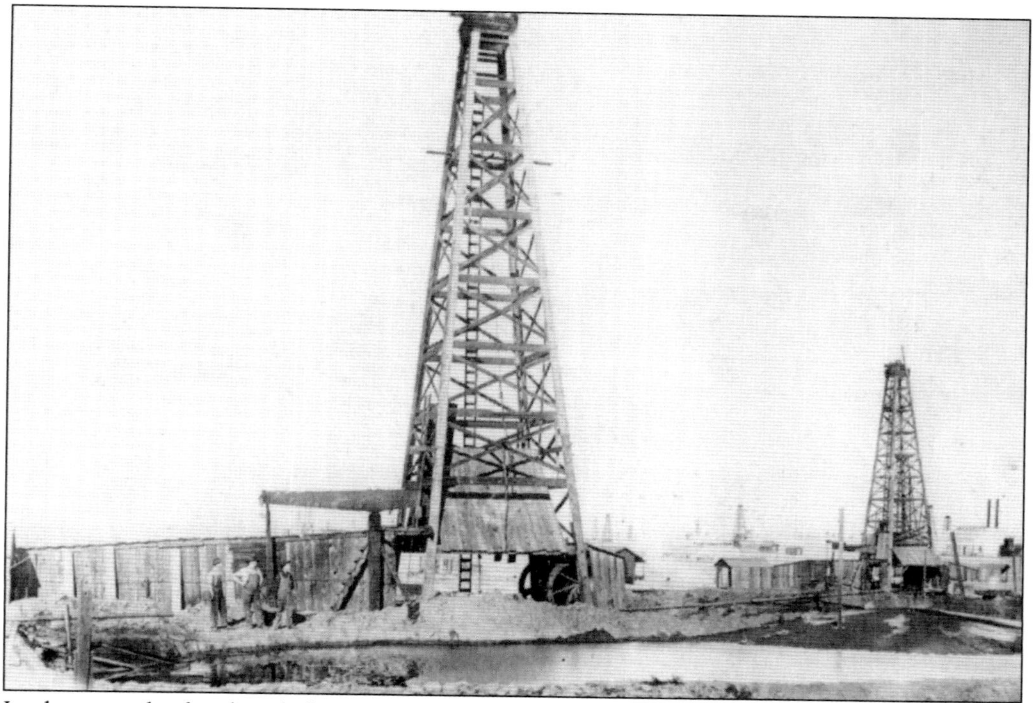

In the past, the familiar drilling rigs were of a different type. Those used today must be more advanced to deal with the ability to drill horizontally as well as directionally.

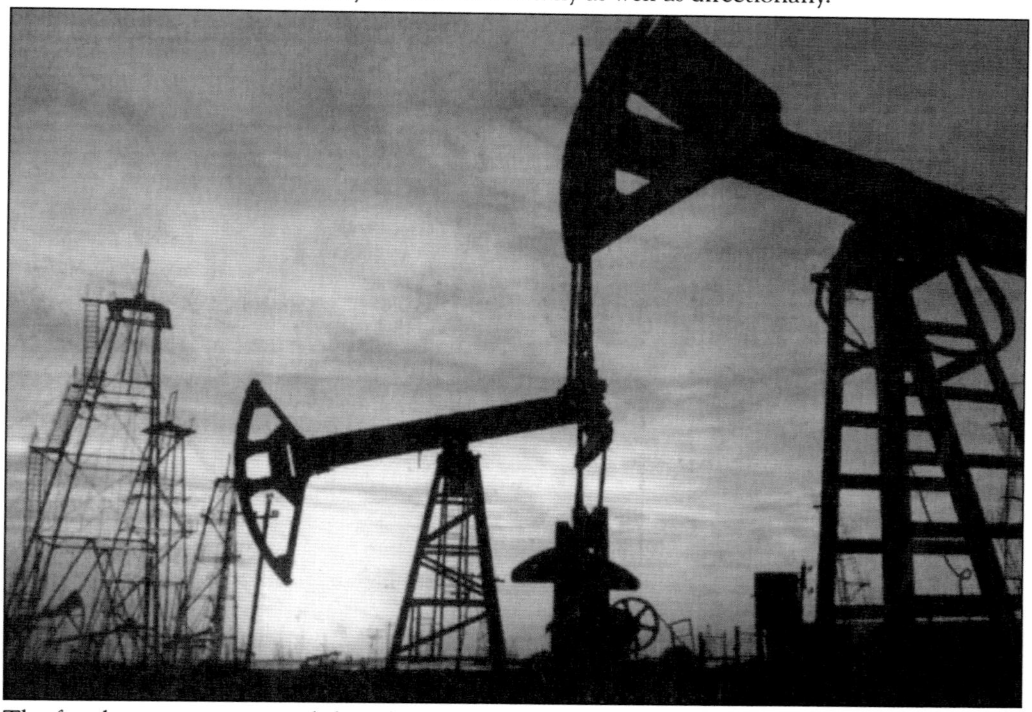

The familiar pumpers around the oil well sites are no longer seen at this time, either. They may be on the scene at some point in the process.

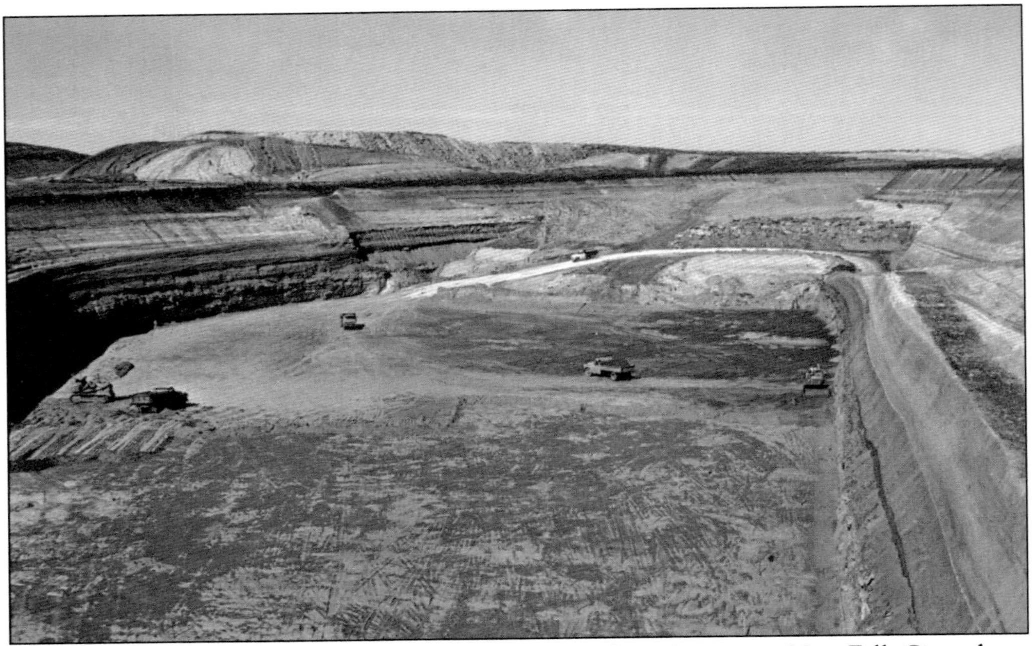

Oil and gas wells were not the only discoveries being made in the county. Near Falls City, a huge area of uranium had been found at about the same time as the earlier production of petroleum. It was very welcomed at the time, as the government needed other fuel alternatives while emphasizing national security. Today, that very same area has been reopened and its ore may be stored for future power plants.

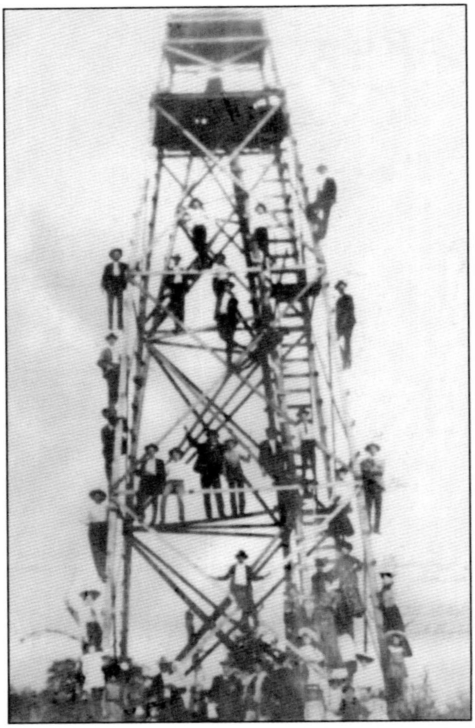

Factors in the search for oil and gas finds deal with many aspects of land, soil, past finds, and even topography of certain areas. Although geodetic surveys are done to seek the highest places to figure distances between two points, perhaps the curvature of the land itself could expose the best places for drilling. The 1920s survey tower pictured here was said to have shown that the Hugh Ruckman Ranch near Ecleto was the highest point in the county.

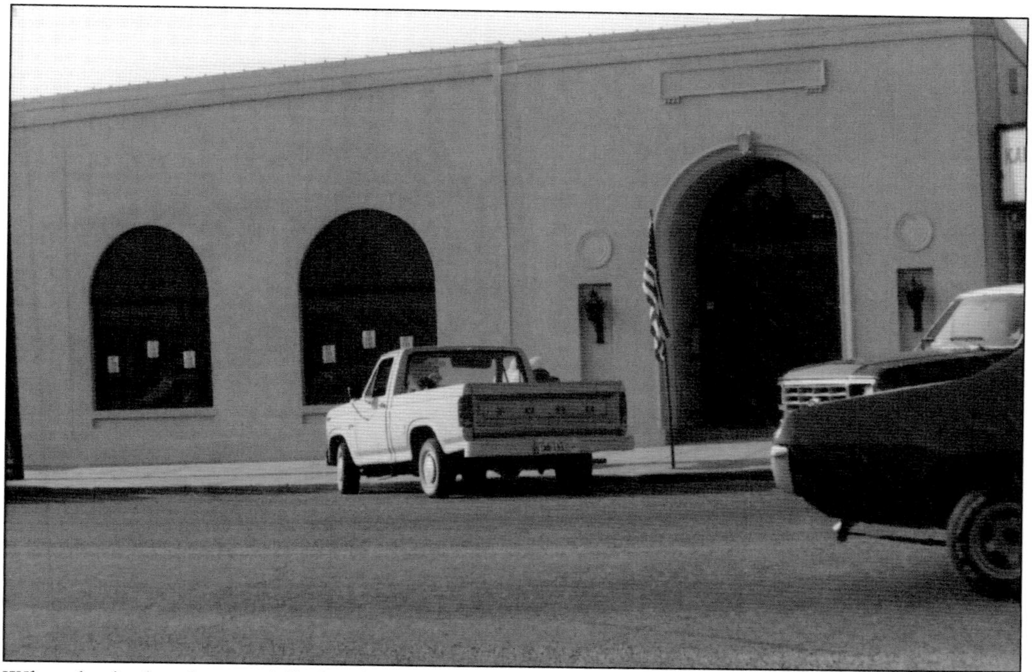

What do the local townsfolk do when the sudden arrival of hundreds of people working with the petroleum industry crowd the roadways, cafés, hotels, and motels? They go on with their lives, celebrating their newfound riches and share at the local stores and the tax office!

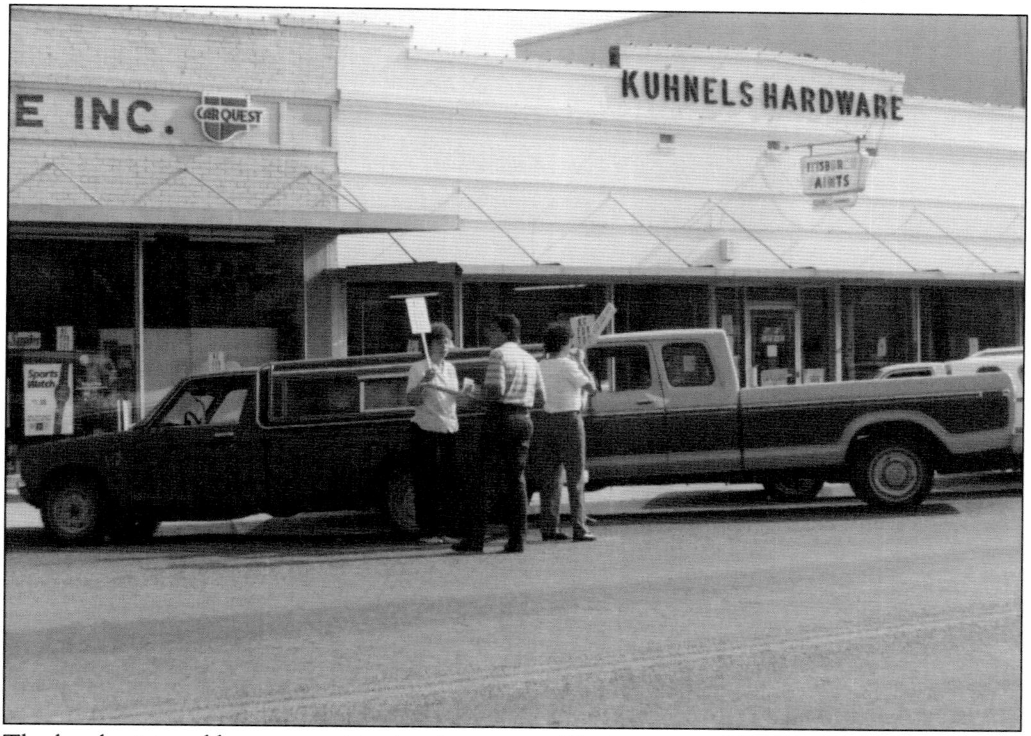

The locals pictured here are petitioning for a cause. Their signs say "KC for TOC."

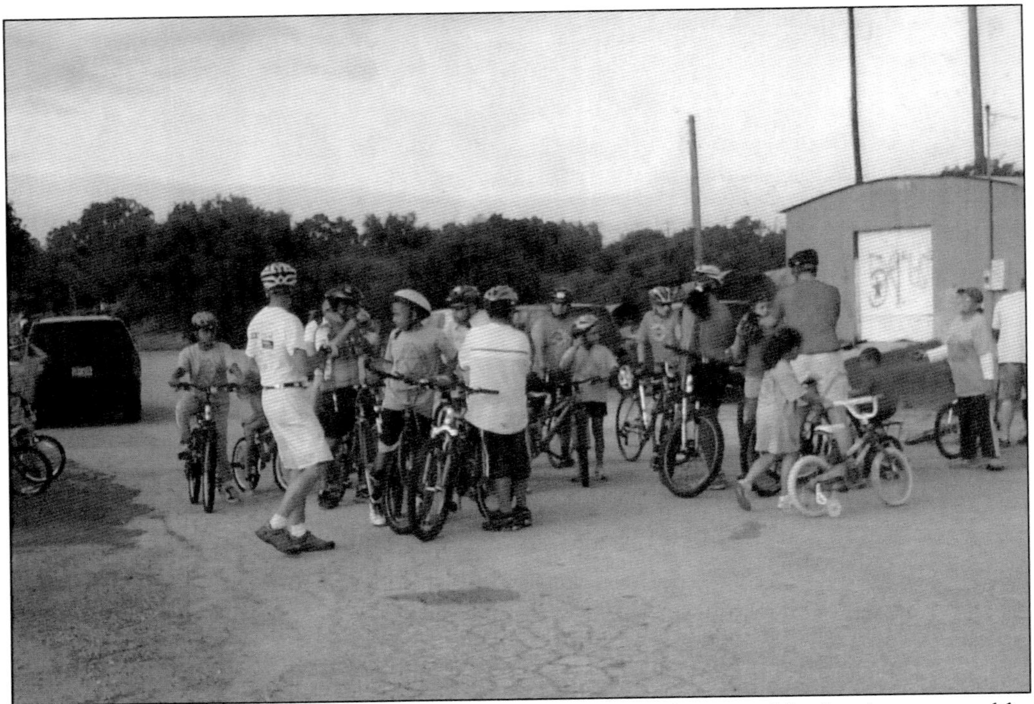

Good exercise can let off a lot of steam and frustration through some of the local programs, like the annual Fitness Day. Getting lined up is the first thing to do.

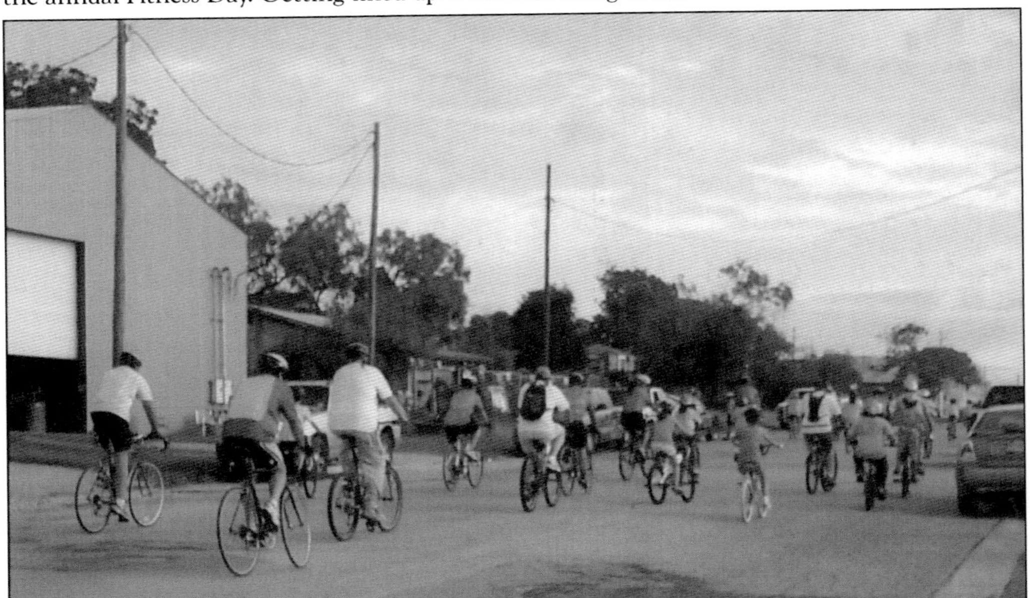

They're off! Since horses no longer race through town, this is the best thing to do! Young and old enjoy bicycling during Fitness Day.

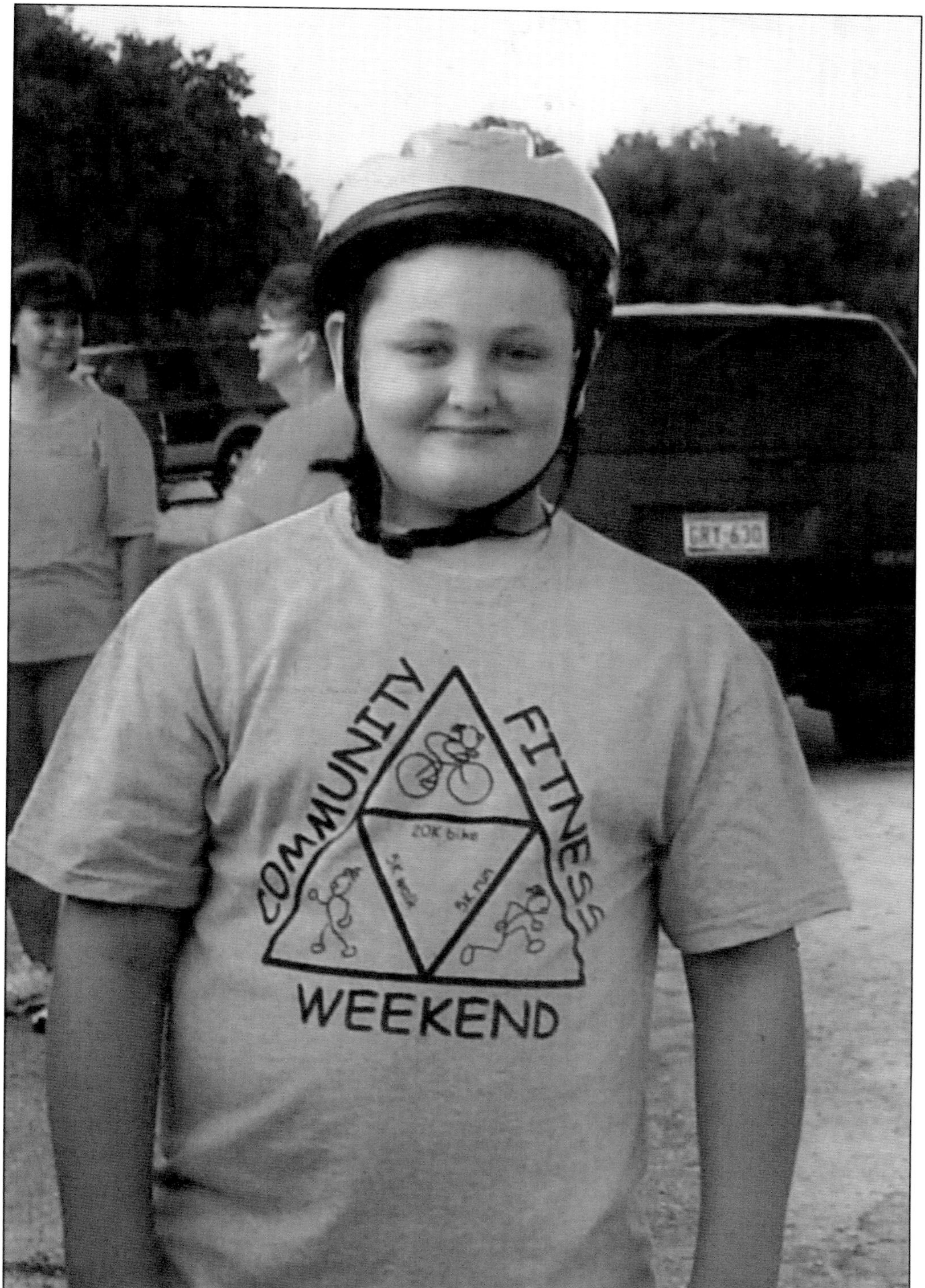

Is there any doubt that this young man is proud to be part of the event? Kyle Kellner smiles for the camera, ready to go.

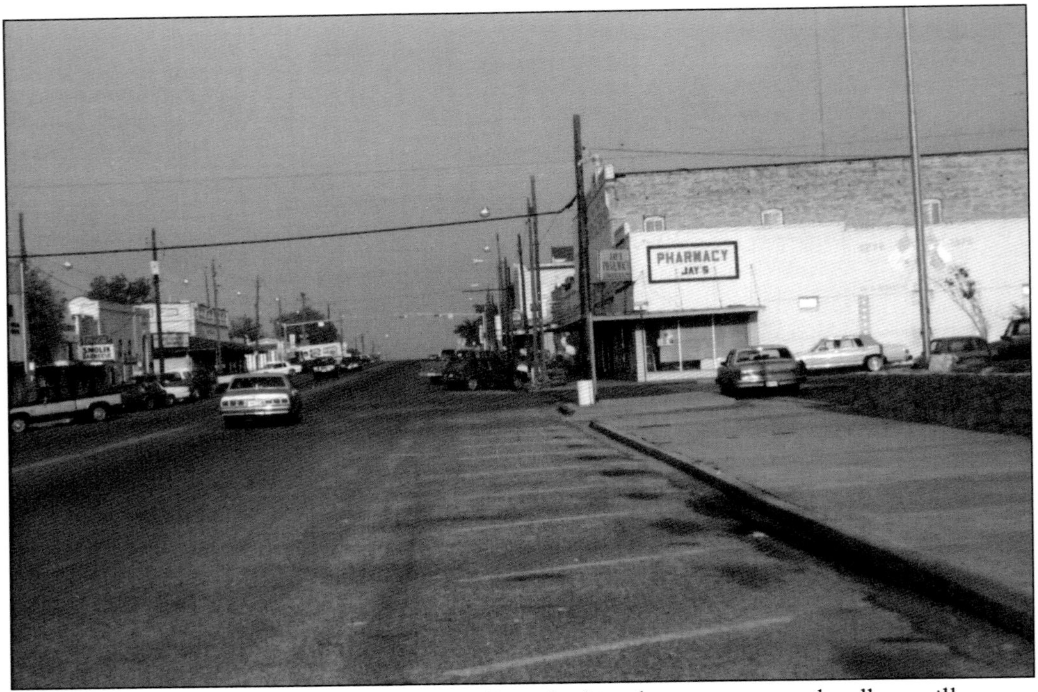

Through these streets of downtown Karnes City, the bicyclers, runners, and walkers will go.

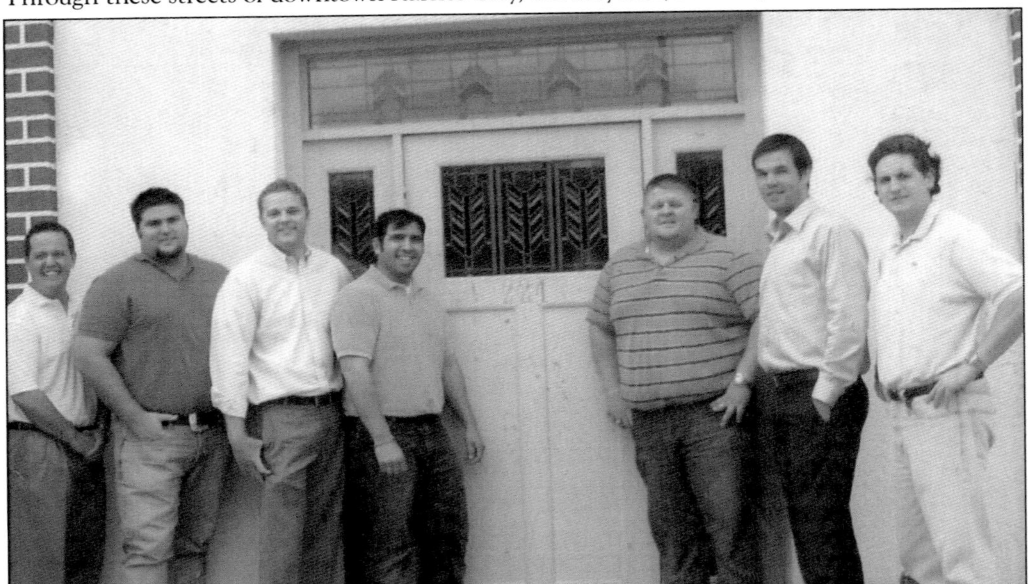

One of the blessings of having the oil and gas companies come to the county is that they need spaces to work from. They often take old and unused buildings and turn them into nice offices, like the Dale Acquisition Group, who are standing outside a renovated office in Kenedy.

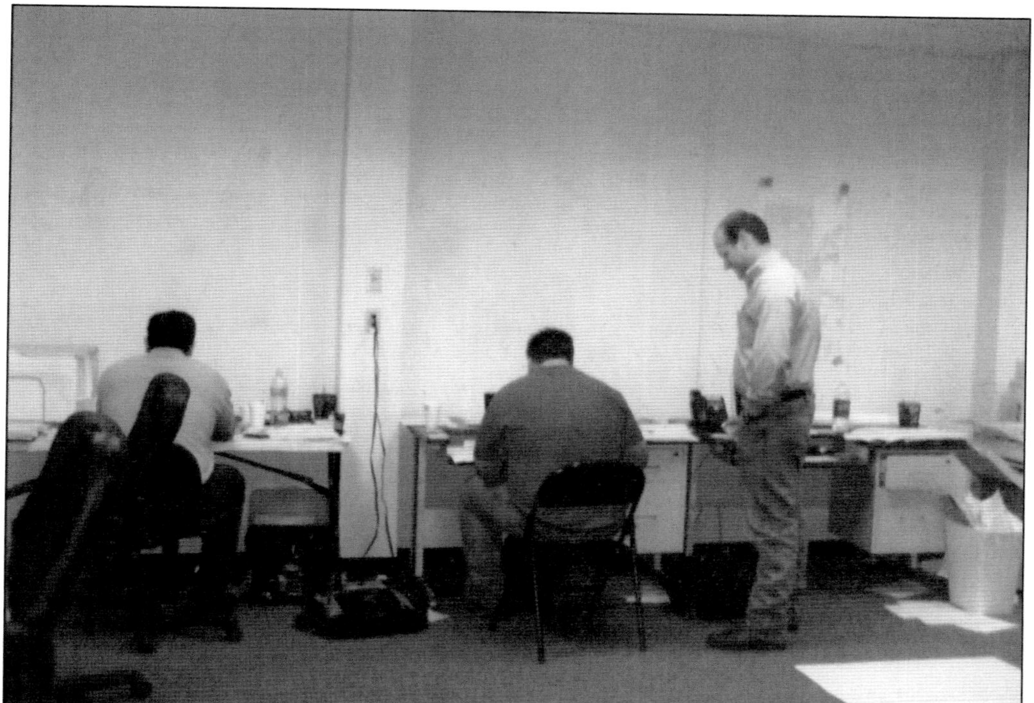

Interior renovations provided lots of room for the landmen and Blake Williams to oversee the work and research for petroleum rich property owners they want to explore.

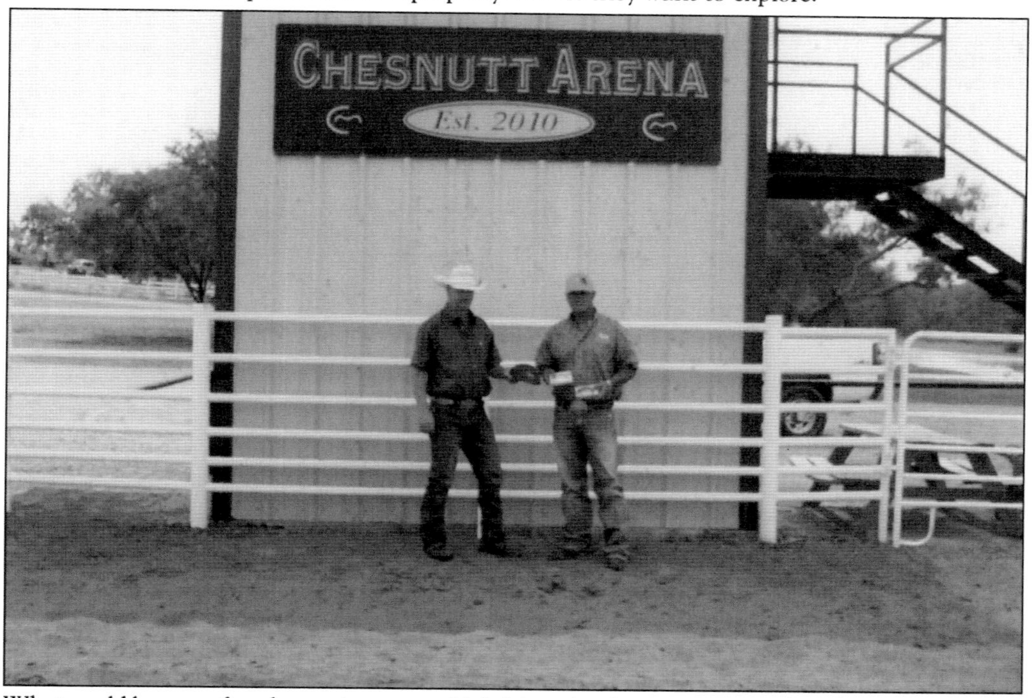

What could be more fun than going to an old-fashioned rodeo arena to watch real ropin' and ridin'? The Chesnutt Arena recently opened in Kenedy and makes South Central Texans very happy.

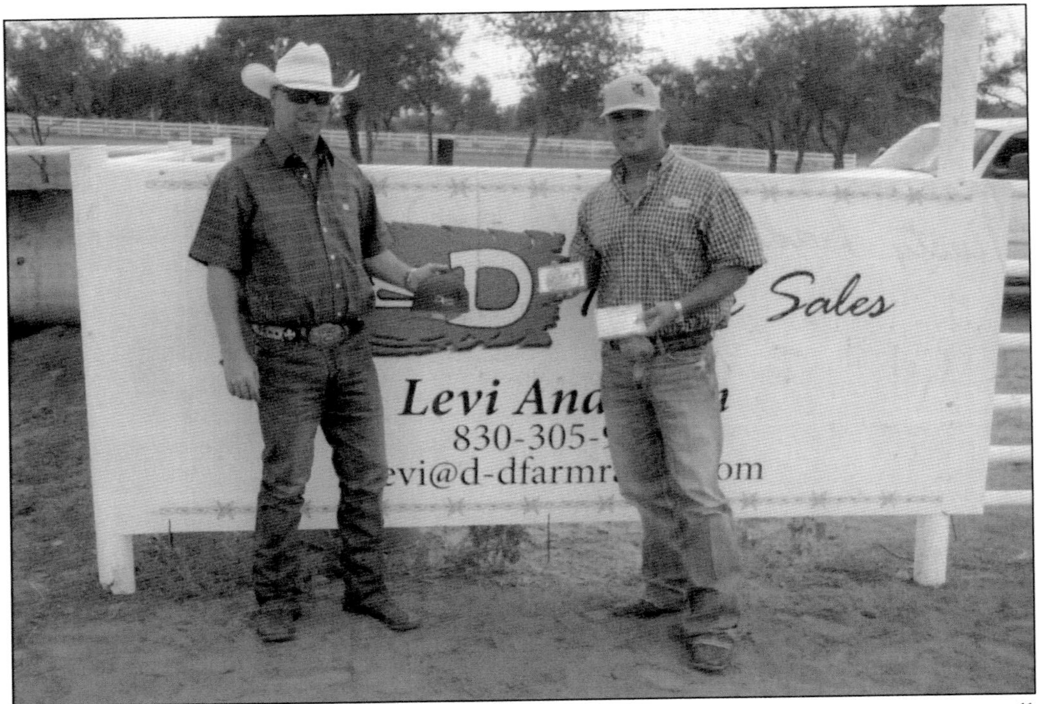

The owners are glad to see the enthusiasm once again for what used to be in almost every small community: the local rodeo. Many are glad there is now a rodeo in Karnes County. Standing by the sign are Malcolm Chesnutt and Rusty Badillo.

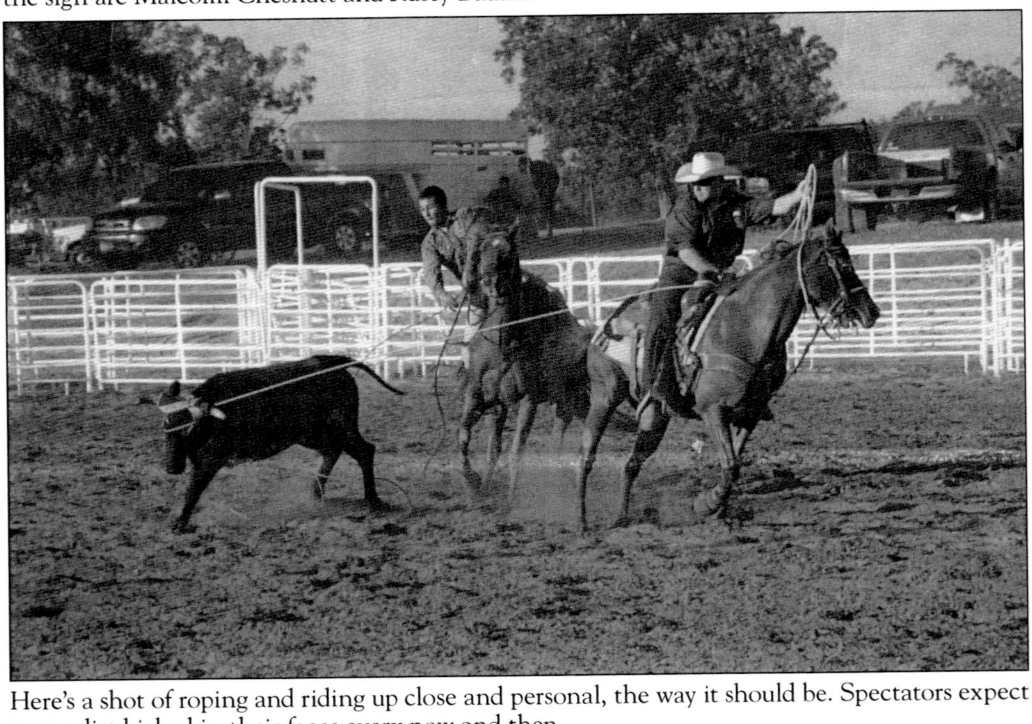
Here's a shot of roping and riding up close and personal, the way it should be. Spectators expect to get dirt kicked in their faces every now and then.

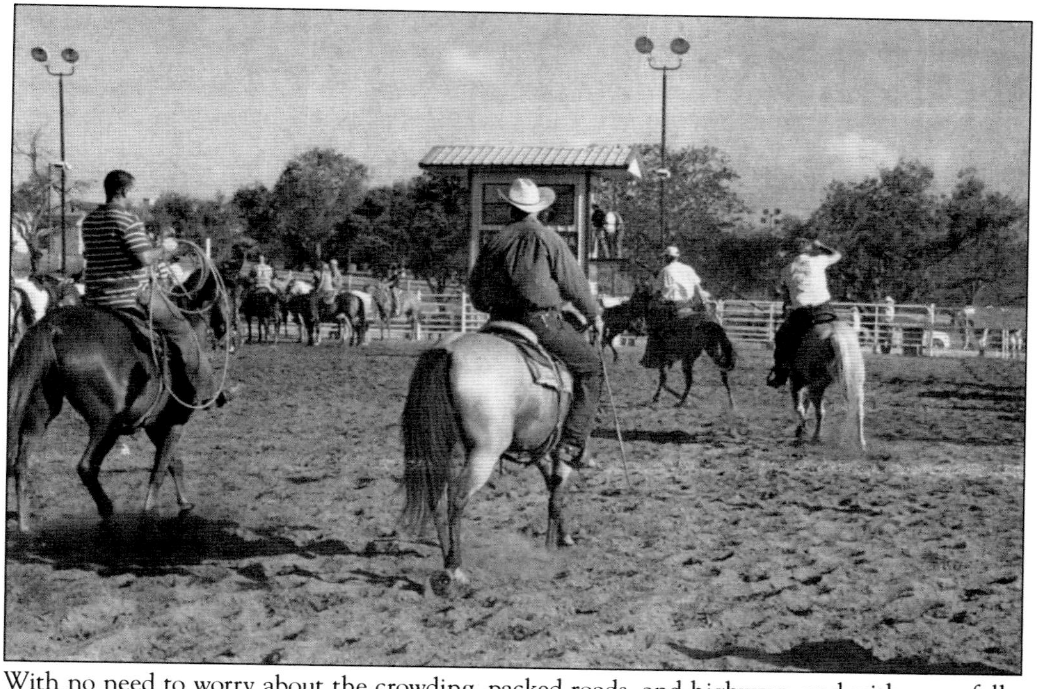

With no need to worry about the crowding, packed roads, and highways, and with some folks having more money in their pockets from soon-to-be oil and gas wells, it really makes Karnes Countians want to celebrate!

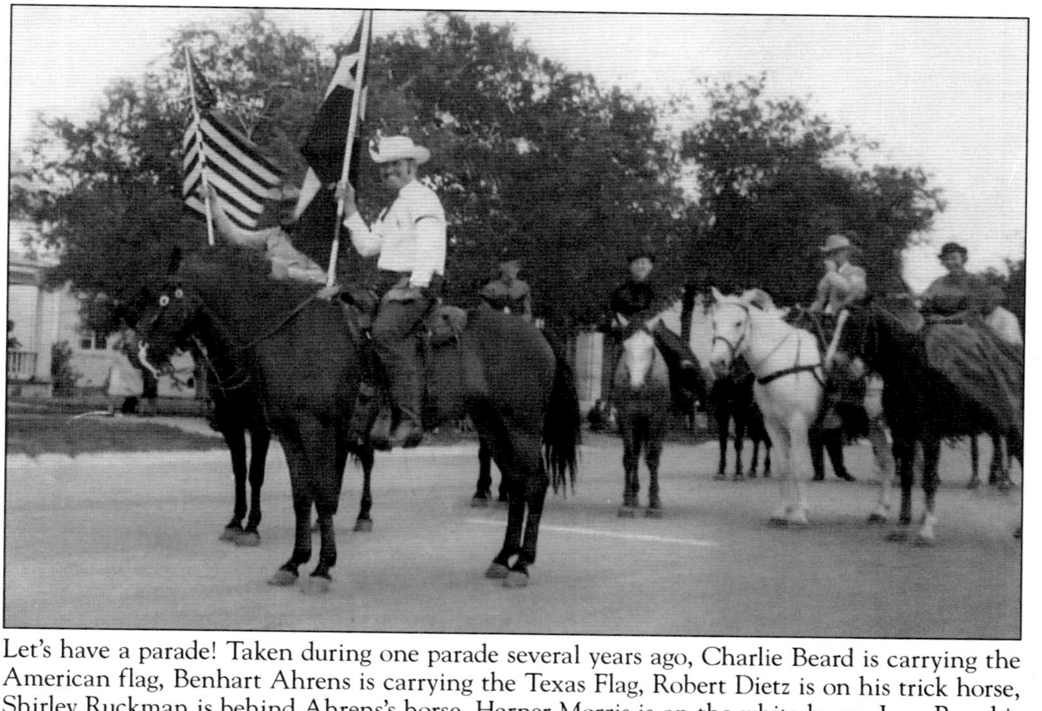

Let's have a parade! Taken during one parade several years ago, Charlie Beard is carrying the American flag, Benhart Ahrens is carrying the Texas Flag, Robert Dietz is on his trick horse, Shirley Ruckman is behind Ahrens's horse, Harper Morris is on the white horse, June Beard is to the right of Morris, and Margie Best is on the grey horse.

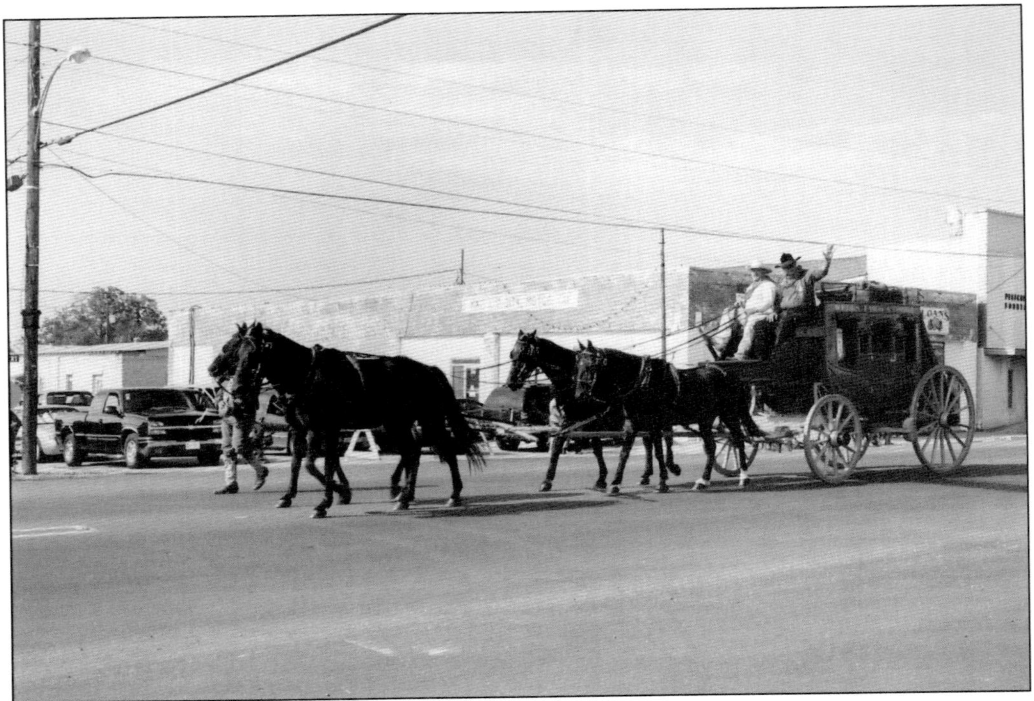

Every year, Karnes City has a wonderful kick-off parade for the Lonesome Dove Fest, soon going into its 19th year.

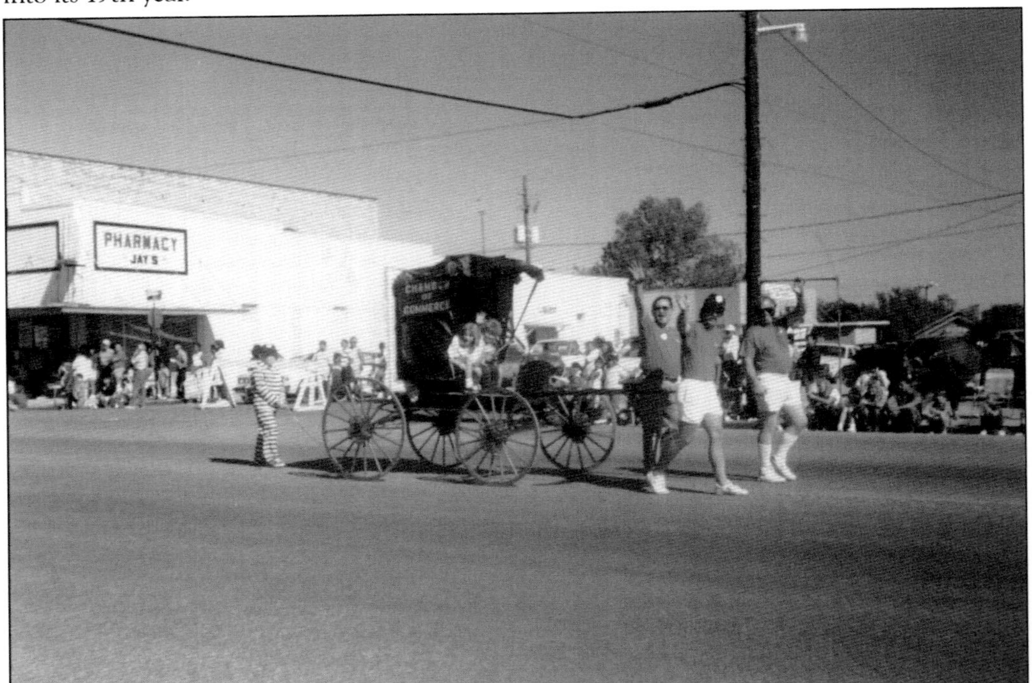

Carriages of all shapes and sizes are a part of the celebration that kicks off the hunting season and the gathering of hunters from all over the county to congregate here in our county.

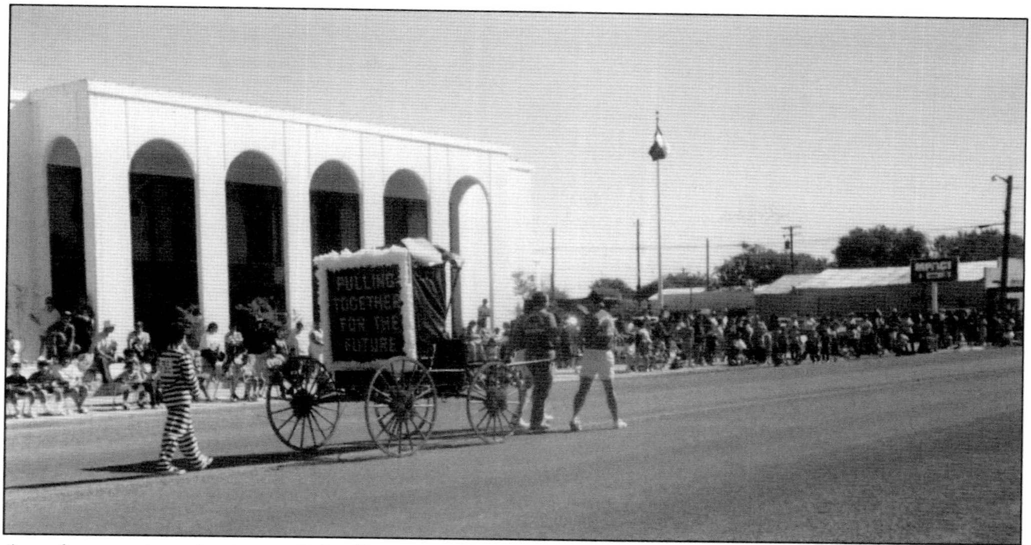

Another carriage is pictured, "pulling together for the future."

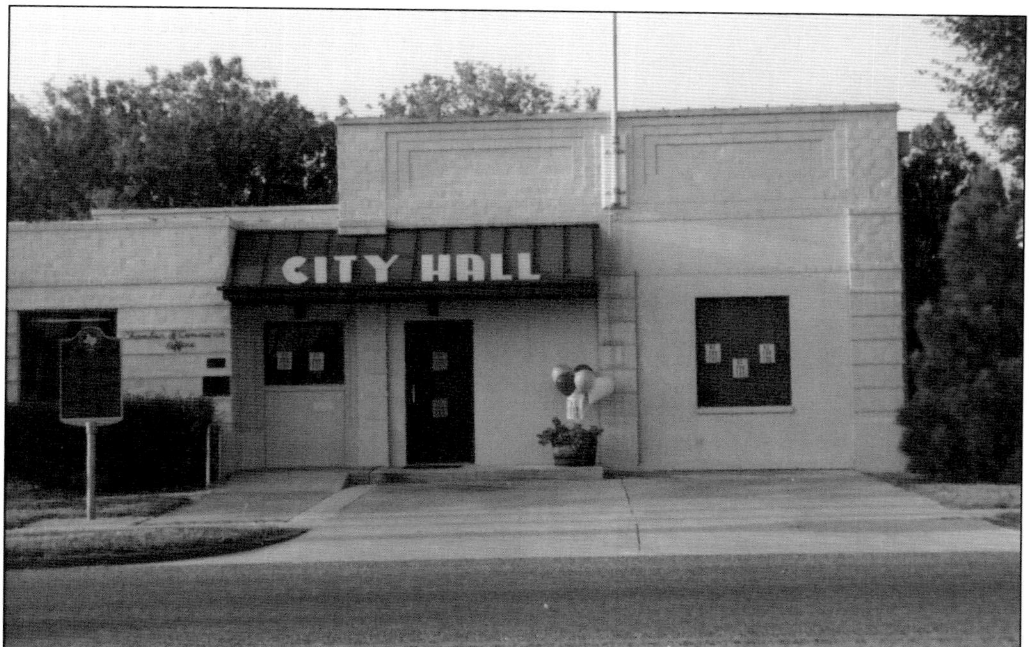

Karnes City Hall awaits that next big event. The biggest of all occurs in September with the now famous Lonesome Dove Fest.

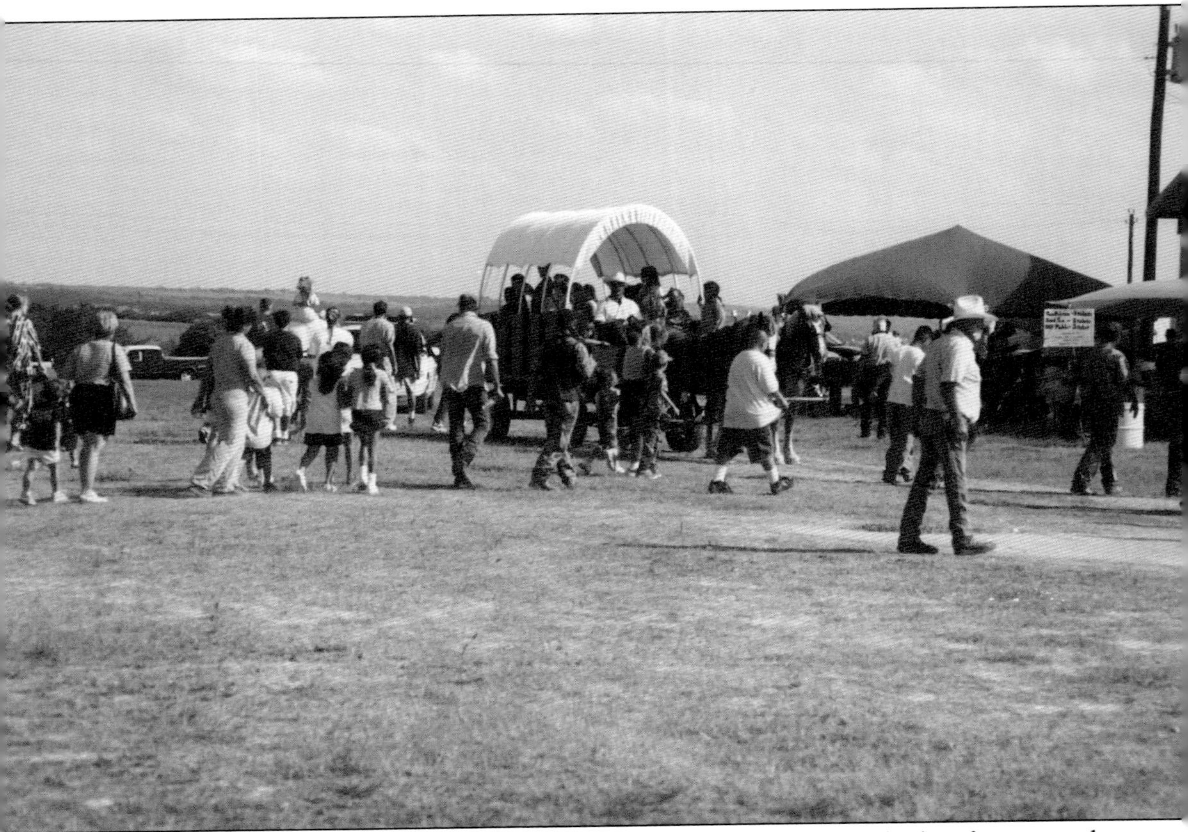

The covered wagon heads for the site of the Lonesome Dove Fest. In the last few years, the festival has been held at the Karnes County Youth Show Barn, about halfway between Karnes City and Kenedy.

Nine

How Far Have We Come?

Karnes County is a lively and vibrant place at this time. Once again, there is a boom of oil and gas exploration going on, thanks to the recent large discovery of Eagle-Ford shale. Rigs continue to spring up daily on the surrounding landscape, with some right on the edge of busy highways. Citizens are adjusting to the accompanying scramble to construct or provide more housing and more facilities to house additional industries, local restaurateurs, businesses, and food markets to provide food and supplies to the newcomers. Most community members are pleased with the increased activity and look forward to the promise of bigger and better events to celebrate our growth. One of the biggest events held each year is the Lonesome Dove Fest that precedes the opening of quail, dove, and deer-hunting season. Reports have been given that it grows larger every year, with the latest estimate of people coming to our county being over 10,000 who travel here to enjoy the festivities accompanying the hunting prospects. With our county already bursting at the seams with newcomers, it should be quite an exciting time for sure. Throughout our history, we have had some outstanding dignitaries to visit and celebrate our distinctive past and present. Two of those in the past were then Texas governor George W. Bush and Pope John Paul II. Governor Bush was here to give accolades to Karnes Countians for soil conservation efforts and the Pope was here to honor the very first Polish settlers' descendants on their anniversary of settling in Panna Maria, Texas. We have had some strange distinctions as well, like the shooting of a wild, often rampaging elephant that had trampled a woman in another small town while traveling through with a circus. Black Diamond met his fate upon the decision of the circus owner between Karnes City and Kenedy just off Highway 181. There is a marker there to show where it took 55 gunshots to bring him down. Living in a small town can be very exciting.

Nearly all of the images relating to the Lonesome Dove Fest are from Randy Witte and his Lonsome Dove Fest Committee.

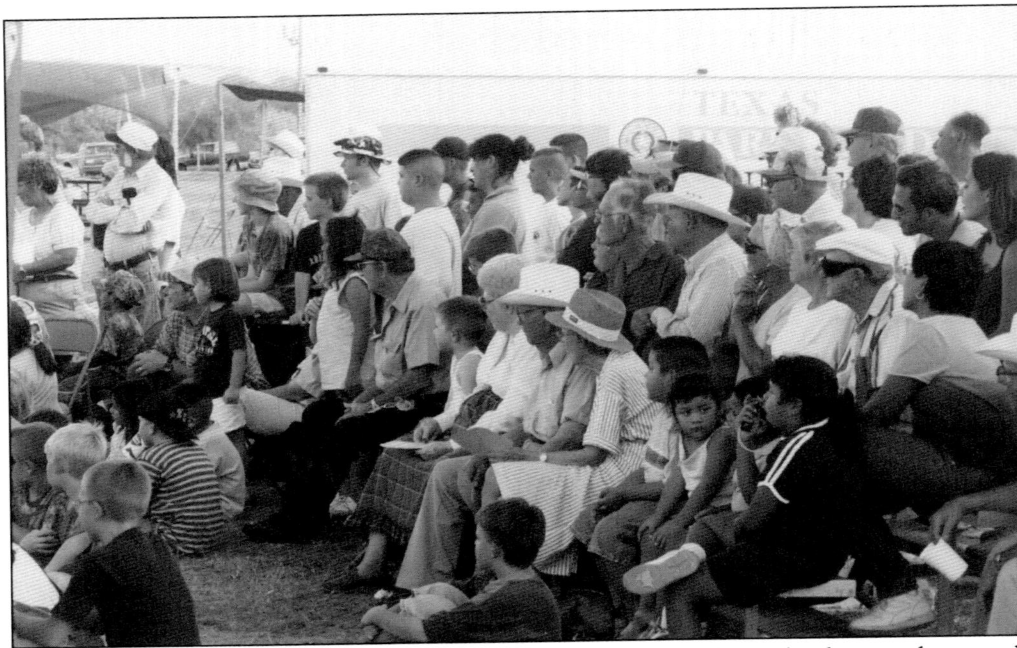

The crowds have already gathered. There is a lot to see and do at the fest, so the crowds arrive early.

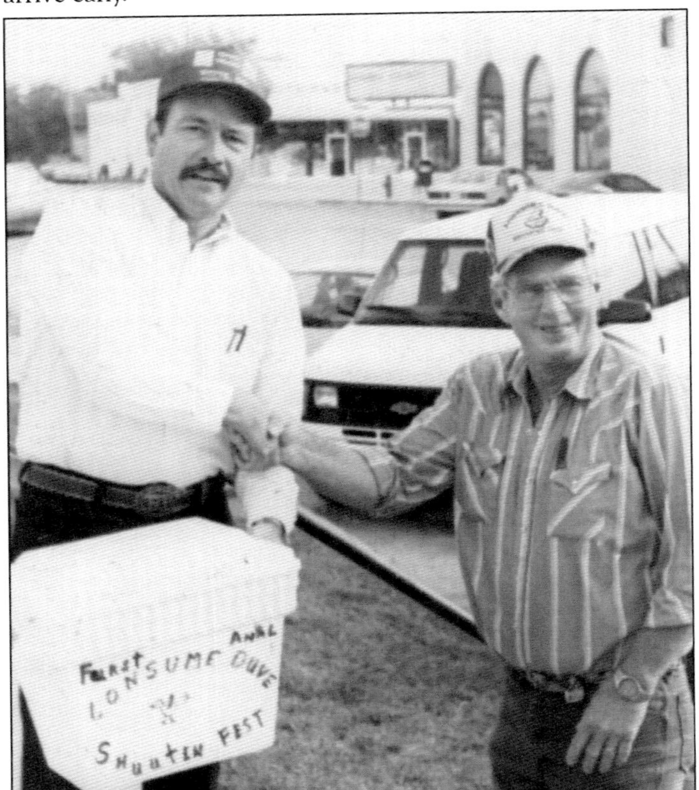

Even though history seems to be repeating itself, we have really come a long way in many areas. The fall Lonesome Dove Fest will be bigger and better than ever with the leadership of Randy Witte and his crew. Pictured here are Randy and his late friend Glen Worthy. Check the mailbox for one of the very first advertisements for the fest at its early beginnings.

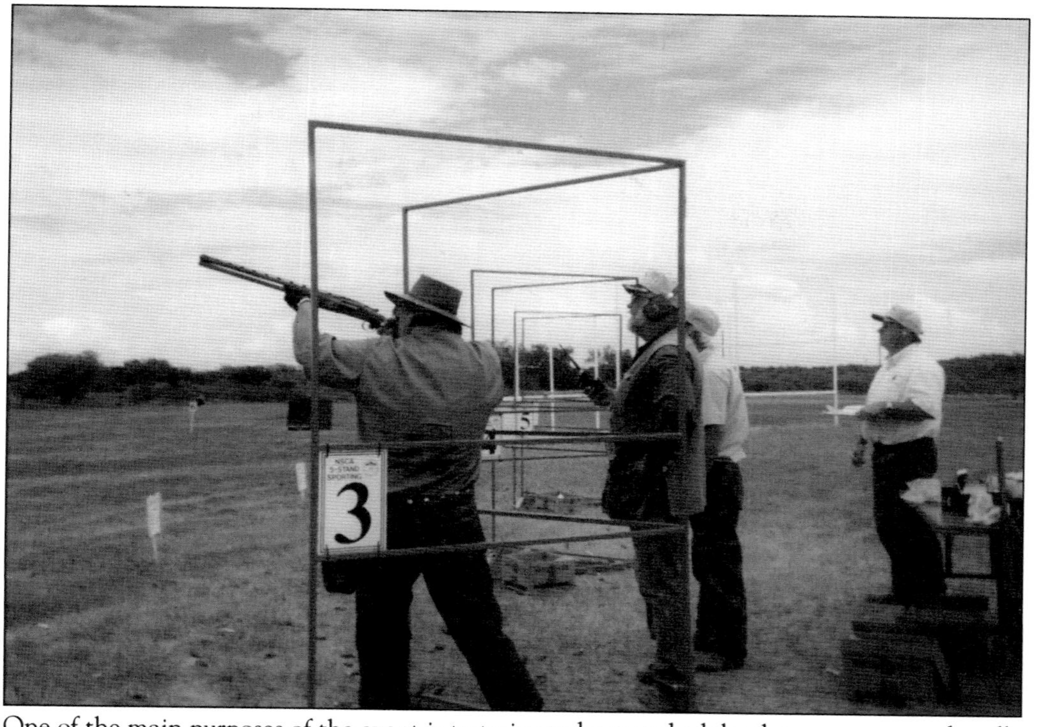

One of the main purposes of the event is to train students and adults the proper way to handle firearms, fishing gear, and even animals.

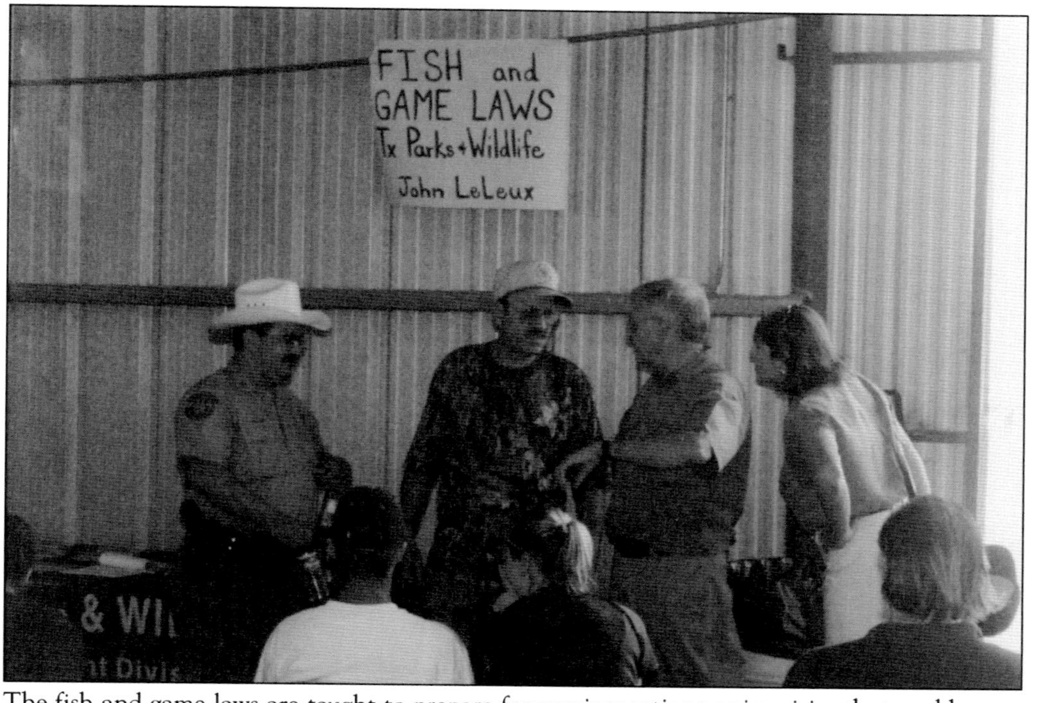

The fish and game laws are taught to prepare for any inspections or inquiries that could occur on a hunting or fishing trip.

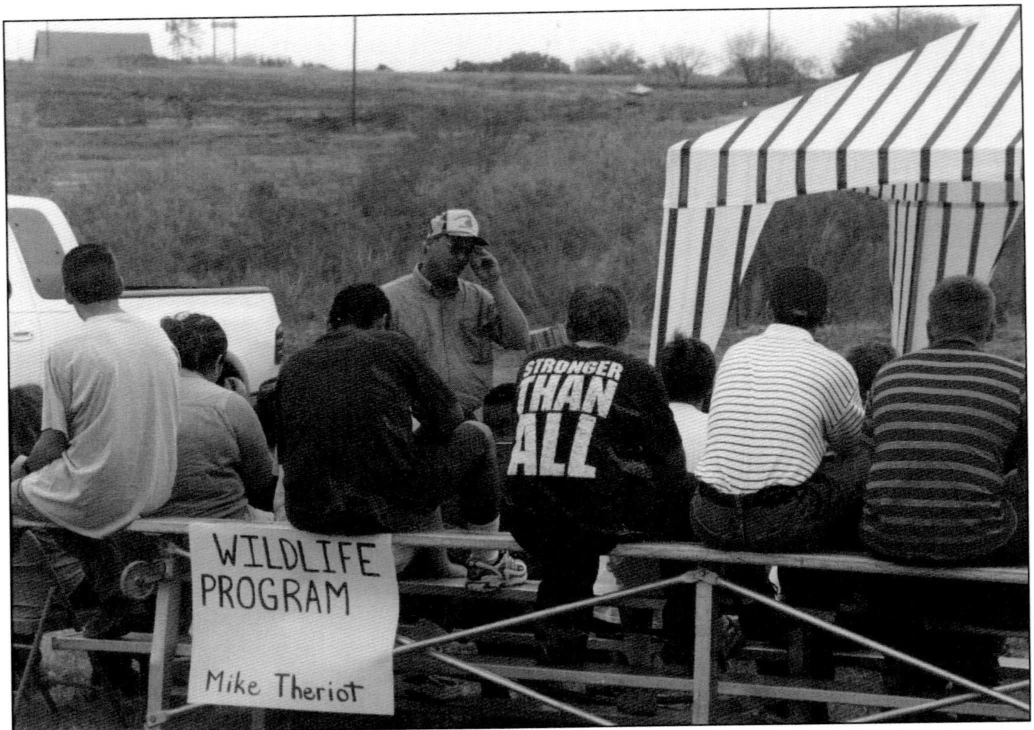

It also includes sharing their skills with others interested in the same things, including baking, barbecuing, and hobbies like rock climbing.

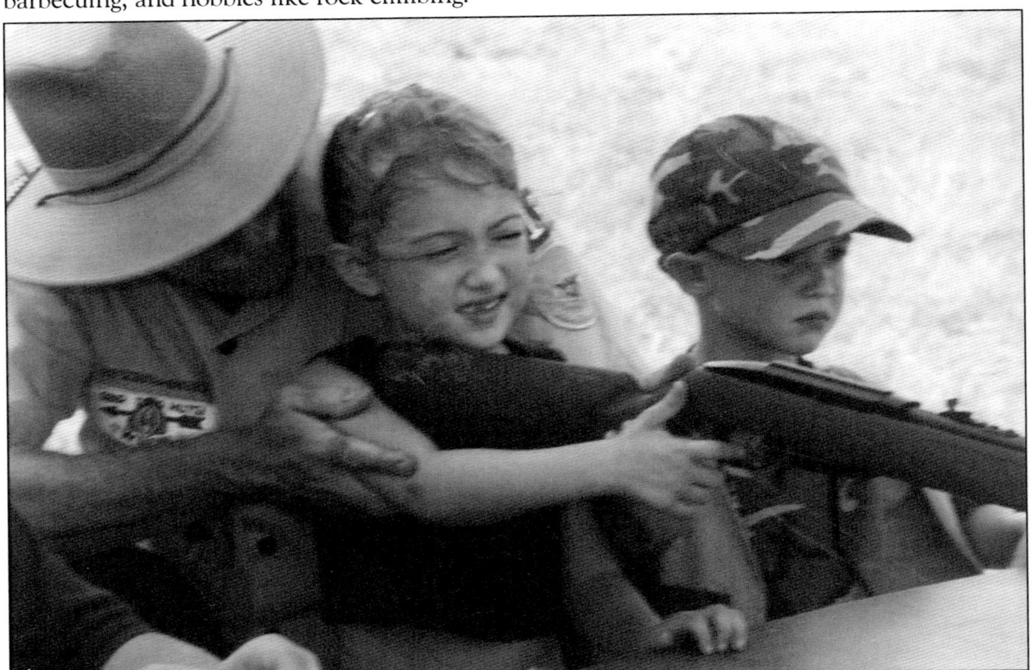

Firearm handling and training starts at a very early age in this area. Many youngsters look forward to going on deer hunts as soon as they are able to handle and control a gun.

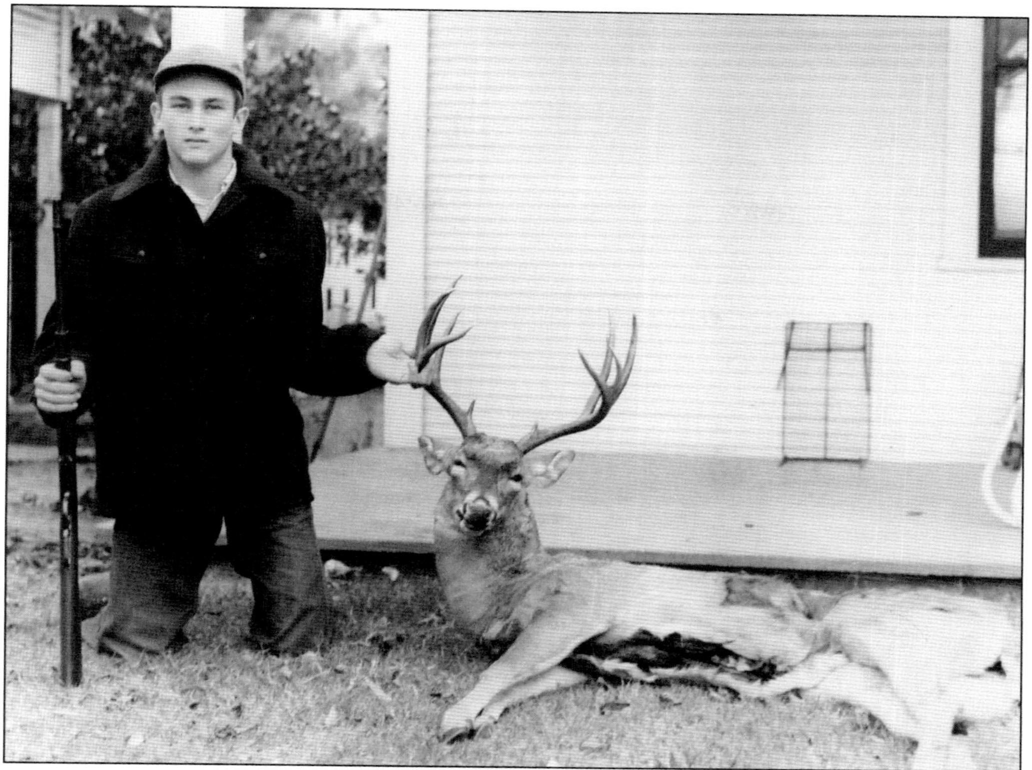

It is not long before they have learned the skills they need and bring home their first buck, just as Ralph Person shows off his prize kill in this picture. Part of the skills learned are how to properly clean and keep the dead animal until it can be processed at a meat preparation plant.

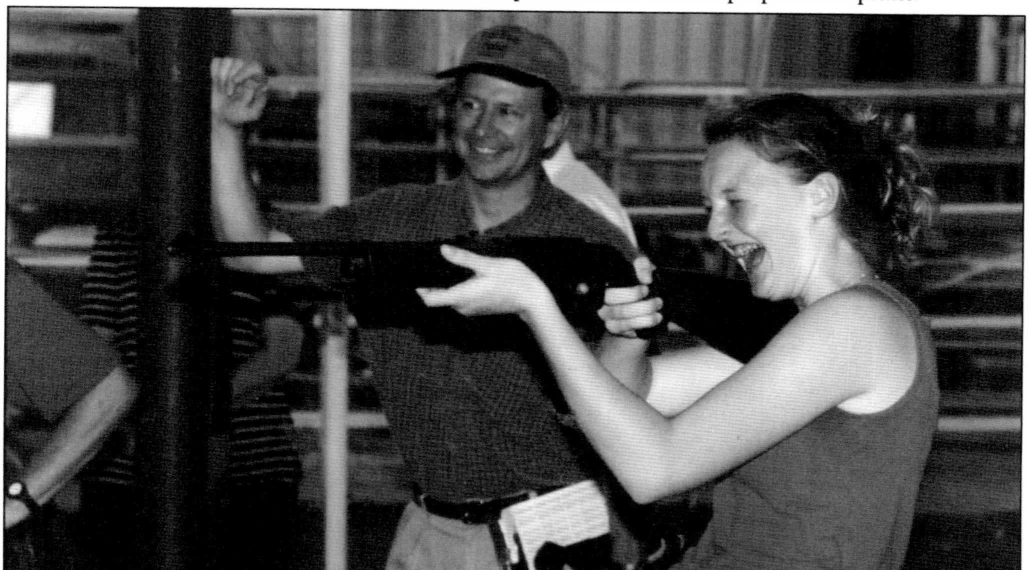

It is no longer a sport just for young men. Young ladies seem to be more and more interested in learning how properly to shoot and handle situations they might find in hunting areas.

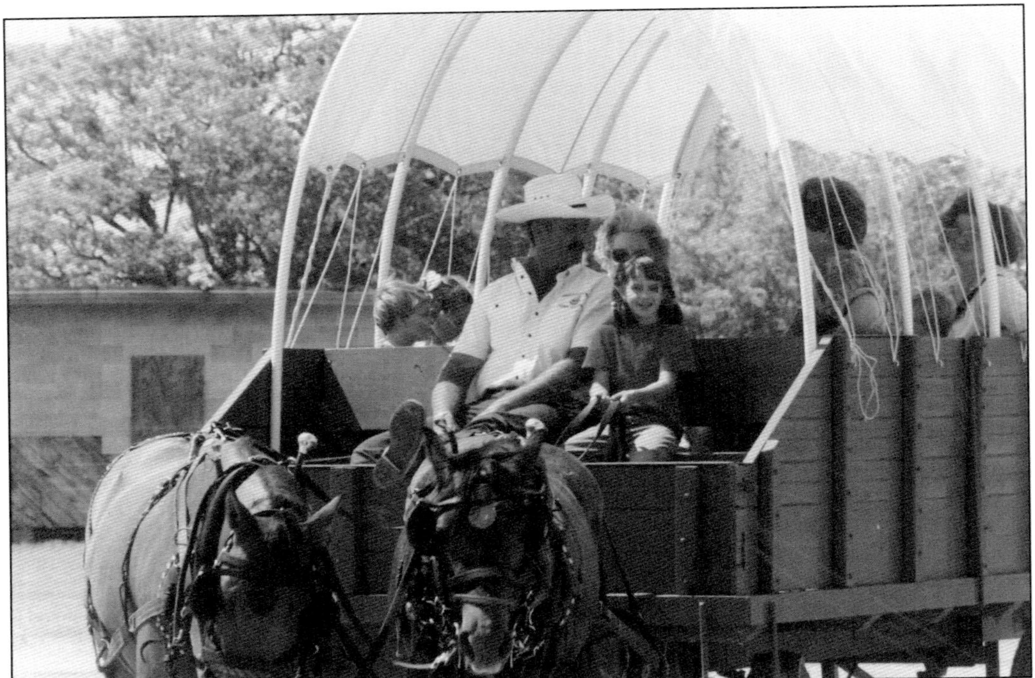

There are also a lot of other fun-filled skills to try a hand at, like handling a wagon and team of horses.

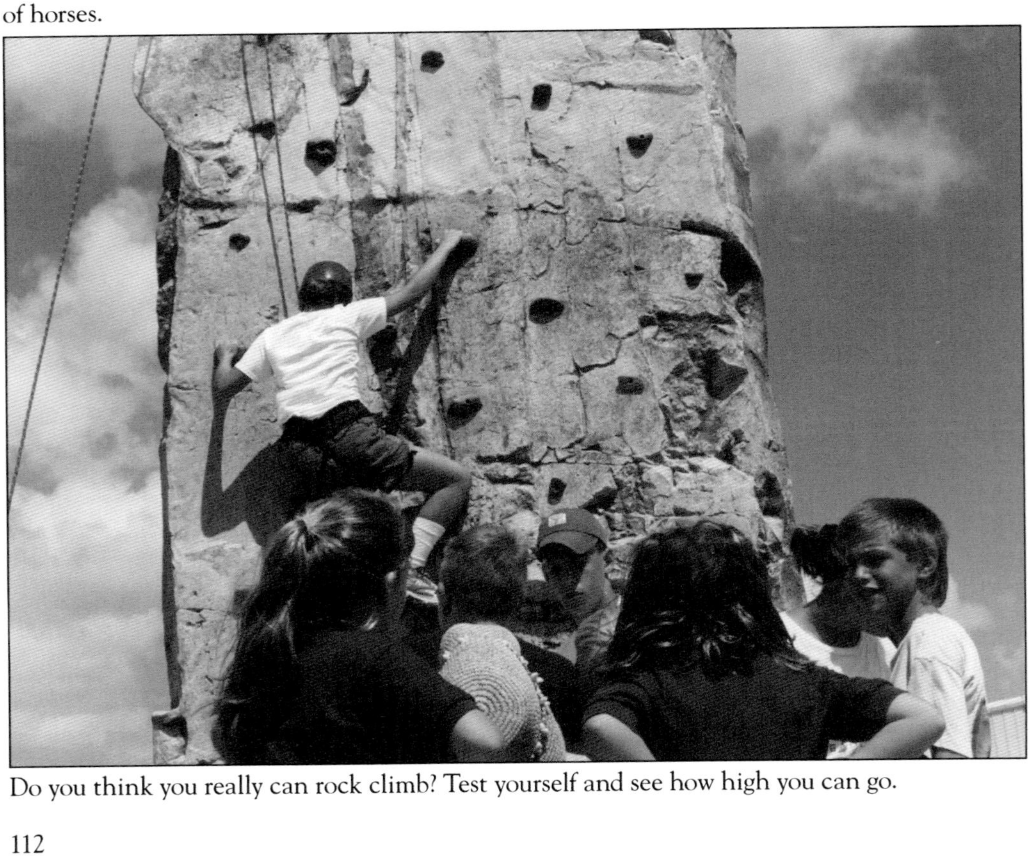

Do you think you really can rock climb? Test yourself and see how high you can go.

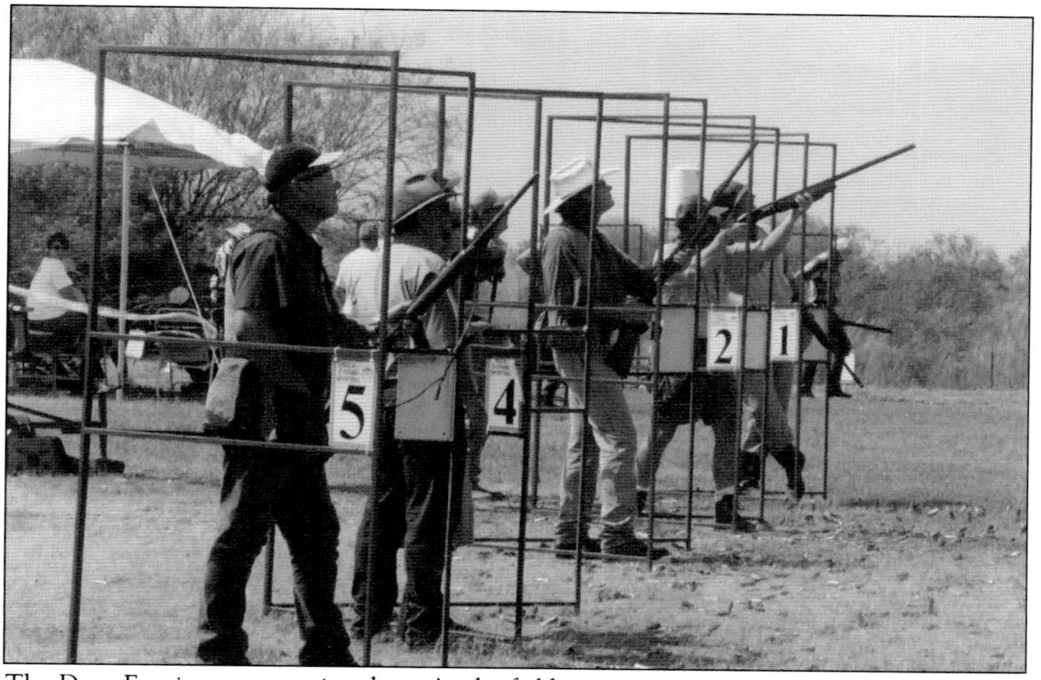

The Dove Fest is a pretty noisy place. At the field cages, practicing and shooting skeet, most wear earplugs.

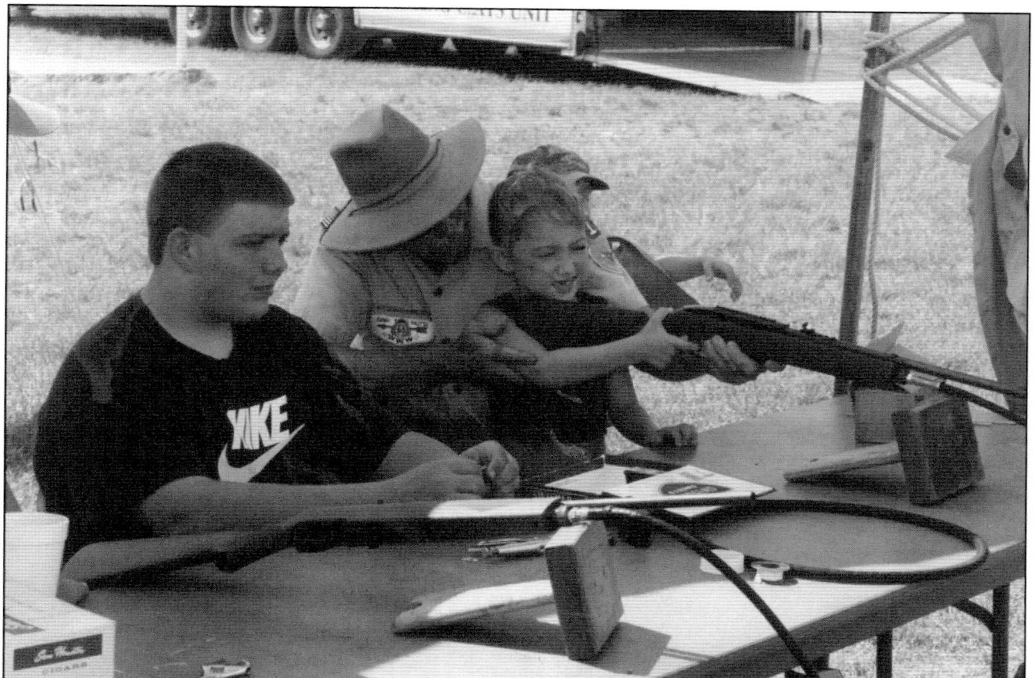

For some, it may take practice, practice, practice, but that is the part of the reason and success of the Lonesome Dove Fest. It has been reported by *Texas Monthly* that the growth and popularity of the event has increased. They now estimate at least 10,000 people are now attending.

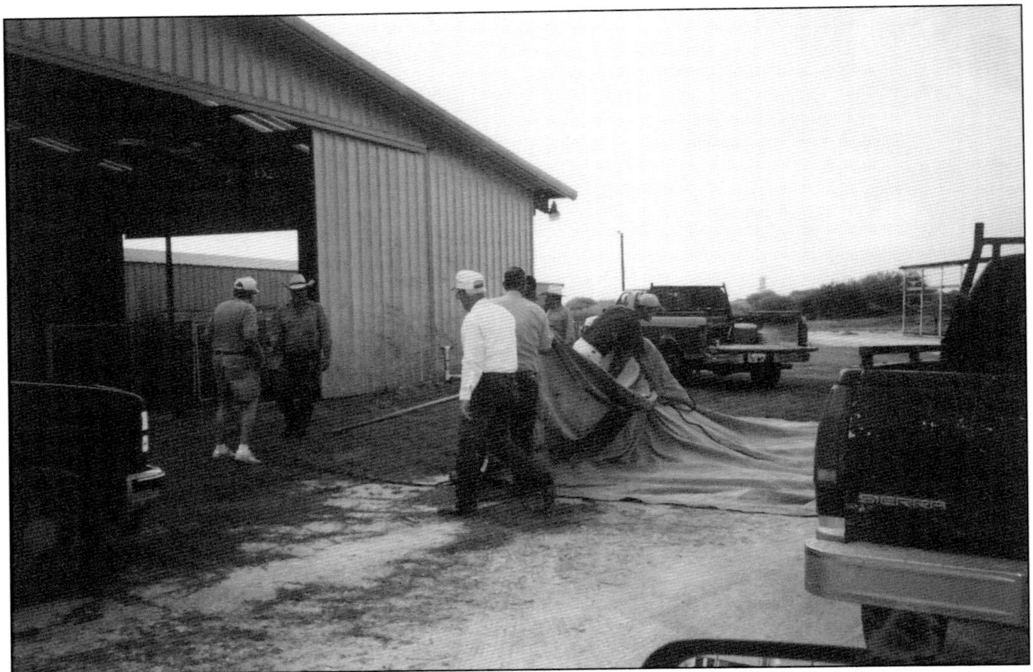

The very first fest was held in a farmer's field in an even smaller town than Karnes City, named Coy City. However, as the event grew and when rain would occur, a new place was sought, and thus, the Show Barn emerged.

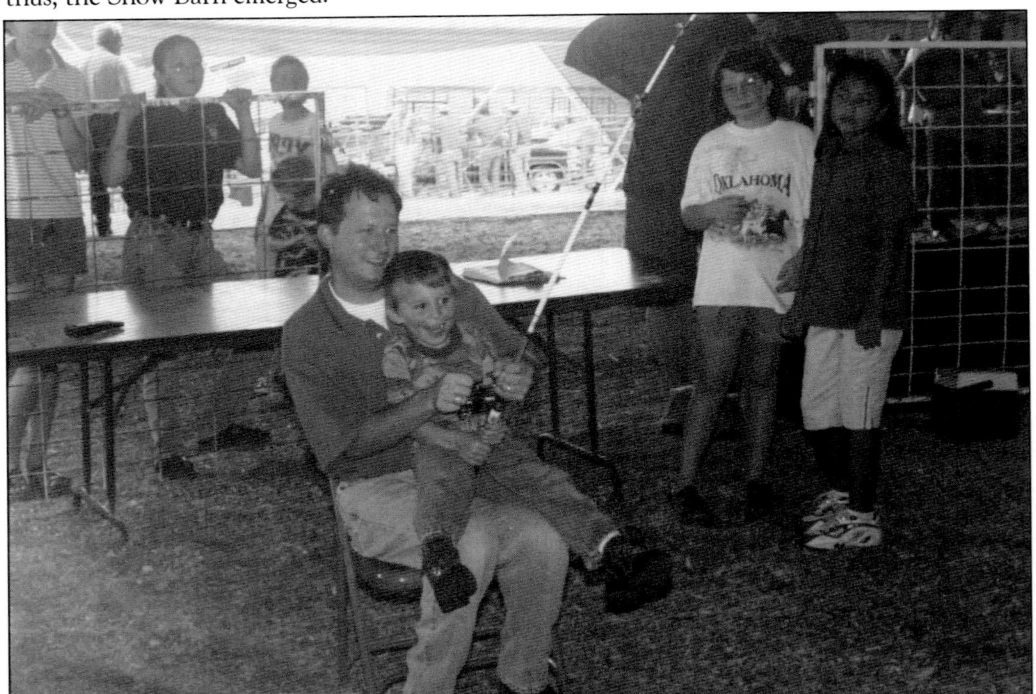

It was soon found that one could learn to fish well in an enclosed building if the need occurs to stay out of the rain or for other reasons.

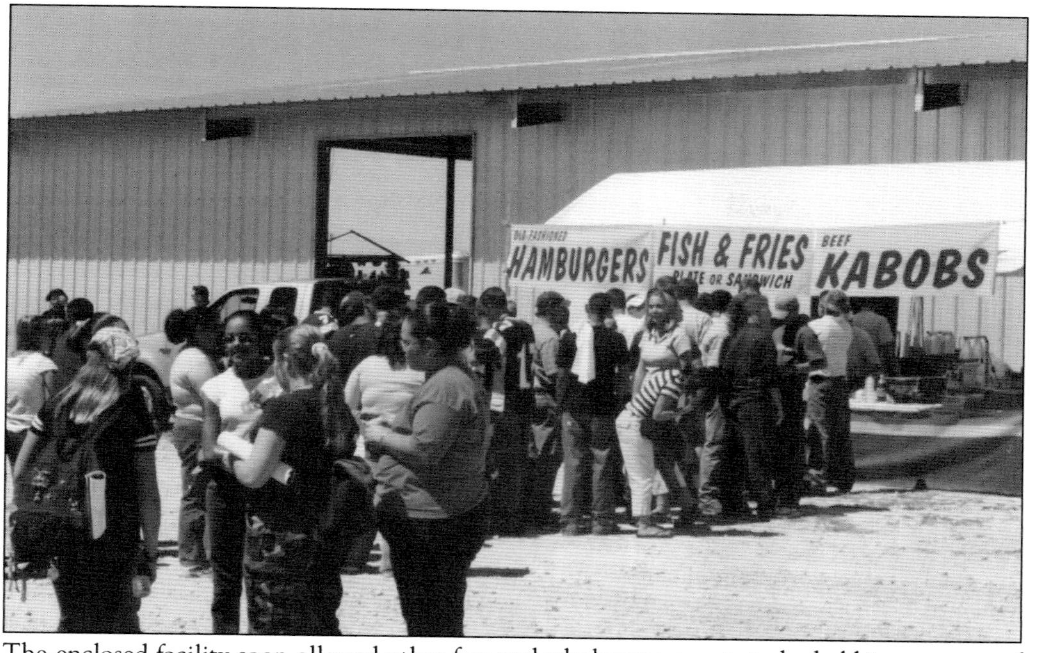

The enclosed facility soon allowed other fun and wholesome events to be held in any type of weather. The fest includes good eats, dancing to acclaimed bands, and country singers to listen to. Thus, it has grown in its offerings for a large variety of the community to come and enjoy the two day event.

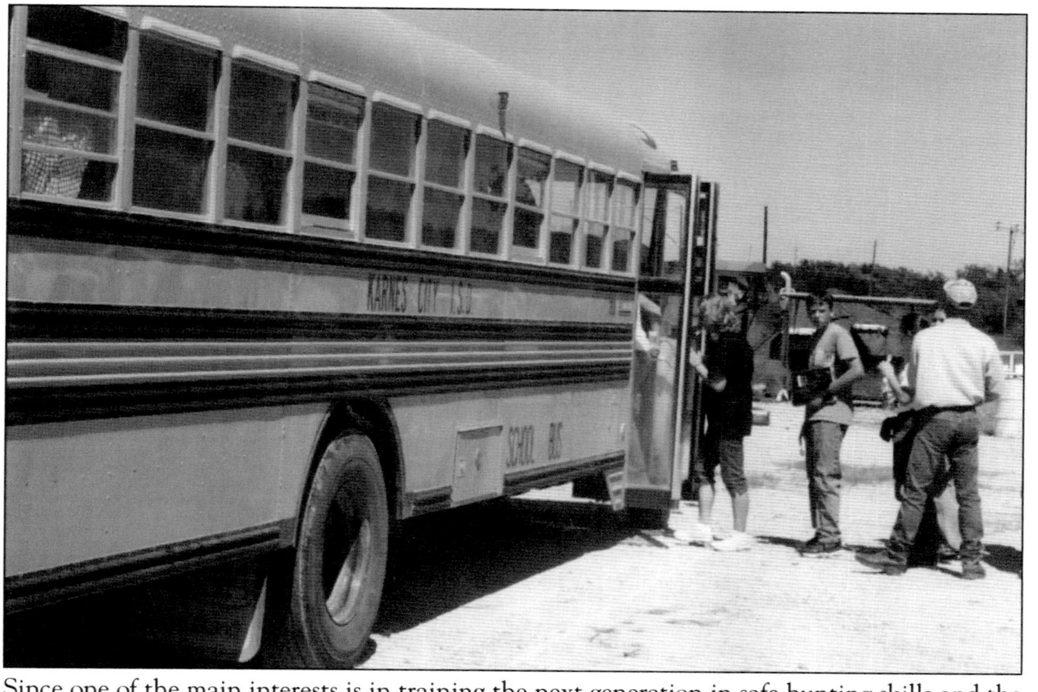

Since one of the main interests is in training the next generation in safe hunting skills and the regulations that go with it, local schools let out usually half a day on Fridays and transported the students by school bus to and from the event.

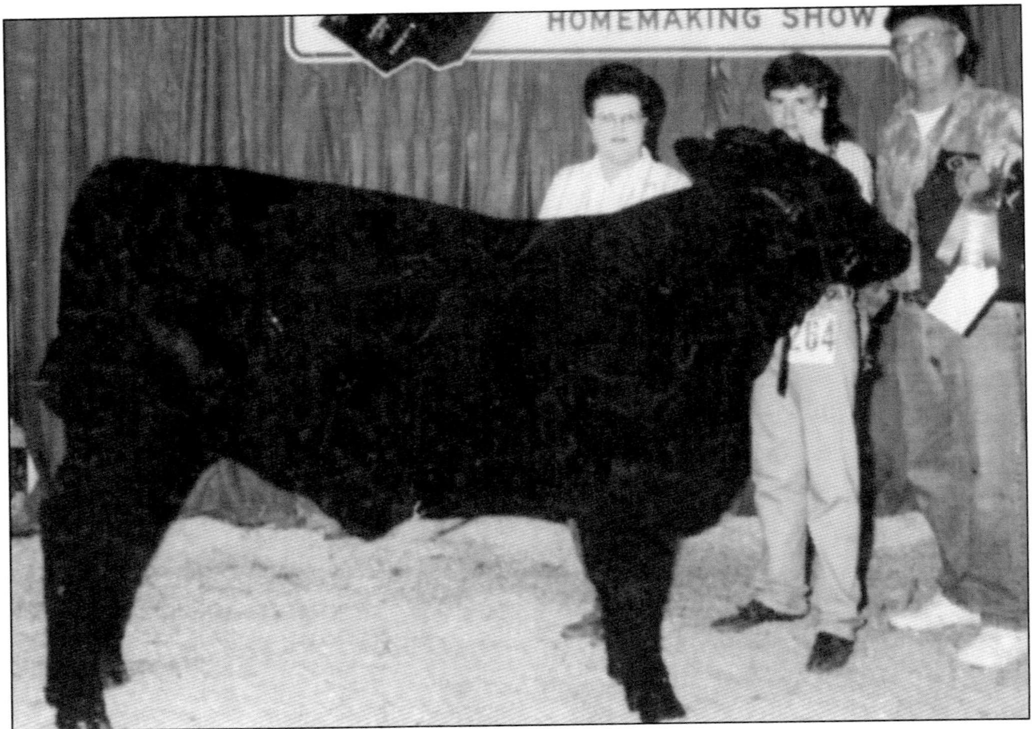

The students find it fascinating to see and learn about different live animals in case they want to try their hand at raising an animal through the agricultural programs taught at school. Those animals can be shown at the local livestock show and auction events.

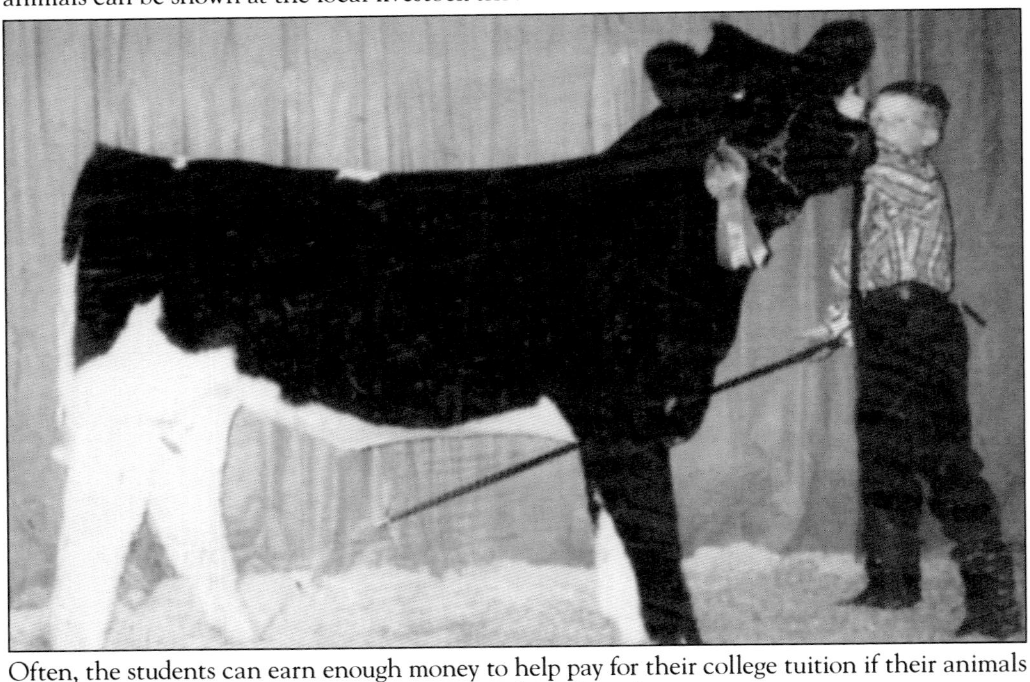

Often, the students can earn enough money to help pay for their college tuition if their animals place well in the auction when the time comes for selling them.

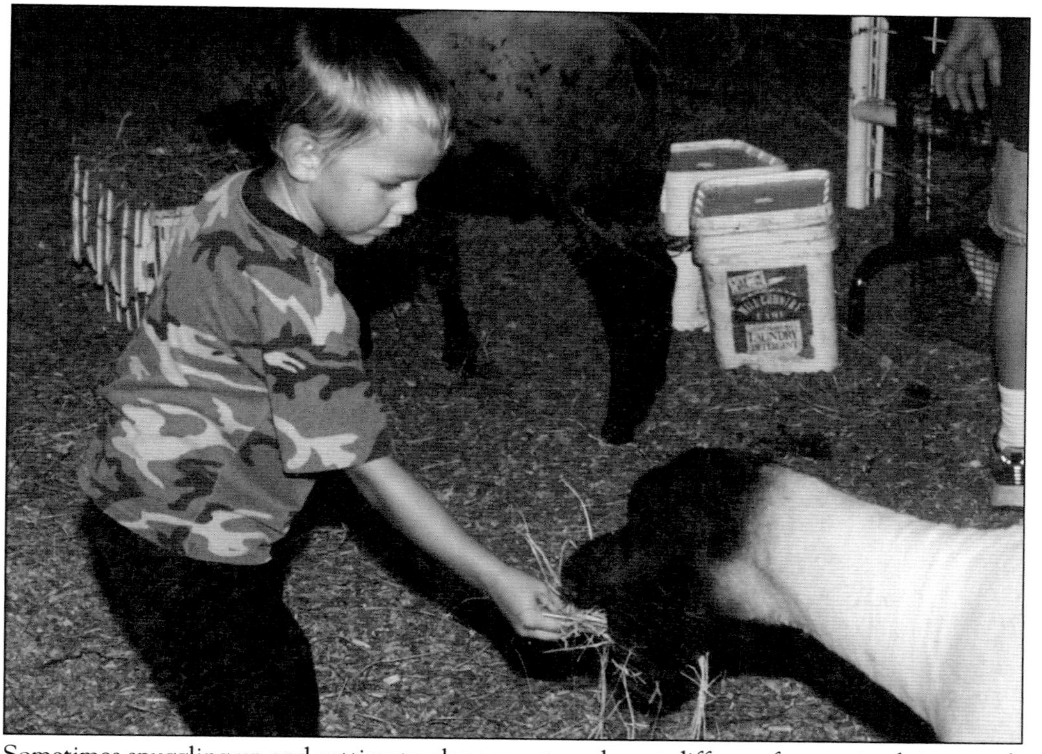

Sometimes snuggling up and getting to observe pets and meet different farm animals is enough of a reason to visit the Show Barn.

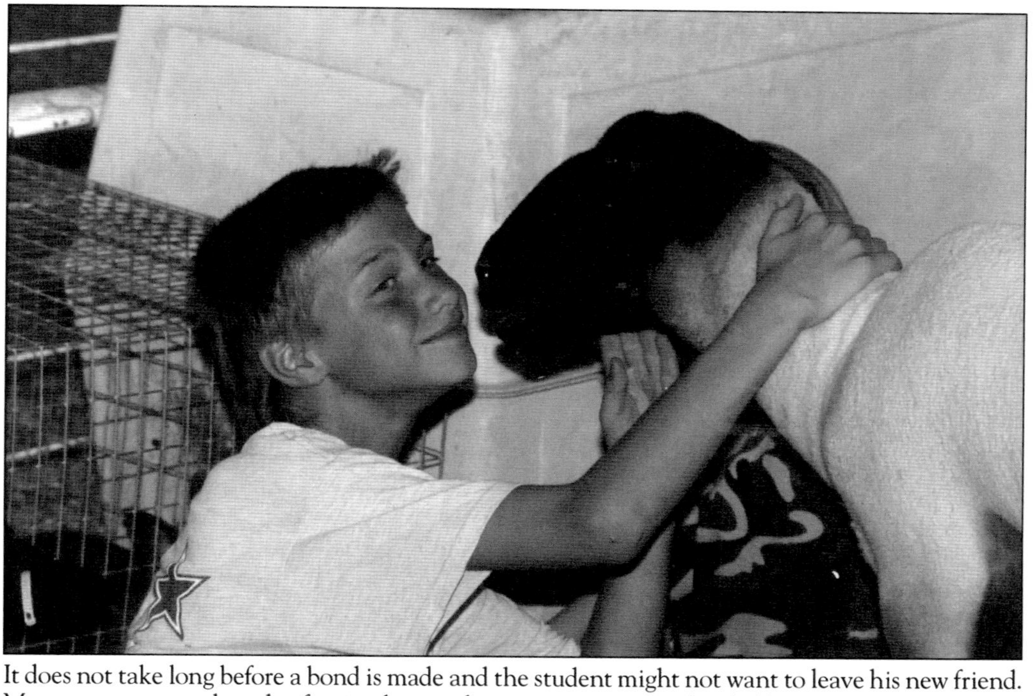

It does not take long before a bond is made and the student might not want to leave his new friend. Many types or new breeds of animals are a learning experience for children and adults.

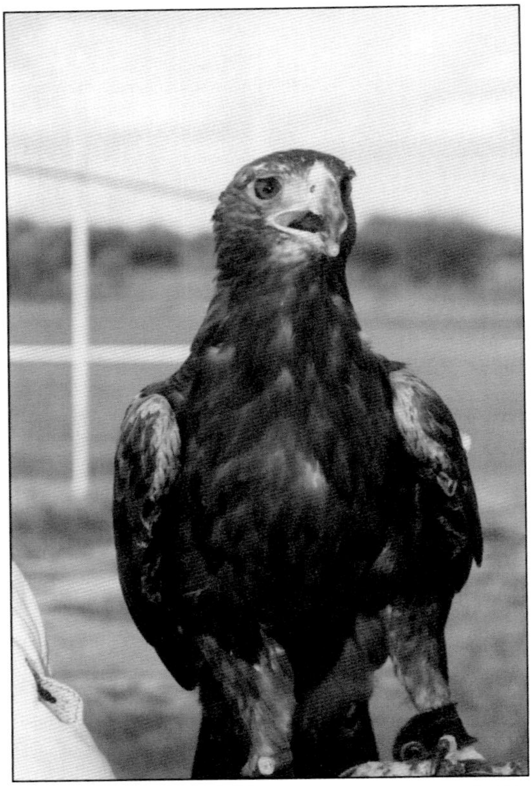

Seeing this creature heading toward a person might make them want to seek safety. But it, too, is a lesson to be learned in case one needs to handle a situation upon meeting one.

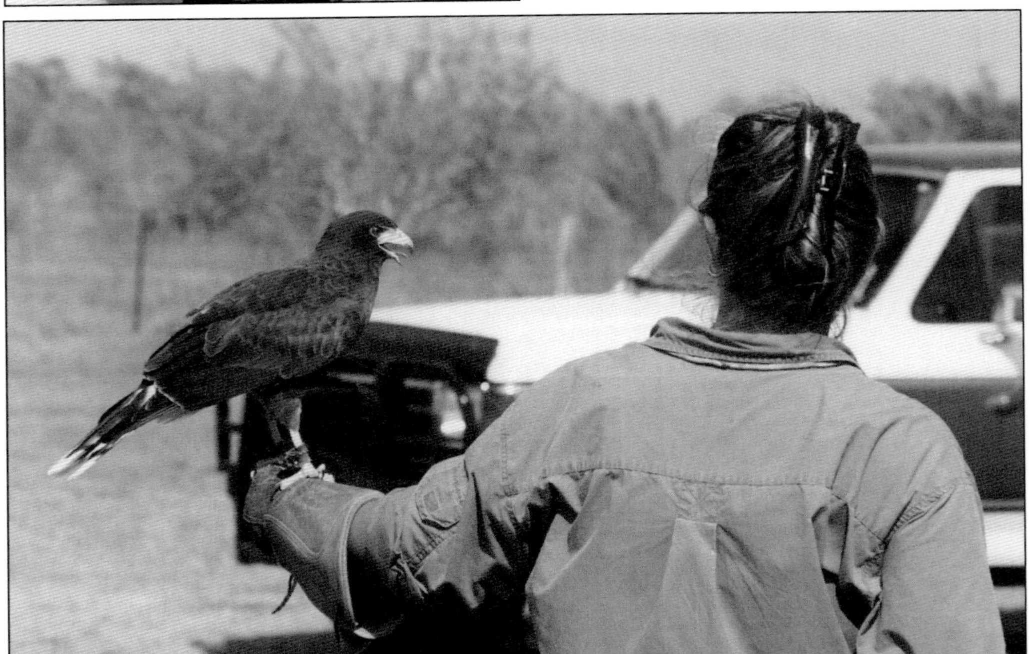

The handler of the bird showed how it should be taken care of to any interested bystander. The bird and his trainer proved to be of great interest to many attending the Dove Fest.

The bird in this photograph looks like it had a mind of its own and wanted to fly away. The noise from the gunfire may have made it wish it were somewhere else.

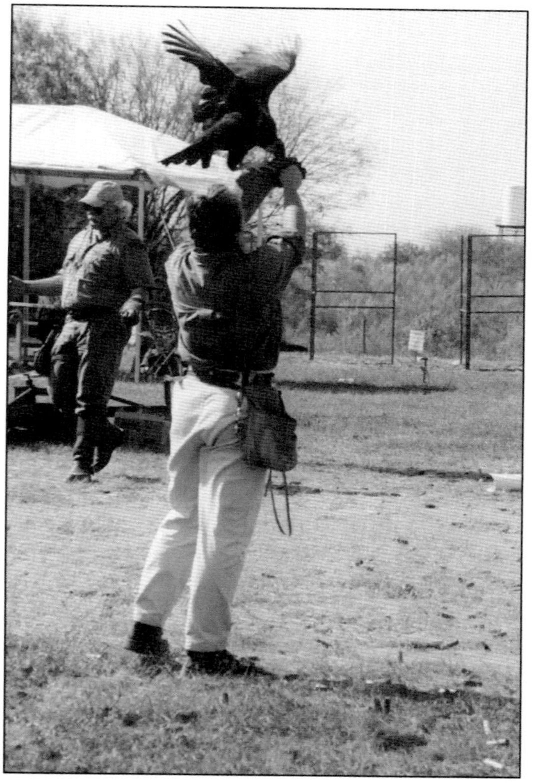

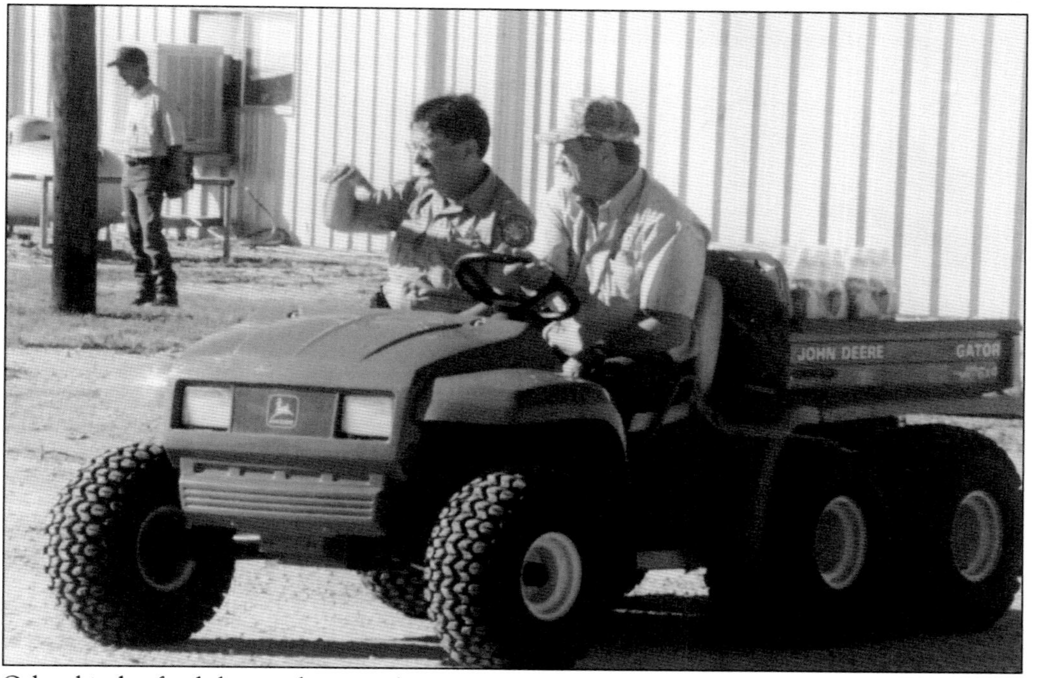

Other kinds of exhibits and items of interest are at the fest as well. The latest equipment and hunting gear are available, and some can even be bought there.

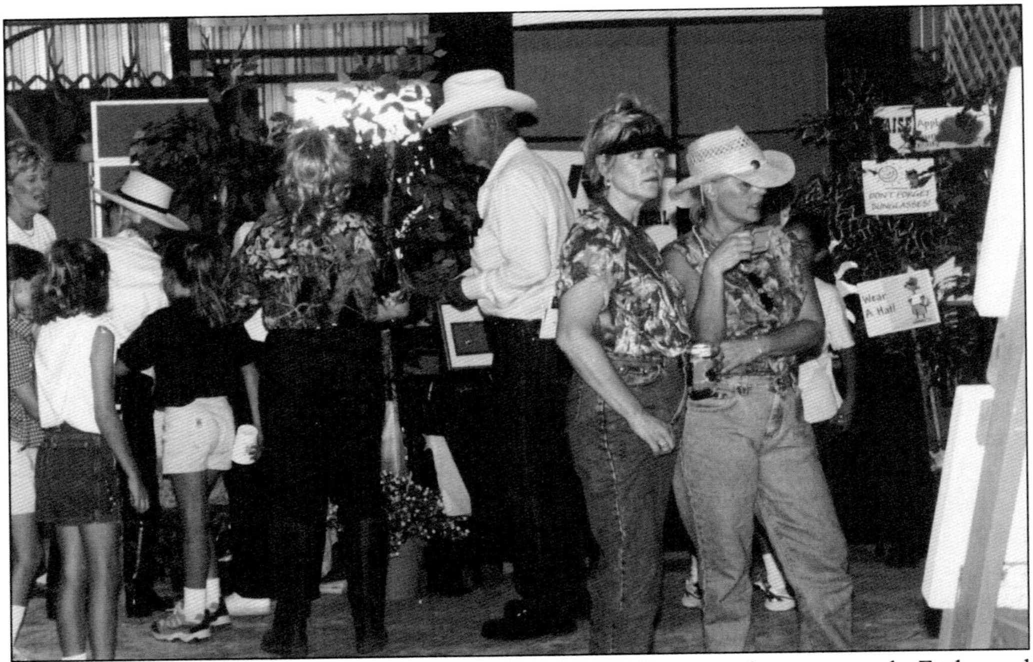

Of course, good food and beverages are available at the fest. It is a good way to spend a Friday and Saturday in September. Also, information on available hunting leases can be found there.

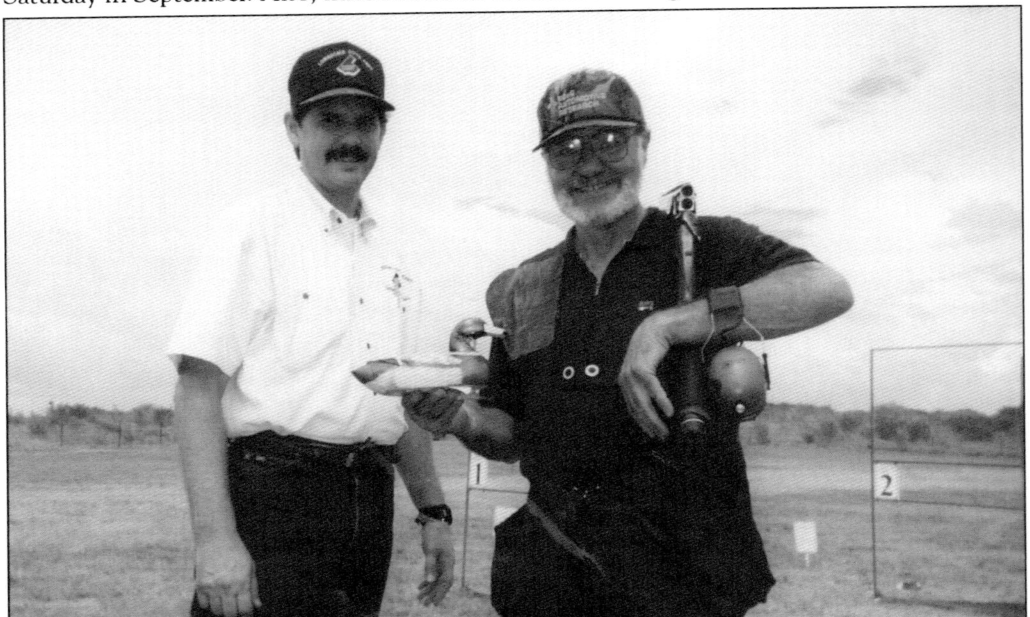

Those interested in taking part in the activities at Lonesome Dove Fest should plan ahead and make some reservations, especially now with the extra oil and gas personnel in the Karnes County area. In this photograph, David Carothers and Jim Harris are checking to see if they have arrived in time.

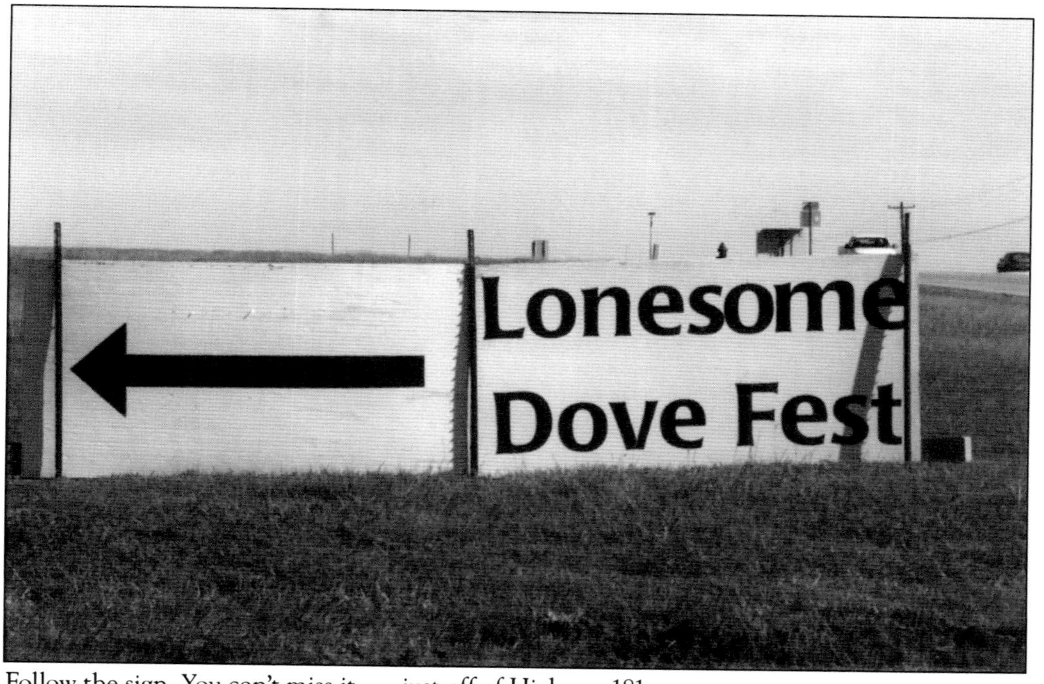

Follow the sign. You can't miss it . . . just off of Highway 181.

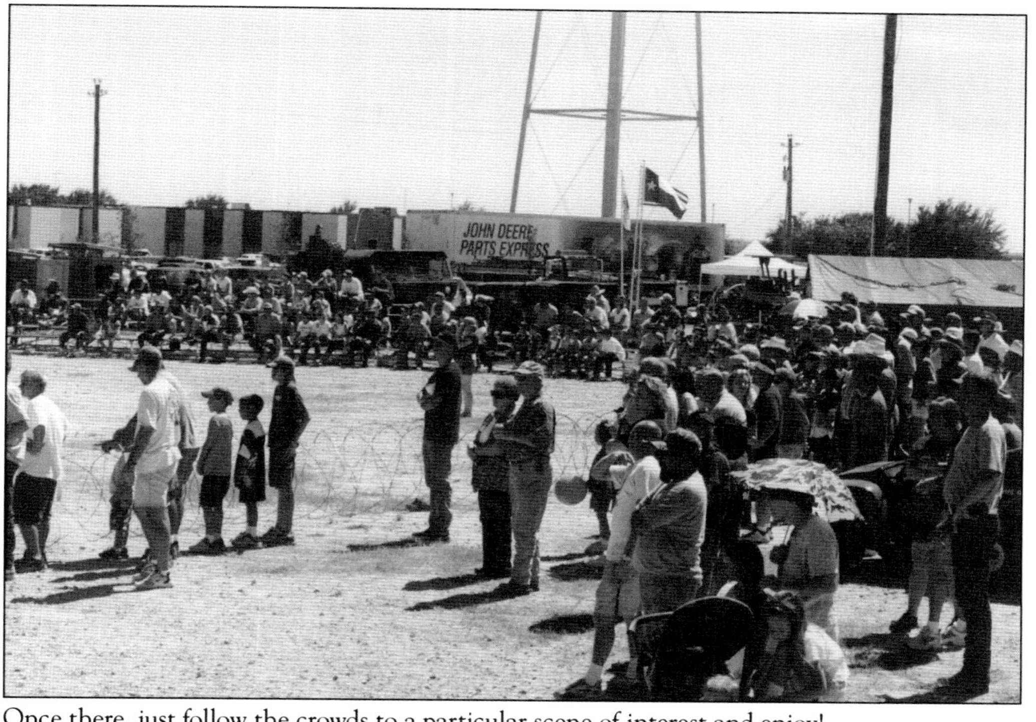

Once there, just follow the crowds to a particular scene of interest and enjoy!

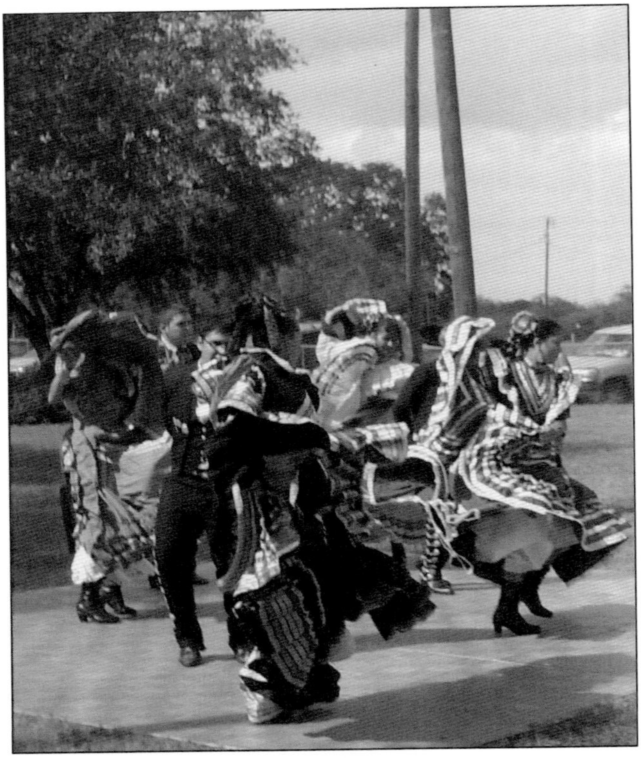

Other social events that connect to Karnes County's interests and history also occur. One such event is held at the Helena Courthouse Museum during the late summer called the Indian Summer Festival. There are exhibits on the courthouse grounds and there is access to the museum to see the historical data and pictures. Food and ethnic dances are performed at different times of the day. A folkloria is shown here.

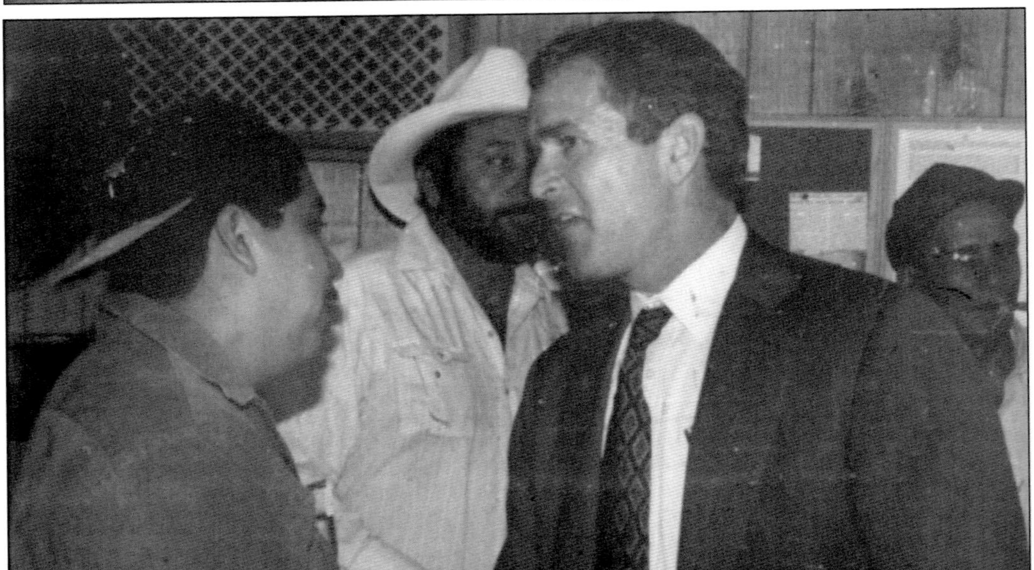

Historical happenings still occur in our county, even in the present. Not too long ago, then governor George W. Bush visited on several occasions. One visit was to sign proclamations thanking our county for participating in an annual Pony Express Christmas Courier Run along the corridor honoring the heroes of the past.

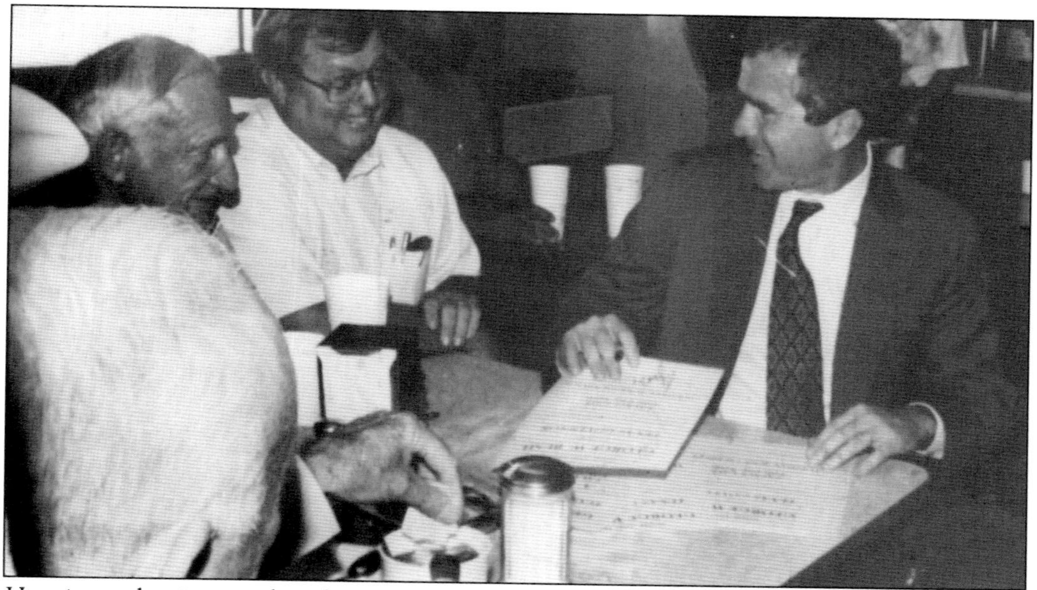
Here is another image taken during the same event.

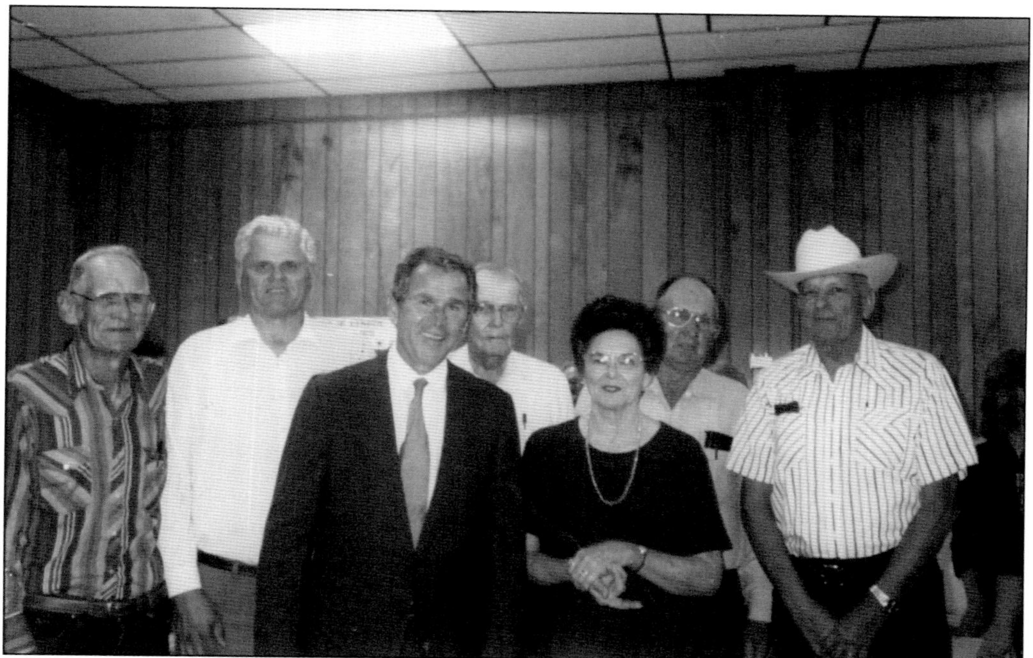
In another visit by Governor Bush, he thanked those in our farming and ranching business for their work in soil conservation in Texas. Standing with Governor Bush are Albert Banduch, A.W. Fenner, Sis Regmund, and Leo Jarzombek.

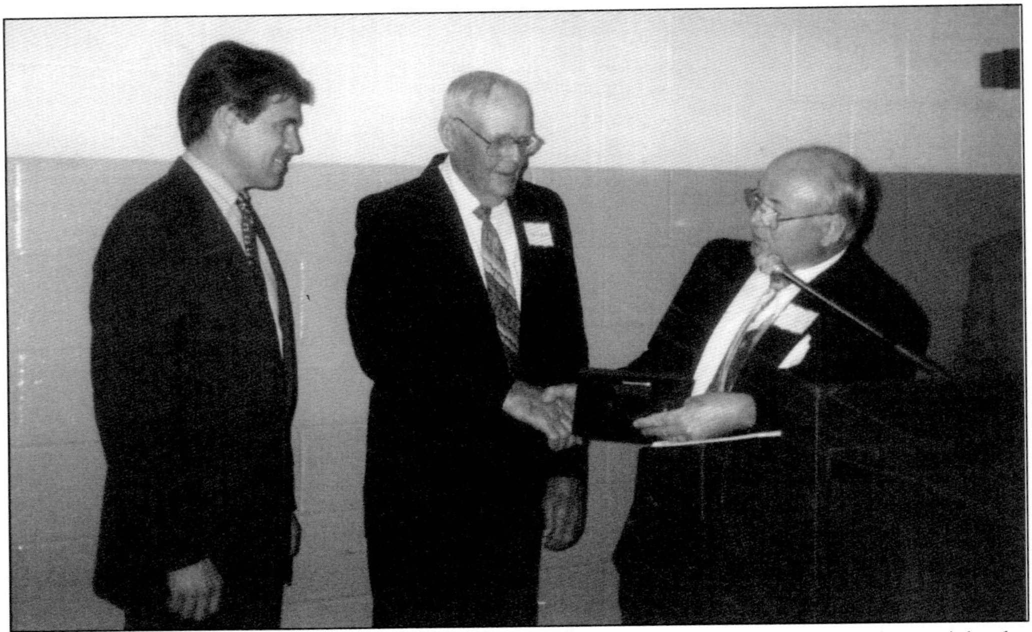

In this image is soon-to-be-governor Rick Perry with Arthur Fenner and Alfred Pawelek, the Karnes County judge, for the 1994 Conservation Award.

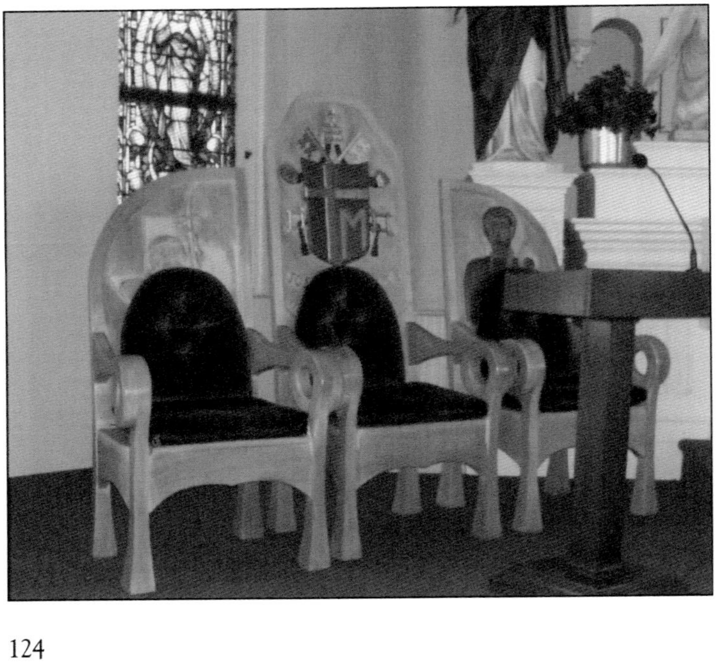

As honorary decrees go, none could be more important to the people of Karnes County, and especially the Panna Maria area, then when Pope John Paul III visited with a delegation of parishioners of the Immaculate Conception Church in 1987. They visited on the anniversary of their founding the first Polish community in the United States in Karnes County, Texas. He presented the church with three beautiful chairs for the occasion.

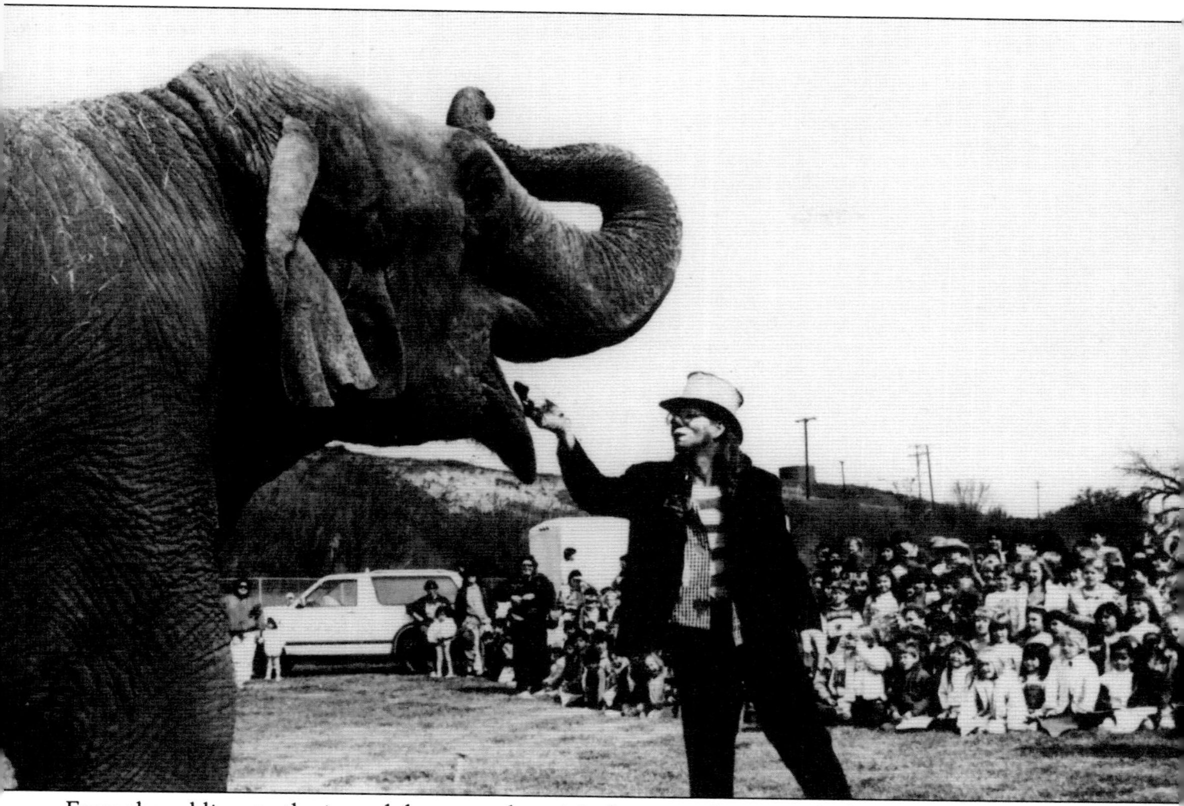

From the sublime to the incredulous, another visit that caused a stir and a little notoriety was the visit by the nine-ton elephant, Black Diamond, to Kenedy, Texas, in 1929. He had gone berserk earlier and killed a woman in a rampage in Corsicana, Texas. By the time they got him chained and back on the route the circus was taking, the owner John Ringling decided it was time to put him down. They stopped about halfway between Kenedy and Karnes City just off Highway 181. With volunteers firing their weapons, it took 55 shots to kill him.

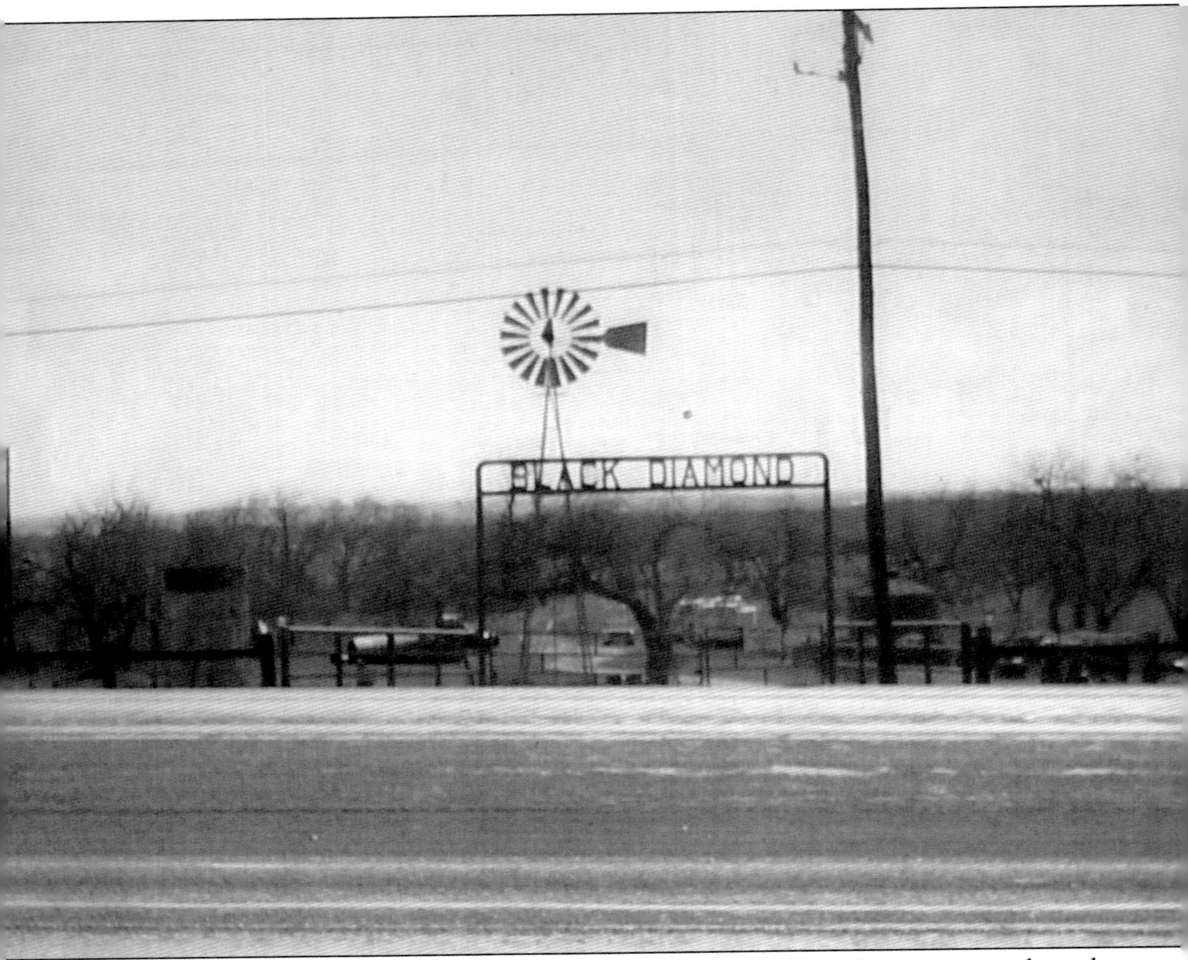

The people in Karnes County put up a sign just off Highway 181 at the exact spot where the elephant Black Diamond was shot 55 times by volunteers in 1929. He was shot at the request of the circus owner, who was traveling with him and other elephants at the time. He was supposed to be buried there, but the hole they made was not big enough to hold the massive carcass.

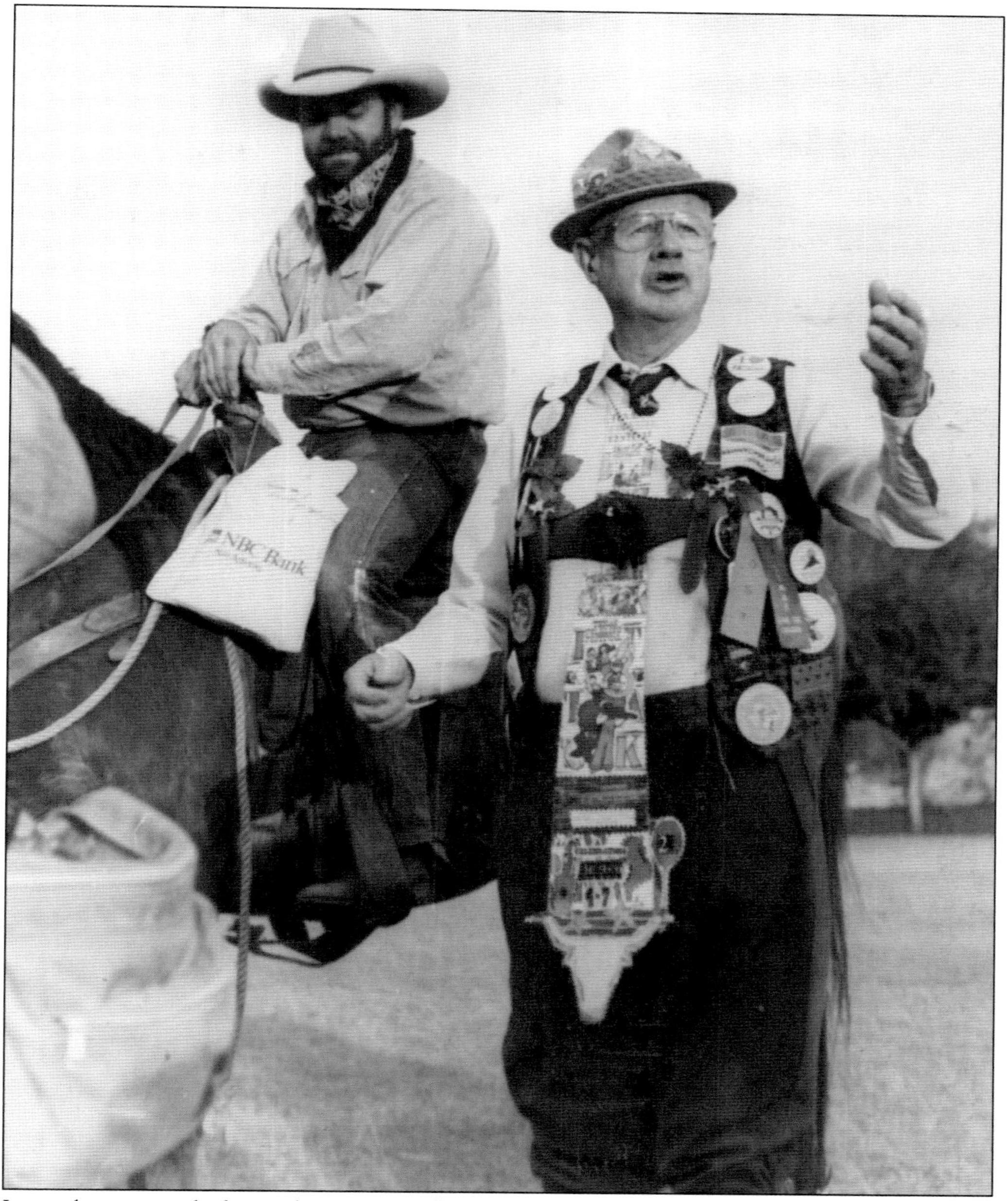

It can be extremely fun to live in a small town like Karnes City. Pictured above is Professor Katzenjammer, better known as the prolific author of many books about Texas, Karnes County's Robert Thonhoff. Professor Katzenjammer enjoyed and spent many years going to the San Antonio Folklife Festival to tell the tall tales he knew about our area and the history of Texas. Our county has wonderful tales to tell and people who love to tell them.